DARKEST BEFORE THE DAWN

Studies in Chinese Christianity

G. Wright Doyle and Carol Lee Hamrin,

Series Editors

A Project of the Global China Center

www.globalchinacenter.org

Previously published volumes in the series

Carol Lee Hamrin & Stacey Bieler, eds., *Salt and Light: Lives of Faith That Shaped Modern China*, volume 1

Carol Lee Hamrin & Stacey Bieler, eds., *Salt and Light: More Lives of Faith That Shaped Modern China*, volume 2

Richard R. Cook & David W. Pao, eds., *After Imperialism: Christian Identity in China and the Global Evangelical Movement*

Carol Lee Hamrin & Stacey Bieler, *Salt and Light: More Lives of Faith That Shaped Modern China*, volume 3

Lit-sen Chang, *Wise Man from the East: Lit-sen Chang (Zhang Lisheng)*

George Hunter McNeur, *Liang A-Fa: China's First Preacher, 1789–1855*

Eunice V. Johnson, *Timothy Richard's Vision: Education and Reform in China, 1880–1910*

G. Wright Doyle, *Builders of the Chinese Church: Pioneer Protestant Missionaries and Chinese Church Leaders*

Jack R. Lundbom, *On the Road to Siangyang: Covenant Mission in Mainland China 1890–1949*

Brent Fulton, *China's Urban Christians: A Light That Cannot Be Hidden*

Andrew T. Kaiser, *The Rushing on of the Purposes of God: Christian Missions in Shanxi since 1876*

Li Ma & Jin Li, *Surviving the State, Remaking the Church: A Sociological Portrait of Christians in Mainland China*

Linda Banks and Robert Banks, *Through the Valley of the Shadow: Australian Women in War-Torn China*

Arthur Lin, *The History of Christian Missions in Guangxi, China*

Linda Banks and Robert Banks, *They Shall See His Face: The Story of Amy Oxley Wilkinson and Her Visionary Work among the Blind in China*

Robert Banks and Linda Banks, *Children of the Massacre: The Extraordinary Story of the Stewart Family in Hong Kong and West China*

DARKEST BEFORE THE DAWN

A Brief History of the Rise of Christianity in China

RICHARD R. COOK

PICKWICK *Publications* · Eugene, Oregon

DARKEST BEFORE THE DAWN
A Brief History of the Rise of Christianity in China

Studies in Chinese Christianity

Pickwick Publications
An Imprint of Wipf and Stock Publishers
199 W. 8th Ave., Suite 3
Eugene, OR 97401

www.wipfandstock.com

PAPERBACK ISBN: 978-1-7252-9715-9
HARDCOVER ISBN: 978-1-7252-9716-6
EBOOK ISBN: 978-1-7252-9717-3

Cataloguing-in-Publication data:

Name: Cook, Richard R., author.

Title: Darkest before the dawn : a brief history of the rise of Christianity in China / Richard R. Cook.

Description: Eugene, OR: Pickwick Publications, 2021. | Studies in Chinese Christianity. | Includes bibliographical references.

Identifiers: ISBN: 978-1-7252-9715-9 (paperback). | ISBN: 978-1-7252-9716-6 (hardcover). | ISBN: 978-1-7252-9717-3 (ebook).

Subjects: LSCH: Christianity—China—History. | Christianity—China—19th century. | Christianity—China—20th century. | Christianity—China—21st century. | Mission—China.

Classification: BR1285 C66 2021 (print). | BR1285 (ebook).

10/25/21

To PF

She laughed at me

when I took a knee

(alas, not her cultural tradition),

but I am forever grateful she said yes.

Contents

Preface | IX
Introduction | XIII

Part One: Pre-Protestant Missions (Beginnings–1807) | 1

1 Alopen and the First Christian in China | 4

2 Marco Polo, Kublai Khan, and the Franciscan Friars | 16

3 Matteo Ricci, the Jesuits, and the Emperor of China | 21

**Part Two: Protestant Missions and Chinese Angst
   (1807–1900)** | 33

4 Robert Morrison, the British, and Liang Fa | 36

5 The Opium Wars, the Taipings, and Hong Xiuquan | 45

6 Sowing the Seed: J. Hudson Taylor
   and the China Inland Mission | 62

7 Reaping the Whirlwind: Boxer Uprising | 76

8 Missions Compounds (An Excursus) | 92

Part Three: Independent Chinese Churches (1900–1949) | 103

9 New China: A Christian Civilization . . . without Christ? | 105

10 New Enemies of Christianity: May Fourth Era | 118

11 Cross Currents: Nationalism, Fundamentalism,
    and Global Christianity | 133

12 Rethinking Imperialism | 149

13 Real Lives: Wang Mingdao and John Sung | 160

Part Four: From 1949 to the Present, and Prospects for the Future (1949–Present) | 171

14 A Land without Missionaries: The Rise
of the Chinese Communist Party | 174

15 A Land without Christians: Victory from the Tomb | 181

16 Out of the Dark Shadows, into the Light
of the Global Stage | 194

Bibliography | 209

Preface

Field Note: On The Woes of a History Teacher

My eight-year-old daughter, Leah, sat in the backseat of my van with her good friend on the way home from school. To make conversation, I asked her friend, "What does your father do?" She hemmed and hawed, and, apparently, she did not really know. Curious, I later asked Leah, "When asked about your father's occupation, what do you say?" She also hesitated, and stammered, "Well . . . I say you are . . . a . . . kinda like a . . . teacher." To help her, I interjected, "You can say I am a history teacher." She dropped her eyes to her lap and responded, "No . . . then they will think you are boring."

I teach history.

Each semester as I teach a class, I commonly face two noteworthy obstacles. First, many students take their seats that first day already convinced that history is boring. I concede that textbooks often do not engender a love for history, and perhaps lackluster history teachers themselves can contribute to students' disinterest, but history itself is not boring! I assure students that the study of history, which includes the story of YHWH's interaction with humanity, is endlessly fascinating. Second, students are always surprised that I am not Chinese. When new students register for a class taught by Professor Ke Litian (柯立天老師), they do not expect to encounter me, a Caucasian foreigner. For the first year or two of my teaching career, my Chinese students intimidated me, especially those with extensive knowledge of Chinese Christianity. However, I realized that I could truly benefit from the abundant experiences of these students who had first-hand knowledge of the Chinese churches from all different parts of China, Taiwan, and the global diaspora. In return, I find that my students also welcome my unique

Western evangelical perspective to Chinese topics. This book developed organically from my teaching experiences and hundreds of hours of lively classroom interaction. The breathtaking sweep of the story starts in ancient China, and it culminates with a thriving Christian church in the twenty-first century. Like my classes on Chinese church history, the narrative in this book begins with a brief description of ancient Chinese history and culture, and it concludes with the maturing Chinese churches poised to take the lead in global missions to the unreached peoples around the world.

Magic occurs each semester in my classroom as we encounter together the drama of fallible human missionaries planting gospel seeds into the soil of China, and watching those seeds, as they take root, transform a people. I liberally season my lectures on church history with anecdotes, relevant current events, and personal experiences. Students often guide conversation into areas they would like to continue exploring, and so I customize my lectures each semester. I also offer suggestions of relevant readings to broaden their knowledge. Moreover, as a missiologist and missionary myself, I regularly urge students to consider missiological implications of church history events as well as current developments.

This passionate desire to bring Chinese church history to life, and the outgrowing of that desire which manifests in my classroom teaching, have resulted in this book. It is a labor of love for those who are eager to learn more about the work God has done and is accomplishing in the nation of China, whether those who want to learn are missionaries, students, or lay people.

The book is decidedly Evangelical and favors this point of view for our story. Thus, for example, after the arrival of Protestant missionaries in China, the rich storyline of the Roman Catholic Church drops out of my narrative. Although my perspective is Evangelical, I believe other readers with different perspectives and faith backgrounds will still find useful insight. The story of Protestant and Evangelical Christianity in China is unique, but many of the political, social, and religious dynamics faced by the missionaries and the indigenous Chinese churches will interest all students of Chinese history and culture.

There are several people I must thank. I deeply appreciate support from G. Wright Doyle and Carol Lee Hamrin, the editors of the series *Studies in Chinese Christianity*. The volumes in the series continue to provide valuable insight into Christianity in China. Wright Doyle, in particular, provided extensive notes on the draft and engaged with me in delightful conversation on numerous topics. Casey Houseworth has carefully read and corrected the manuscript, but even more, she has added insight and judicious feedback. I appreciate the rich support I have received from Logos Evangelical

Seminary, and I want to express gratitude to my seminary colleagues. I sent early drafts of several chapters to former colleagues at Trinity Evangelical Divinity School, and I greatly value the comments I received from David Pao, Scott Manetsch, and Craig Ott. I especially appreciate the consistent encouragement I have received over many years from Eckhard Schnabel. My mom, Alice Feher, also read and commented on an early version of the complete manuscript. Most of all, I want to thank my students from Logos Evangelical Seminary and Trinity Evangelical Divinity School, as well as students from the classes I have taught in San Jose, Taipei, Paris, and Moscow. Their eager participation in conversation has profoundly shaped the material in this book.

Introduction

IN SUCH A BRIEF book on such a vast story as the history of Christianity in China, I had to strategically choose my material. I limited myself to sixteen chapters, divided into four parts.

Part One contains the pertinent events for this history before the arrival of Protestant missionaries in 1807. Chapters 1–3, which comprise Part One, cover the first three instances when Christian missions work entered China, during the Tang, Yuan, and Ming dynasties, respectively. Although the seed was planted during these vibrant eras of Chinese history, it does not seem that the full potential of the gospel was yet realized on Chinese soil.

Part Two opens with the arrival of Robert Morrison and Chapters 4–8 depict the Protestant missionaries in the volatile context of nineteenth century China. These chapters include an underlying focus on the small beginnings of the indigenous church that the missionaries planted during this instability.

The young and fragile indigenous church becomes the open focus of the narrative in Part Three. Chapters 9–13 cover the fast-moving and action-packed first half of the twentieth century. Indeed, this time period includes the Boxer uprising in 1900, the fall of the Qing Dynasty marking the death of the Imperial system, the rise of the warlord era, the May Fourth era, the presidency of the Christian Chiang Kai-shek, the Sino-Japanese War, World War II, and the victory of the Chinese Communist Party in 1949. The indigenous churches took root in Chinese soil in the midst of these cross currents.

As for me, I like to view the chapters from Part Three through the eyes of Wang Mingdao. He was born in 1900, pastor of the largest church in Beijing in the 1940s, and after a long imprisonment, he became a renowned living martyr in the 1980s. He died in 1991, at 91 years old, just as I embarked on my PhD studies. He became the focus of my dissertation, and I find twentieth century Chinese history more riveting when viewing it through the eyes of a participant. For instance, when students first stormed Tiananmen Square on May 4, 1919, unleashing the May Fourth Movement of the 1920s, I like to consider the episode through the eyes of Wang who was a college age student living in Beijing.

Part Four begins in Chapter 14 with the severe persecution of the Christian churches in the 1960s and 1970s, a dark period of suffering. We are relieved to discover in Chapter 15 that the churches not only survived the testing but had burst forth with new life by the 1980s. Chapter 16 concludes with the story of the indigenous Protestant churches after 2000, and it includes a prospectus and a challenge for the future.

In the chapters of this book, I attempt to replicate the classroom experience. Over the years, I have adapted material based on student feedback, and I present content I have found most effective. I have tried to keep academic footnotes to a minimum. I also intersperse numerous "Field Notes," in which I share my stories and experiences. Each chapter concludes with "Reflection Questions" and "Suggested Readings." In addition to wrestling with Chinese church history, these features of the book encourage readers to also think missiologically and contextually. I believe this book fits into a course on Chinese Church History, but it could also provide insight for other courses, such as Chinese History, Global Christianity, Missions History, Introduction to Missions, and Contextualization.

As an example of this encouragement for further thought, let me provide one sample "Reflection Question." Under the Japanese occupation of China from 1937–1945, the Japanese authorities required all foreign journals to print four pro-Japan slogans on the cover. Wang Mingdao (who was forty years old in 1940), who wrote, produced, and funded his own Christian journal, refused to print the slogans on his cover. Here is one Reflection Question from Chapter 13:

> The Japanese occupation forces in Beijing required all foreign journals to print four slogans on the cover. Why do you think the Japanese authorities presumed Wang Mingdao's journal *Spiritual Food Quarterly* to be foreign? Do you consider it foreign or indigenous? Explain your answer.

I find this question—and students' responses to it—very telling. After so many years of studying Chinese history and focusing on Wang, I still marvel at his insight and his pluck. My impulse is to agree uncritically with the Japanese presumption that Christianity is "foreign" in China. Wang, conversely, boldly personified an opposing view. I trust that reflection on such questions can challenge our presumptions and enlarge our view of the Kingdom of God. I hope readers will find the material in this volume engaging. Ancient China, with its opulent culture and manifold traditions, provides a lush backdrop for the story of Christianity. Christianity, with its designer missionary DNA, was destined to arrive on China's shores. This book tells that story. The deepest darkness could never snuff out the light of the gospel, and the revival of the churches today reveals the profound grace and unrelenting power of God.

PART ONE

Pre-Protestant Missions (Beginnings–1807)

WHERE DOES THE STORY of Chinese church history begin?

The logical place to begin might be with the first arrival of Christianity in China, and numerous textbooks and courses do begin with the arrival of the Nestorian[1] Christians in the seventh century during the Tang Dynasty. However, the church started by Alopen did not survive. Likewise, the Roman Catholic mission work inaugurated in the thirteenth century by the Franciscan missionary John of Montecorvino during the Yuan Dynasty did not survive. Later, Roman Catholics would need to plant churches once again in the sixteenth century during the Ming Dynasty.

In this book, the first chapter will cover the story of Alopen and the Nestorians during the Tang Dynasty, and the second chapter will move on to the Yuan Dynasty and the arrival of the Franciscans.

A second sensible starting point might be the story of the arrival of the Jesuit missionary Matteo Ricci into China in the sixteenth century. His missionary endeavors, begun in 1582, planted the Roman Catholic Church in China that survives today. Chapter 3 tells of the efforts of Ricci and the Jesuits.

Another way to conceive of the story, however, is to see Chinese Christianity as continuous with early church history. Thus, a study of Chinese church history could start during the early church, the first three centuries of Christianity. The story of the early church raises intriguing questions for Chinese Christians today. For instance, why did the gospel first go to

1. I am following the convention in Chinese church history of referring to this as the "Nestorian" Church, but it is also known as the Assyrian Church of the East.

1

the West rather than the East? There is scholarship that shows that the Silk Route was open during the first century, and so it is not impossible that Christian missionaries could have traversed from Jerusalem all the way to China. The apostle Thomas is reported to have gone as far as India in the first century, but there is no record of any missionaries moving on to China.

By the fourth century, the Roman Empire had adopted Christianity, and yet the gospel still had not spread to China. What was God's plan for China? China, it seemed, was ripe for a new religion, and Buddhist emissaries from India had successfully planted Buddhism in China during the first and second centuries because the Silk Route was, in fact, open. Buddhism persisted in China for several centuries, and during the seventh and eighth centuries, during the Tang Dynasty, Buddhism became part of the indigenous religious culture in China. If Christianity had spread to the East rather than the West during the first few centuries, one can imagine a very different world today.

Chinese church history ultimately begins with the birth of the church at Pentecost in Acts 2. From its very beginning, Christianity was a missionary faith. Paul, the missionary to the Gentiles, carried the Christian church from the Jewish believers into the Gentile world. In the book of Acts, Christianity was already set on a trajectory to expand to all nations around the entire globe. The very nature of Christianity and the church assured the eventual arrival of Christianity to the shores of China. And, of course, the church in China is part of a universal and catholic church that stretches back to the book of Acts. Everything that happened in the book of Acts is part of Chinese church history.

Finally, it is also essential to note that Chinese Christianity did not merely emerge out of the expansion of missionary outreach into the country; but, more importantly, the gospel that was planted produced an indigenous church that grew out of Chinese soil.

To understand Christianity in China, one needs also to understand Chinese history and culture. Like any people group, the Chinese people viewed the gospel through indigenous eyes. When the gospel arrived in the land, it had to interact with Chinese people and a Chinese culture which were completely unfamiliar with its message. In that exchange, both China and the universal Christian church were to be transformed.

This book tells that story. Missions history is an extraordinary saga that involves the unpredictable interaction of foreign missionaries with indigenous peoples who are enmeshed in a different worldview and culture, often radically so. The story of the arrival of Western missionaries onto the shores of China was destined to produce a remarkable tale. This tale does not begin with the landing of the missionaries upon foreign soil, but it has its origins in the ancient history of the land and people receiving those missionaries.

SUGGESTED READING FOR PART ONE

Millward, James A. *Eurasian Crossroads: A History of Xinjiang*. New York: Columbia University Press, 2007.

Ruokanen, Miika, and Paulos Huang, eds. *Christianity and Chinese Culture*. Grand Rapids: Eerdmans, 2010.

Thong, Chan Kei, and Charlene L. Fu. *Finding God in Ancient China: How the Ancient Chinese Worshipped the God of the Bible*. Grand Rapids: Zondervan, 2009.

GENERAL BOOKS ON CHINA AND CHINESE CHRISTIANITY

Each chapter provides a small list of recommended books relevant to the time and subject matter discussed, and below are some of the best comprehensive books on Chinese History and Chinese Church History.

Aikman, David. *Jesus in Beijing*. 2nd rev. ed. Oxford: Monarch, 2006.

Bays, Daniel H. *A New History Christianity in China*. West Sussex, UK: Wiley-Blackwell, 2012.

Charbonnier, Jean-Pierre. *Christians in China: A.D. 600–2000*. Translated by M. N. L. Couve de Murville. San Francisco: Ignatius, 2007.

Fairbank, John King, and Merle Goldman. *China: A New History*. 2nd ed. Cambridge, MA: Belknap, 2006.

Latourette, Kenneth S. *A History of Christian Missions in China*. Taipei: Ch'eng Wen, 1973.

Moffett, Samuel Hugh. *A History of Christianity in Asia: Beginnings to 1500*. Vol 1. Maryknoll, NY: Orbis, 1998.

———. *A History of Christianity in Asia: 1500 to 1900*. Vol. 2. Maryknoll, NY: Orbis, 2005.

Spence, Jonathan D. *The Search for Modern China*. 3rd ed. New York: Norton, 2012.

1

Alopen and the First Christian in China

CHINA BOASTS OF FERTILE soil in many ways. The geography, history, and culture vary brilliantly and colorfully. The arrival of the gospel through foreign missionaries would certainly transform and enrich Chinese civilization. From ancient times, Christianity was also destined to be shaped by this people. Through centuries of excruciating effort, a tender indigenous church would be born in the land.

This chapter begins with a glimpse into ancient China, commenting on its rich culture and remarkable history before the arrival of Christianity. Next, we explore New Testament Christianity, with its designer DNA intended to multiply and mature around the world. Although the faith might have traveled from Palestine toward China in the first and second centuries, it instead eventually put down its roots in the Roman Empire. The second part of the chapter then turns to the momentous arrival of Christianity in the Chinese Empire during the Tang Dynasty in the seventh century as it tells the story of the Nestorian Christians and the first Christian in China.

BEFORE CHRISTIANITY ARRIVED IN CHINA

In the first century, the stage for the dramatic arrival of Christianity into China was being set. Under the influence of the Apostle Paul, Christianity emerged as an indomitable missionary faith, while under the administration of the great Han Dynasty emperors, China enjoyed a golden age. The meeting of China and Christianity was inevitable.

History and Culture of China

Long before the arrival of the gospel, the story of China was one of the longest, most complex, and most fascinating stories in the world. Chinese people, steeped in thousands of years of Chinese language, culture, and their own worldview, would inevitably understand the message of the Christian gospel only through their own unique cultural lenses. The arrival of the Christian gospel in China was a pivotal moment because the gospel enriched an already vibrant culture. Missionaries tapped into deep cultural forms when, for instance, they translated the Greek word *Logos* into Chinese as *Tao*, such as in John 1:1, "In the beginning was the Word (*Logos, Tao*), and the Word was with God, and the Word was God." (太初有道，道與神同在，道就是神。) Claiming that the Tao had become incarnate in Jesus, the missionaries suggested a deep connection between China and the God of the Bible.

Chinese culture, philosophy, and religion is multilayered and complex, and the following information contains only a small sample of the rich fabric of Chinese civilization. The brief bullet points can only offer a hint of the immensity of cultural material available to the missionaries and Chinese Christians, hinting at the myriad potential points of contact between Chinese culture and Christianity. Just as Chinese Christians today must seek to contextualize their Christian faith, throughout history missionaries and Chinese Christians have had to wrestle with issues arising out of Chinese culture, philosophy, and religion.

- In China, political philosophy and organization varied over time, but there are some elements that might be considered foundational and somewhat consistent. During much of Chinese history, authority was centralized in the Son of Heaven, the Emperor, and the organizing ideology was Confucianism. Of course, Confucianism itself is diverse and often contested, but it also to some degree offered a shared sense of purpose. (*Does Christianity undermine or enhance that shared sense of purpose?*)

- Family morality, or filial piety (*xiao*孝), was the linchpin to the Chinese system. It held the whole system together under a strict hierarchy. The hierarchy included, for instance, age over youth and male over female. The three bonds consist of loyalty on the part of subject to the ruler, the filial obedience on the part of son to father, and chastity on the part of wives to husbands (but not husbands to wives). (*In what ways are Chinese ideals of filial piety consistent with biblical teaching?*)

- The religious world of China has always been diverse and complex. Confucius (551–479 BCE) was not the first in the so-called Confucian tradition, but he did have profound impact. Mencius (372–289 BCE) also provided a rich contribution. Key ideas included "*li*" (禮) (proper behavior according to status) and humanism. Taoism also developed a rich tradition, and Tao can be translated "the path," or "the way." Tao, as mentioned, became the translation of the Greek word Logos, or Word, in John 1. "In the beginning was the Tao, and the Tao was with God, and the Tao was God." The Legalist school *fajia* (法家) provided a system of punishments and rewards that served to strengthen the state over the family. In cosmology, some additional key concepts included *Tian* (天) which is translated heaven, and *qi* (氣) which is sometimes translated pneuma, ether, or "life force." (*Do these ideas continue to animate Chinese culture and people in Modern China today? Can theologians incorporate these ideas into an orthodox Christian theology?*)

- Buddhism was brought to China from the outside, but it became Sinicized and considered part of Chinese culture. The great age of Buddhism in China was from the fifth to the ninth centuries, when it held wide appeal. As the practice of Buddhism became widespread, it was infused with many folk religious practices and beliefs. Buddhist millennial movements arose numerous times, sometimes fomenting large-scale rebellions, and these rebellions caused the Emperor and the central government to fear and often suppress grassroots religious movements. Both Buddhism and Taoism tended to be largely decentralized, and thus highly suspect to the centralized government. (*If the Christian church wants to contextualize itself in China, does it want to look like Buddhism? Would a highly contextualized Christianity become indistinguishable from indigenous folk religions?*)

These points are offered only to whet the appetite, and Chinese language, Chinese culture, Chinese religion, and Chinese philosophy were never static. There was constant change through eras of turbulence and violence as well as during the magnificent reigns of some of the great dynasties, such as the Han Dynasty, the Tang Dynasty, the Song Dynasty, the Ming Dynasty, and the Qing Dynasty. Further, there may have been even greater change after the fall of the dynastic imperial system in 1911 and the rise of the Chinese Communist Party in 1949. China provides endlessly rich and fertile subjects for research. Even today, Christianity has only begun to be translated adequately into Chinese culture.

New Testament Christianity

When the first non-Jewish people came to faith in Jesus Christ, it was not necessarily self-evident that they would not need to first convert to Judaism. Today, of course, we know that Gentile believers were not required to receive circumcision and follow Old Testament law, but there was a faction of Jewish Christians who insisted that the Gentiles should be circumcised and enter the Christian church through the door of Judaism.

Field Notes: On Gentile Believers

If this faction had won the day, then we can only guess what Gentile Christians might look like today. I imagine Christians from China, the United States, Africa, India, and all parts of the world would look something like the ultra-Orthodox Jewish people do today. We might all have full beards, long ringlets of curly hair flowing down the side of our cheeks, and a wonderful variety of unusual hats!

Paul, the Apostle to the Gentiles, opposed that faction and vigorously argued that Gentiles can enter the church without passing through the door of Judaism. In Romans 1:16–17, he stressed that God brings salvation to everyone who believes, first to the Jews, but then also to the Gentiles. In Acts 15, at the Jerusalem Council, Paul successfully argued that Gentile believers should be free from the Law, and of particular importance, he pointed out that the Gentile believers, just like the Jewish believers at Pentecost, had received the sign of the Holy Spirit.

Gentile Christians were permitted not only to maintain their own language, history, and culture, but even to celebrate it. They were not required to adopt the Hebrew language and the idiosyncratic features of Jewish culture. The Gentile believers were, on the one hand, called to speak prophetically against pagan practices and corrupt facets of their home culture, but they were also freed to become champions of the positive and virtuous characteristics, those which were in harmony with biblical principles, of their familiar and beloved traditions. When the Protestant missionaries arrived in China in the nineteenth century, their goal, properly understood, was never to "civilize" or "westernize" the people, but to empower the indigenous believers who had received the gift of the Holy Spirit to contextualize the Christian faith for themselves.

Christianity and China in the First and Second Centuries

China has often been a closed country, looking inward. At various times in history, however, China has also been open to contact with the outside world. What about during the apostolic age? Is it possible that Christianity could have entered China in the first century?

During the apostolic period, China was, in fact, tentatively looking toward the West. Around 128 B.C., the Han Emperor Wu-ti (武帝) established a route for trade with the areas as far away as the borders of Greco-Roman Syria. Commerce then prospered until about the time of the birth of Christ, but around AD 25, there was a short period of disunity and the Western regions of China splintered and the trade routes were closed. Thus, during the first few decades of the apostolic church, it would have been impossible for missionaries to travel over a land route to China from Roman or Persian Asia.

However, Emperor Ming-ti (明帝, AD 57–75) again consolidated China, pushing into Central Asia. By AD 87, caravan trade across Asia again prospered. There was a "Chinese Peace" of the East like the *Pax Romana* of the West. Trade flourished between the East and West, and yet Christian missionaries did not seem to have penetrated China.

The Silk Road was open, but the first historical record of Christian missionaries attempting to travel east to China was the Nestorians in the seventh century. There is credible evidence that St. Thomas did establish a church in India in the first century, but most historians agree that he did not make it as far as China.

Instead, Buddhist missionaries from India arrived in China. The White Horse monastery (白馬寺) in Luoyang might have been established as early as AD 65, just as Emperor Ming-ti was establishing the Chinese Peace. While historians are not sure about the earliest arrival of Buddhism in China, the historical records are clear that An Shih-kao (安世高) arrived in China by AD 148. While Christianity does not appear to have traveled along the Silk Route into China during the first and second centuries, Buddhism arrived and began to take root in China at about the same time that Christianity became settled in the Roman Empire.

NESTORIAN CHRISTIANITY IN THE TANG DYNASTY

The first documented arrival of Christian missionaries was in the seventh century. The Nestorian church raises several tricky theological and historical issues. The Nestorian church today is better known as the Assyrian Church of the East. They were declared heretical at the Council of Chalcedon in AD 451. Thus, they have existed outside of both the Roman Catholic Church and the Eastern Orthodox Church since that time. If they are a heretical group, should they be included in a course on Chinese church history? The narrative of the arrival in AD 635 of Christian missionaries from Persia into the Chinese capital, which was lost for centuries to history until redis-covered by the Roman Catholic missionaries in the sixteenth century, is a spellbinding tale, but is it part of the story of the church? While they have been officially considered heretical, in the past century many theologians and church historians have taken a fresh look at Nestorius, and the "Nesto-rian" church that has sometimes been labeled with his name.

Field Notes: On Teaching Church History in Taiwan

The first semester I taught at a seminary in Taiwan I was assigned to teach Church History. I had just completed my MDiv and ThM degrees at a seminary in the United States, and in my Church History class, we focused mostly on the developments in the church related to Western Christianity. As I was preparing my course, I wondered if the focus for students in Taiwan should be different. I did check the rest of the curricu-lum for my seminary, and I noticed that in addition to "Church History" students were also required to take a course called "Chinese Church His-tory." Thus, I decided that the "Church History" course was intended to fo-cus more on Western Christianity. Then, I wondered, why would Chinese students in Taiwan be required to learn Western Christianity at all? The answer, however, was obvious. The Chinese Protestant churches in China and Taiwan are an outgrowth of the Protestant missionary movements which trace their roots through the Evangelical revivals, the Reformation, and back to Augustine and the early church. When I taught my course that first semester, I taught it with tremendous confidence that students needed to learn this material.

Several semesters later I was asked to teach the "Chinese Church History" course. Familiar with the material the students had already learned in the "Church History" course, I began to think through what I should teach in Chinese Church History. As I began to prepare lectures on Nestorian Christianity of the Tang Dynasty, I became hesitant. In what way is Nestorian Christianity in China relevant to Chinese Protestants today? Since the church completely died out, is that church in any way related to Chinese Protestant Christianity today? If not, then why would a Chinese Christian want to know or study the story of the Nestorians?

> *My response is that if anybody came to saving faith in Jesus Christ during the Tang Dynasty, then that person is part of the universal church and a part of the history of the church. I enjoy suggesting to my Chinese students, who are aware that the Tang Dynasty (618–907) is my favorite era in Chinese history, that when I get to heaven, the first people I hope to meet are Chinese Christians from the Tang Dynasty!*

Today, some theologians would agree that perhaps Nestorius was not treated fairly during his lifetime or in the historical record. It was his Christology that was deemed heretical, but, in fact, the real opposition to him might have been political rather than theological. At that time in the fourth and fifth centuries, when the church was struggling to define the relationship between the full humanity and the full divinity of Jesus Christ, Nestorius offered a theological formulation that was declared heterodox, but, at least to some degree, might be understood as within the boundaries of the final orthodox formulation agreed upon at Chalcedon. Like all the church fathers before Nicaea and Chalcedon, Nestorius was searching to make the best sense of the biblical teachings, and perhaps Nestorian Christology could be considered orthodox, at least within the pre-Chalcedon timeframe.

In the context of Chinese church history, the critical question might be whether enough information of the gospel was presented by the Nestorian missionaries to the Chinese people during the Tang Dynasty. Research must still be completed and could be focused on three different phases of the mission. First, were Nestorius and his Christology orthodox? After his excommunication for heresy in 451, Nestorius was forced into exile and his writings were destroyed, and therefore much of his theology must be pieced together by reading the writings of his enemies. Second, was the church in Persia through the fifth to eighth centuries, which was eventually referred to as the "Nestorian Church," an orthodox church? Through those centuries, did the church hold to the same beliefs, did it veer away from orthodoxy, or, perhaps, did it become more orthodox? Finally, were the missionaries who traveled to India and then to China from Persia orthodox, and what was the message they preached? More specifically, was there enough information available from the gospel for a Chinese person in the seventh century to come to a saving faith in Jesus Christ? Today, Chinese Christian historians might be the best equipped to investigate these questions, particularly concerning the details of the message that was preached in China during the Tang Dynasty.

There is, of course, one Nestorian written document that is abundantly available. In fact, it is a gorgeous monument that is copied and posted in countless locations around the world: the Nestorian Tablet. The Nestorian Tablet was erected in AD 781 in the capital Chang'an (modern Xi'an) and, with an extensive text, it tells the story of the arrival of Christianity in China in AD 635. The limestone block is over 9 feet tall (279 cm) and since 1907, it has been in the Beilin Museum (碑林) in Xi'an.

The writing on the tablet is invaluable history, and the history of the large tablet itself is also marvelous. It was buried, probably in AD 845, during the religious suppression of that era. The tablet, and thus the story of Nestorian Christianity in China, was lost for centuries. It was only found again next to a Buddhist temple during the late Ming Dynasty around AD 1625, and originally upon discovery it was probably presumed to contain a Buddhist text. According to the account from a Jesuit missionary at that time, the area governor set the newly discovered tablet on a pedestal. Local intellectuals took an interest in the text and one Chinese scholar, who may have been a Catholic converted by the Jesuit missionary Matteo Ricci, recognized the content as Christian. The text was then published, and the Jesuit missionaries had an opportunity to read and eventually visit the tablet. They were astonished to learn there had been Christian missionaries in China in the Tang Dynasty. They prepared a Latin translation that soon made its way to Europe, and it was first published in French in 1628.

The story inscribed on the tablet tells us that Alopen arrived in China in AD 635. At that moment, and throughout much of the Tang Dynasty, China remained open to outside influences. Buddhists had been welcomed and invited to translate their sutras openly in China, and the Nestorians were also granted the same opportunity. They were allowed to translate the bible and to establish a church in China that persisted for several generations. The Tang Dynasty enjoyed a flourishing of Chinese culture and this might have been an ideal moment for the introduction of Christianity into China.

Field Notes: On the Need for Christian Scholars

If I have time during Chinese church history class, I like to take the students on the "world's shortest field trip." We walk on campus to view a copy of a rubbing of the Nestorian Tablet. When I am teaching the class with both Chinese and non-Chinese students, I enjoy giving the Chinese students an opportunity to translate the tablet for their classmates. The large characters at the top of the tablet are familiar and easy to translate, and my students enjoy the opportunity to show off! However, as they begin translating the very first line of the actual text of the document

> *they usually get stuck right away. The classical Chinese language and the Syriac and foreign influences on the text make it extremely difficult to decipher. The Chinese student serving as the translator invariably starts to laugh, and the Chinese students confess they cannot read anymore. I believe I accomplish three goals on this brief excursion. I get the students out of the classroom for a bit of fun, I succeed in getting them to look closely at one of the most important artifacts in Chinese Christianity, and I demonstrate the need for linguistically accomplished scholars to work on the diverse resources related to Chinese Christianity.*

Today, English translations of the Nestorian Tablet exist, and it is possible to make an examination of the content. Although it is probably impossible to assert with any certainty, based on the brief quotes below, I cautiously suggest that there seems to be enough information about the gospel in the short excerpts for a person to come to saving faith in Jesus Christ. For instance, examine this statement on the eternal Creator God:

> Behold the unchangeably true and invisible, who existed through all eternity without origin; the far-seeing perfect intelligence, whose mysterious existence is everlasting; operating on primordial substance he created the universe, being more excellent than all holy intelligences, inasmuch as he is the source of all that is honorable.[1]

In this next statement, there are several cardinal truths concerning the Trinity and the Incarnation:

> Thereupon, our Trinity being divided in nature, the illustrious and honorable Messiah, veiling his true dignity, appeared in the world as a man; angelic powers promulgated the glad tidings, a virgin gave birth to the Holy One in Syria . . .[2]

There is also reference to the New Testament, as well as baptism:

> Twenty-seven sacred books [the number in the New Testament] have been left, which disseminate intelligence by unfolding the original transforming principles. By the rule for admission, it is the custom to apply the water of baptism, to wash away all superficial show and to cleanse and purify the neophytes.[3]

---

1. Wylie, "Translation of the Nestorian Inscription," 11.
2. Wylie, "Translation of the Nestorian Inscription," 12.
3. Wylie, "Translation of the Nestorian Inscription," 12.

There is also reference to worship and the pursuit of holiness:

> . . . they fast, in order to perfect themselves by self-inspection; they submit to restraints, in order to strengthen themselves by silent watchfulness; seven times a day they have worship and praise for the benefit of the living and the dead; once in seven days they sacrifice, to cleanse the heart and return to purity.[4]

The text of the tablet does not identify the converts, but perhaps the information provided does indicate the likelihood of the conversion of the first Christian in China.

Unfortunately, under the leadership of a new emperor in AD 845, the Nestorian church was persecuted mercilessly. The target of the persecution was Buddhism, but apparently at that time Nestorian Christianity was often indistinguishable from Buddhism. Some historians suggest the Nestorian churches may have been over-contextualized, adopting too many Buddhist terms and symbols, and the Nestorians were thus persecuted together with the Buddhists. Further, it appears the Nestorians relied too heavily on the Imperial house for their presence in China, and when the government removed their favor, they were not able to survive.

The tablet itself also suggests another problem. At the time of its writing in AD 781, more than one hundred years after the arrival of Alopen, many of the names of church leaders listed appear to be foreign, not Chinese, suggesting that an indigenous Chinese leadership was not properly prepared. When the foreign leadership was eradicated from China, the Nestorian church collapsed, because they had not developed an indigenous Chinese clergy that could survive.

However, Buddhism did survive in China beyond this period of persecution. In contrast to Christianity, Buddhism became an established and indigenous part of Chinese culture during the open era of the Tang Dynasty. I find it striking that China might have become a Christian nation, a state that has a sanctioned church and recognizes a form of Christianity as its official religion, before Russia; the remarkable story of the conversion of Prince Vladimir and Russia does not occur until AD 988.

Christianity, nonetheless, did not disappear completely from the region. Significantly, the Nestorians survived on the borders of China, particularly among the Uighurs and the Mongols. When Roman Catholic missionaries arrived in China in the next era, during the Yuan Dynasty of the thirteenth century, they were surprised to find Nestorian Christians within the Chinese court. As we will see, after the Mongol conquest of

---

4. Wylie, "Translation of the Nestorian Inscription," 13.

China led by Genghis Khan, a small contingent of Nestorians were able to return to the Chinese capital. And, from this position of power, they were able to work to oppose the new Roman Catholic missionaries. We turn to that story in the next chapter.

BRIEF EXCURSUS REGARDING CHRISTIAN SCHOLARSHIP ON CHINESE CHRISTIANITY

In class I sometimes lightheartedly refer to this as my "rant."

Who, other than Jesus, is the greatest figure in the New Testament? While many people choose Paul, or Peter, or Mary, very few people think to name Luke. Nonetheless, Luke should not be overlooked. Of course, I love Paul because he was a missionary. But how much would we know of the ministry of Paul if not for the work of Luke? Luke, the historian, is the faithful researcher who meticulously gathered the information in order to write the Gospel of Luke and the Acts of the Apostles.

I believe scholars, including historians, can provide an invaluable service for the kingdom. For instance, to recover more detail of the story of the Nestorians during the Tang Dynasty would be a remarkable contribution to the church and our understanding of God and his kingdom. I especially encourage Chinese scholars to consider taking up this extraordinary challenge. In addition to proficiency in classical Chinese, a scholar would probably need to know Latin, Persian, Syriac, and several other Middle Eastern languages. Libraries and archives in China, as well as other parts of the world, will need to be carefully scoured for each small fragment of information. But the information may exist somewhere, and there might be a fascinating story to be recovered.

Over the last fifty years the church has grown so rapidly in so many places, and we also need researchers to document the events of this growth; I fear the story of these churches might be lost otherwise. Researchers, I am convinced, need to heed the call, like Luke, and record the stories. Alas, I do acknowledge that evangelists, missionaries, and church planters like Paul are a critical need for the church today, and I also acknowledge that we need many more evangelists than we do historians, but I do pray that there would be a small group of faithful and effective scholars preserving and publishing research to the glory of God.

REFLECTION QUESTIONS

1. I have Chinese friends who have wondered out loud why God waited so long to bring the gospel to China. Why didn't their grandparents, great-grandparents, or earlier ancestors have an opportunity to hear the gospel? How would you answer that question? (Why might God wait so many centuries for the gospel to take root in China?)

2. Why might some Chinese Christians hope to find evidence that Christianity entered China in the first century?

3. Why might Buddhism have become established during the Tang Dynasty in China, but not Christianity? Can we perceive the wisdom of God in this?

4. Is Nestorian Christianity part of the story of today's Chinese Protestant history? Explain your answer.

SUGGESTED READING FOR CHAPTER 1

Brashier, K. E. *Ancestral Memory in Early China*. Cambridge: Harvard University Asia Center, 2011.

Lewis, Mark Edward. *China's Cosmopolitan Empire: The Tang Dynasty*. Cambridge, MA: Belknap, 2009.

Ten Elshof, Gregg A. *Confucius for Christians: What an Ancient Chinese Worldview Can Teach Us about Life in Christ*. Grand Rapids: Eerdmans, 2015.

2

Marco Polo, Kublai Khan, and the Franciscan Friars

THE NAME MARCO POLO is familiar in the United States and in China, but his role in Chinese church history is not well known. His story was only possible in the volatile and fluid context of the thirteenth century, and only an improbable combination of historical factors allowed the Venetian Marco Polo to arrive in the court of Kublai Khan, the Mongolian emperor of the short-lived Yuan Dynasty. Kublai Khan invited Marco Polo to relay to the Pope an invitation for Christian missionaries from Europe to enter his kingdom. The arrival of the Franciscan monk John of Montecorvino in 1294 represented the second time Christianity entered China.

YUAN CHINA AND THE MONGOL EMPIRE

The Yuan Dynasty in China was an outgrowth of the great Mongol Empire (1206–1368), a vast empire unified and ruled by Genghis Khan which spread all the way from Roman Catholic Europe to Mongol-controlled China. During the Crusades, Europe and parts of the Middle East were locked in a centuries-long deadly conflict, often resulting only in a stalemate. Three civilizations were vying for supremacy, all three of which had roots in the ancient Roman Empire. The Roman Catholics in the West maintained an uneasy alliance with the Eastern Orthodox of the Byzantine Empire. Their common enemy was the Muslims, who occupied large swaths of territory formerly part of the Roman Empire. Islam stretched from northern Africa to Palestine, including Jerusalem, and into Persia.

Into that uneasy standoff among Western Catholicism, Eastern Orthodoxy, and the Muslim world, a fourth actor burst on the scene in the thirteenth century. Swarms of Mongolian horsemen swept across the continent with electrifying speed, gaining control of the Middle East, and spreading to the eastern borders of Germany. The expansive Mongol conquest occasioned the intermingling of numerous people groups, perhaps most notably the mass migration of the ethnic Turks. This particular people group was recruited into the Mongol armies, and they settled in Asia Minor, becoming the core of the Ottoman Empire by the fifteenth century. Throughout Asia, the Mongol Empire facilitated the rise of Islam, which accompanied the collapse of Asian Christianity. In China, both Islam and Buddhism were strengthened.

The Mongols' spectacular global conquest was short-lived, but its influence on China and the world was permanent. Ancient civilizations and people groups were brought into contact, and those connections created new opportunities for communication and travel. Thus, for instance, travelers from Venice could safely traverse all the way to China.

Genghis Khan died in 1227, and the Mongol Empire quickly fragmented. Kublai Khan, the grandson of Genghis Khan, grasped control in northern China and officially proclaimed the Yuan Dynasty in 1271. His territory eventually included most of present-day China, including Mongolia and Korea. The Yuan Dynasty, then, is both an imperial dynasty in Chinese history as well as the successor to the Mongol Empire.

The arrival of Kublai Khan in the Chinese capital reintroduced Persian, or Nestorian, Christianity into China. Kublai Khan's mother, Sorkaktani, was Nestorian. Although he had a Nestorian Christian mother, and was familiar with her faith, Kublai Khan never became Christian. In one intriguing incident, according to Marco Polo, one of Kublai Khan's cousins, Prince Naian, mounted a rebellion in 1287, fighting under a standard that bore the insignia of a Christian cross. (Prince Naian might be likened to the young Constantine, who also used Christian symbols as he began his consolidation of power in Rome in the fourth century.)

Kublai Khan suppressed the rebellion, but he refused to censure the Nestorians. When some people mocked the defeated Nestorians and the cross, Kublai apparently interceded, arguing that God would surely protect the "right," and that he, Kublai, therefore must be right. The cross should not be mocked, he argued, because the cross would not help the disloyal Prince Naian, but it would protect the righteous. Thus, he, Kublai Khan, was shown to be the righteous.

MARCO POLO AND THE POLO BROTHERS

The *Pax Mongolica*, or Mongolian Peace, brought Roman Catholicism to the doors of China. In 1260, the brothers Niccolò and Maffeo Polo sailed from Western Europe, through much of Asia, and then arrived in China. Once there, they found their way to the Court and Kublai Khan granted them an audience. According to some accounts, Kublai asked them to bring one hundred Christian missionaries from the West on their return trip to China.

In 1271, Marco Polo joined his father and uncle on their return to China when he was only seventeen years old. The Chinese may have thought that the Polos appeared in China out of nowhere, but there was in fact the wider global context that could explain their arrival. The Crusades, the rise of Venice as a major maritime power, and the establishment of the Mongolian empire all were part of the story.

Venice had emerged as a thriving port city during the Crusades, providing logistical assistance to the Crusaders and facilitating trade with the short-lived Crusader states in Palestine. Thanks to growing wealth and prestige, Venice, along with several other Italian city-states, began to build some of the most advanced ships in the world, and they amassed extensive knowledge of navigation. Therefore, during the Mongolian era, it was possible for them to travel with relative safety from Venice all the way to Yuan China.

Marco Polo remained in China from 1271 until 1295, and twenty-four years later he returned to Europe with many riches and fabulous stories of the great and ancient Empire located on the far side of the world. Through his stories and writings, Marco Polo became a key cultural ambassador between China and Western Europe. Unfortunately for missions and Christianity in China, apparently only two of the one hundred missionaries requested by Kublai Khan ever made it to China.

Field Notes: On The Importance of Readiness

The story serves as a solemn reminder to the church in all ages that it is of utmost importance to be prepared always to take advantage of opportunities for missions and the gospel. This instance appears to be a case where the church was not ready, and thus it missed the opportunity. When the Roman Catholic missionaries finally did arrive, Kublai Khan had already died. If those missionaries had been dispatched earlier, or if Kublai Khan had still been alive, perhaps the history of Roman Catholicism in China might have been different.

JOHN OF MONTECORVINO AND THE FRANCISCANS

In 1294, the Franciscan missionary John of Montecorvino (d.1328) arrived in China, but he did not arrive until shortly after the death of Kublai Khan, who died at seventy-eight years of age in February of 1294. Nonetheless, John of Montecorvino was permitted to remain in China. He established churches in several cities and quickly baptized six thousand Chinese converts. He translated the New Testament and the Psalms into the language of the Court, which may have been Mongolian.

John also purchased young Chinese boys in order to baptize them and then teach them Greek and Latin. While at first glance the purchase of young indigenous boys might not seem like an appropriate mission strategy, it is worth considering the broader context. In Yuan Dynasty China, the boys were probably children of impoverished families or they were orphans, and, likely, the cultural norm was for children in this situation to join the families of wealthy people. Therefore, the missionaries can be seen as merely carrying out a culturally appropriate practice.

John of Montecorvino was consistently hindered by the Nestorians who held high positions in the Mongol Court. The Nestorians who had been expelled from China at the end of the Tang Dynasty returned with the Mongols, and during the Yuan Dynasty they had more influence and status than they did during the Tang Dynasty. The Christian witness in China was divided, and a similar division between Roman Catholics and Protestants would arise with the arrival of Robert Morrison, the first Protestant missionary to China, in 1807.

At the time of John's death in 1328, he and his colleagues had seen approximately 100,000 Chinese people become adherents of the Roman Catholic Church in China, but again the church did not survive. The church all but disappeared with the rise of the Ming Dynasty in 1368, and when the Jesuits arrived around 1600 near the end of the Ming Dynasty, there were no remnants of either Nestorian or Roman Catholic Christianity.

CONCLUSION

The missionaries did build the church and minister to thousands of people, but the church did not survive. Even if the one hundred missionaries had arrived earlier, before the death of Kublai Khan, and converted the emperor himself, the church might not have survived the demise of the Yuan Dynasty. If the church is reliant on the favor of the emperor or the state, it remains vulnerable to regime changes. In the case of the Yuan Dynasty, the Mongol dynastic family was expelled and replaced by Zhu Yuanzhang (朱元璋), who established the new Ming Dynasty in 1368. He represented a popular xenophobic movement of Han Chinese people who resented Mongol rule, and they pressed for the revival of traditional Confucian civilization. Even if the Emperor Kublai Khan himself had converted, it is doubtful the church would have survived. Nonetheless, the Franciscan mission represented the second time Christianity entered China. During both the Tang Dynasty and the Yuan Dynasty there were opportunities for individual Chinese to respond the gospel message of Jesus Christ, no doubt providing a precious few with the gift of saving faith.

Field Notes: On Missions Strategy

In seminary classes, I enjoy discussing missions strategy. As will be seen in the next chapter, the Jesuits who arrived in China about two hundred years later targeted the emperor and the ruling elite. They reasoned that the conversion of the emperor, as the head of a Confucian hierarchical state and society, could convert the nation. Their thinking is logical and persuasive to many of my students, but this case study of Christianity during the Yuan Dynasty challenges the Jesuit approach.

REFLECTION QUESTIONS

1. If Kublai Khan had embraced Christianity, would that have helped or hurt the Christian churches in China? Would the new Ming Dynasty have preserved any traditions embraced during the Yuan?

2. Was the Yuan Dynasty a hospitable period for Christianity to enter China? Why or why not?

3. Would the conversion of the Emperor, in any period of Chinese history, generally help or hurt Christianity in China? Would it help China? Explain your answer.

SUGGESTED READING FOR CHAPTER 2

Polo, Marco. *The Travels of Marco Polo.* New York: Penguin, 1958.
Weatherford, Jack. *Genghis Khan and the Making of the Modern World.* New York: Three Rivers, 2004.

3

Matteo Ricci, the Jesuits, and the Emperor of China

> *who were from the gentry. Furthermore, Loyola and the Jesuits make a terrific story.*

THIS CHAPTER WILL LOOK first at Ignatius Loyola and the founding of the Jesuits, and then it will turn to the story of Matteo Ricci in China.

IGNATIUS LOYOLA

The story of Ignatius Loyola, the founder of the Jesuits, helps explain the paradox of this order. In fact, both of my views of the Jesuits were probably correct. The Jesuits were both zealous frontline soldiers of the Roman Catholic Reformation, and they were also pious missionaries who faithfully spanned the globe to expand the church.

Loyola was born in Spain in 1491. Thus, he was a contemporary of Martin Luther, who was born in Germany in 1483. Loyola became a soldier, and in 1521 he was wounded by a cannonball in battle, with his leg violently broken in two places. Without the use of anesthetics, doctors pressed his leg into a splint. (Although telling the gruesome story might make us squirm in uneasy pain, I think it is an integral piece to the unique character of the Jesuits.) Unfortunately, the bones did not heal properly, and the doctors needed to re-break the leg. (Whenever I tell this part of the story, listeners begin to wince.) The leg was still not set properly, and they needed to re-break the leg a second time.

Through this excruciating physical agony that lingered for more than one year, Loyola experienced a spiritual reformation. Unlike Luther in Germany, however, Loyola did not move away from the church during this spiritual reformation; rather, he reaffirmed his vow to maintain fidelity to the Pope in Rome.

While recuperating in the hospital, Loyola penned *Spiritual Exercises*, a classic book in church history and one of my personal favorite books on Christian spiritual formation. Although the theology behind the book is unmistakably Catholic, I find it singularly powerful, even for Protestant readers. With deep insights on spirituality, the book resonates with many Protestants in the way that it endeavors to cultivate a personal relationship between the Christian believer and God. The book provides insight into the way Ignatius Loyola and the Jesuits would challenge and change the status quo of Roman Catholic missions.

Spiritual Exercises is a manual for a mentor to lead a student on a spiritual retreat, a retreat that typically lasts 3 to 4 weeks, broken up into a series of exercises. The exercises include the extensive use of imagination.

Field Notes: On Spiritual Exercises

In history classes in the seminary, I have attempted to incorporate simple spiritual exercises inspired by those written by Ignatius Loyola to help my Protestant students get a feel for the spirituality of the Jesuits. For instance, I invite my students to close their eyes and imagine standing in a green field on a sunny day. (In class we only use a few minutes, but when practiced by the Jesuits, each small section of this exercise might last for an hour or more.)

I speak slowly and deliberately as invite them to picture a scene:

"Imagine a cross in the middle of the field . . . Now with that picture clearly in view, consider the form of Jesus on the cross with the sun shining over his head.

"See his stripes, and see the blood as it flows . . .

"After thinking through these images, next focus on the face of Jesus. And then look at his eyes, and see his love as he looks out . . .

"Hear Jesus as he asks you the following questions. Among a series of questions, he might ask, for instance, 'Do you know why I am here? Have you been faithful to me this week?

"Do you love me?'"

The deep spirituality in the *Spiritual Exercises*, I believe, contributed to the personal piety and spiritual vitality of Matteo Ricci.

After his recovery, Loyola went on to the University of Paris to pursue an MA degree in 1528. The story of Loyola gaining admittance at the University of Paris provides encouragement that God can use students who appear the least promising. When Loyola arrived at one of the greatest universities in the world, he had little to recommend himself as a student. He spoke French with a thick and apparently unappealing Spanish accent. He was small, balding, close to forty years old, and he walked with a horrible limp. He also lacked adequate finances, but the University apparently recognized his innate talent and admitted him.

During his studies, he met the eight men who would join him in the founding of the Society of Jesus (Jesuits). In 1540, they traveled to Rome where they were determined to offer themselves to the service of the Pope. They hoped to become missionaries in Jerusalem, but if they were unable to travel as missionaries, they were willing to obey whatever the Pope asked of them. Pope Paul III, a key figure of the Catholic Reformation (also known by Protestants as the "Counter-Reformation"), established the Jesuits in 1540 by papal bull, and in 1541, Ignatius Loyola was elected first Superior General of the order. Among their unique features, the Jesuits added a fourth vow. For centuries monastic movements had adopted three vows: poverty, chastity, and obedience, but the Jesuits also added a fourth vow: obedience to the Pope.

Since it was not possible to travel to Jerusalem at the time, the Jesuits cultivated three core ministries: promoting education, fighting heresy, and conducting missions. Coming out of the University of Paris, many of them were exceptionally intelligent and highly educated. Establishing schools became a priority, and many of the finest universities and educational centers around the world today were founded by the Jesuits. They also became the frontline forces of the Pope in attacking heresy around Europe in the sixteenth century. Therefore, my original impression of the Jesuits as the shock troops of the Roman Catholic persecution of the Protestants was partially correct. But there was far more to the Jesuits, especially in their desire to serve God and in their zeal for missions. In addition to Matteo Ricci, some of the great early Jesuit missionaries included Francis Xavier who went to Japan and Robert de Nobili who went to India.

THE JESUITS AND MISSIONS AND THE "FOURTH VOW"

The Jesuits in China were particularly adept at learning Chinese language and culture, and they were famous for their contextualization. They also bore the imprint of the Jesuits and Ignatius Loyola, Matteo Ricci especially. Not only did the Jesuits embody a deep spirituality, but they also, at least in the early decades, focused their efforts on a spiritual mission and ministry.

Why did the Jesuits add the fourth vow? It might appear that they were "hyper-Catholic" and overly zealous in their fight against heresy. That is, just as Luther and the Protestants were disavowing the Pope, it seemed that Loyola and the Jesuits countered by redoubling their oath of loyalty to the pontiff. But Andrew Ross, in *A Vision Betrayed*, offered an alternative perspective on the fourth vow. Ross provided the context of the fourth vow by first demonstrating the profound spirituality and piety of the early Jesuits. He revealed the powerful ethos of the new religious order. Missionaries like

Xavier and Ricci carried the charisma of the Jesuit order to many parts of the world, including China.

Examining the fourth vow specifically, Andrew Ross pointed out that in 1540, the year Loyola founded the Jesuits, missionary efforts were generally carried out under the direction of the King. Thus, the King of Spain or the King of Portugal directed the missionaries in the New World. Loyola envisioned a new paradigm, and he did not want the Jesuits to be a political arm of the nation and King. He desired a spiritual mission under the direction of the church and the Pope. Hence, the fourth vow arose from that desire. The Jesuits, I would argue, marked the inauguration of a new age in missions, with an emphasis on Christian ministry and spirituality. When Matteo Ricci arrived in China, he did not endeavor to establish a Spanish or Portuguese political or cultural colony; rather, with humility, he learned Chinese language and culture and wore the garb of the Chinese literati.

MATTEO RICCI AND CHINA

Matteo Ricci was born in 1552 in Macerata, Italy, and in 1561 became a student in a Jesuit school. Like many of the Jesuits, he endured extensive training and obtained an excellent education. In 1568, he traveled to Rome to study law, and then in 1573, he enrolled at a Jesuit college in Rome. He studied under Christopher Clavius, a renowned mathematician and astronomer in Europe. In 1578, he reached Goa, a Portuguese colony, where he served as a missionary and a teacher.

In 1582, he arrived in Macau, a Portuguese trading post on the southern edge of China. At that time, during the late Ming dynasty, the foreign missionaries were not permitted into the country. He began the arduous task of learning the Chinese language and culture, eventually becoming a leading Western Sinologist. He also began to seek opportunities to travel north into the heartland of China and then finally to Beijing, the home of the emperor.

Originally, he donned the clothing of Buddhist monks, but in 1594, after realizing that the Buddhist monks did not earn the same respect as the Chinese literati, he decided to adopt the clothing of the literati. Over several years, he successfully worked his way north, arriving in Nanjing in 1598, and in 1601, during the reign of the Wanli Emperor (萬曆帝), his patient persistence was rewarded as he was the first Westerner allowed to reside in Beijing.

Ricci himself provided six reasons for his acceptance in China. The first was his extraordinary ability to read and write Chinese. He translated foundational philosophical texts from Latin into Chinese, and from Chinese into Latin. Second, he exhibited an astonishing memory, which thrilled his friends and associates in China. I personally imagine that he would have been a very popular party guest in Beijing, as he was apparently a master at a particular party game. The host would bring out a large blank poster board, and the other guests would call out random Chinese characters that would be recorded on the board. After two or three hundred characters were carefully written out, Ricci would be asked to turn his back. The large poster would be positioned where the audience could see it, but Ricci could not, and he would then proceed to read, from memory the entire list of 300 characters from the first to the final character! Amazed, the partygoers would naturally applaud the remarkable gift of Ricci. As if that weren't astonishing enough, Ricci would then start from the final character on the list and read all 300 characters backward to the first character! I imagine many of those in the Chinese literati would eagerly attend a party featuring this European guest from afar.

Ricci identified a third reason for his acceptance in China: his knowledge of Western mathematics, a field which was new in China. Interestingly, scholars today are increasing their efforts to clarify the nature of the knowledge of mathematics in China before the arrival of Ricci and the Jesuits. Fourth, Ricci introduced curious objects such as three-dimensional paintings, glass prisms, and clocks. The objects enchanted the emperor, as well as many other people.

These clever gifts served as an effective missionary strategy. Perhaps the clocks even provided a reason why the Jesuits were able to stay in China long-term. After presenting the emperor with the gift of European-made clocks, the Imperial house hired the Jesuits to maintain the clocks, thus requiring the Jesuits' continued presence. They were the only ones who knew how to wind and to maintain the instruments.

The Chinese accepted Ricci for a fifth reason, he claimed, and it was for his talents as an alchemist. The sixth and final reason was the doctrines that he presented. However, he did admit that the majority of the Chinese were not particularly interested in his Christian teaching. In spite of this, he did establish a church. The men known as the "three pillars" of the Chinese Roman Catholic church were: Xu Guangqi (徐光啟, 1562–1633), Li Zhizao (李之藻, 1565–1630), and Yang Tingyun (楊廷筠, 1562–1627). These men were all literati of tremendous learning and influence.

Matteo Ricci was fifty-seven years old when he died in 1610. At that time, foreigners who died in China were required to be buried in Macau, but a request was made for a special burial plot in Beijing. The Wanli Emperor granted the request, and visitors today can view Ricci's tomb in the Xicheng District of Beijing.

THE JESUITS IN CHINA

The Jesuits' missionary objective centered around the conversion of the emperor. Noting the hierarchical nature of Confucianism in China, the Jesuits were convinced that if the emperor were converted, the Chinese people would follow. As men of high intelligence and impeccable education and training, the Jesuits were particularly suited to reaching the intelligentsia in Beijing and the educated gentry around China.

Matteo Ricci died in 1610, but the number of missionaries in China continued to grow. By 1680, there were approximately thirty to forty missionaries in China. During the 1630s, Franciscans, Dominicans, and Augustinians also arrived in China. The Ming Dynasty itself fell in 1644 to the Manchus, and it was replaced by the Qing Dynasty. By the 1690s, the number of missionaries had doubled again.

The new arrivals often disagreed with the Jesuits' missionary objective. The Franciscans, in particular, desired to serve among the poor as they endeavored to follow in the footsteps of the great St. Francis of Assisi. They hoped to aid those who were most helpless in China.

Field Notes: On Missions Strategy

Even today, we might ask if the best strategy to reach China is to first convert the emperor. In my Chinese Church History classes, I find my students initially tend to agree with the emphasis of Ricci and the Jesuits. However, when we examine the alternative model of the Franciscans, some students realize they prefer placing a priority on serving the poor and the people who most need help. There is always lively discussion.

THE RITES CONTROVERSY

In 1692, just as the Jesuits and other missionaries in China were achieving some success, an extraordinary development occurred during the lengthy reign of the great Emperor Kangxi (康熙帝, r. 1661–1722). Christianity during the early years of the Qing Dynasty, at least for a time, was made legal in China. The Emperor Kangxi offered an edict of toleration for Christianity. In the edict, Kangxi indicated an openness to the missionary efforts in China.

In part, the remarkable edict reads:

> The Europeans are very quiet; they do not excite any disturbances in the provinces, they do no harm to anyone, they commit no crimes, and their doctrine has nothing in common with that of the false sects in the empire, nor has it any tendency to excite sedition . . . We decide therefore that all temples dedicated to the Lord of heaven [i.e., the Christian God] in whatever place they may be found, ought to be preserved, and that it may be permitted to all who wish to worship this God to enter these temples, offer him incense, and perform the ceremonies practised according to ancient custom by the Christians. Therefore let no one henceforth offer them any opposition.[1]

By this edict of Emperor Kangxi in 1692, Christianity was legalized in China. Perhaps Kangxi, the emperor himself, was close to coming to Christian faith, but the open period was short-lived. The Rites Controversy, which was in progress, soon changed the mind of the emperor.

The Jesuits were famous for their accommodation of Chinese culture, and the early Jesuits believed Chinese Catholics should be encouraged to worship, or venerate, their ancestors as part of Christian worship. However, by the 1630s, the Jesuits were not the only European missionaries in China. The Franciscans, Dominicans, and Augustinians opposed Jesuit accommodation. They argued that the ancestor rites were a form of idolatry and insisted that the traditions should be prohibited in the Catholic Church. Both sides appealed to the Pope for a final determination.

The Pope could have issued a "final" decision, at least in theory, but, in fact, the Pope was placed in a difficult situation. How was the European pontiff to know the cultural and spiritual significance of ancestor practices in China? Naturally, he had to rely on information from the Catholic missionaries, resulting in a controversy that lingered for years.

The Jesuits, on the one hand, would write a petition to the Pope explaining how the rites merely accommodated a cultural expression and did not involve idolatry. The Franciscans and Dominicans did not agree. They would therefore submit their own petition to the Pope. They provided new information contending that the rites were idolatry. With the snail's pace

---

1. Neill, *History of Christian Missions*, 189–90.

of communication between China and Rome, each correspondence might take months or years, and the popes vacillated.

Initially the Pope favored the Jesuits, and he allowed the practices. However, subsequent decrees agreed with the Franciscans and Dominicans, and the practices involving ancestors were banned as idolatry. The Jesuits, learning of the new decision, again sent a petition. In some cases, the Pope would yet again change the position of the church, causing the Franciscans and Dominicans to file a protest with the Pope once more. Although hard to imagine, the Rites Controversy, as it came to be known, dragged on for over one hundred years!

After that long time period, the final decision of the Pope, by declaration, ruled against the Jesuits. In 1704, during the reign of Emperor Kangxi, and twelve years after the edict of toleration in 1692, the Pope prohibited the practice of ancestor rites in the Catholic Church in China. A representative of the Pope arrived in Beijing in 1705, and in 1706, the Pope's representative met with Kangxi. Kangxi was stunned at the Pope's ignorance concerning Chinese customs and at the ineptness of the Pope's representative. He noted that the representative did not resemble the intelligent and fluent Jesuit missionaries. The fact that the Pope presumed to rule on the practices allowed for the Chinese Christians offended the emperor. Kangxi was convinced that the ancestor rites were simply a form of veneration, and he believed Chinese Christian converts could surely maintain Chinese culture and customs. Who, the emperor wondered, was the Pope to say otherwise?

Not surprisingly, after the Pope issued his final decision against the ancestor rites, the emperor promulgated his own proclamation. Less than thirty years earlier, in 1692, Kangxi had issued his edict of toleration, but in 1721, the long-serving Emperor reversed himself and issued a new decree:

> Reading this proclamation, I have concluded that the Westerners are petty indeed. It is impossible to reason with them because they do not understand larger issues as we understand them in China. There is not a single Westerner versed in Chinese works, and their remarks are often incredible and ridiculous. To judge from this proclamation, their religion is no different from other small, bigoted sects of Buddhism or Taoism. I have never seen a document which contains so much nonsense. From now on, Westerners should not be allowed to preach in China, to avoid further trouble.[2]

Perhaps an opportunity for the conversion of the emperor of China was lost, and the European Pope might be criticized for making this definitive

---

2. Li, *China in Transition*, 22.

ruling with a limited knowledge of Chinese language and culture. The final decision of the Pope in 1704 did stand for over two centuries, but the decision was again revisited in the 1930s. At that time, the Jesuit view of accommodation was ascendant again. Protestants would generally proscribe ancestor practices in the Chinese Protestant churches, but throughout history, they have sometimes adopted various accommodations for Chinese traditional practices. As in the Catholic Church, the issue of Chinese ancestor rites has been contentious in the Protestant churches.

The root cause for the contradictory views on the adoption of ancestor practices might be better understood by contemplating the conflicting goals of the Catholic missionaries. None of the missionaries possessed an insider understanding of Chinese culture and ancestor rites, so they had to rely on their Chinese cultural informants. The Jesuits who were endeavoring to convert the emperor and the Imperial house naturally spoke to the literati, and those resulting views would likely be sophisticated and humanistic. They would tend to reject the folk beliefs of the uneducated masses, and they would assure the Jesuits that the Chinese ancestor practices were strictly a humanistic veneration and respect for family and parents. On the other hand, the Franciscans and Dominicans were working among the uneducated masses. Their cultural informants may well have insisted, based on their own experience, that ancestor practices were in fact religious. They comprised a central part of folk worship and folk practices, and thus they were idolatrous.

It would seem that the Pope's decision against Jesuit accommodation of ancestor practices damaged the growth of Roman Catholicism in China. Shortly after the 1721 decree from Kangxi, the new Emperor Yongzheng (雍正帝, r. 1723–1735) went one step further, declaring Christianity illegal (*xiejiao* 邪教) in China in 1724. Christianity would consequently be illegal in China from 1724 until the 1840s.

CONCLUSION

The Jesuits, the soldier-saints, were not only embroiled in conflict with Rome in China, but also, it turns out, in many parts of the world as well. In 1773, after years of controversy, the Pope ordered the Jesuits to dissolve. Although the Jesuits vowed obedience to the Pope by their fourth vow, they also passionately desired to follow the guidance of God himself, a trait that was instilled in them generation after generation from Loyola's *Spiritual Exercises*. Jesuit missionaries, inspired by their own calling and personal sense of right and wrong, were often a thorn in the Pope's side. After their dissolution in 1773, the Jesuits continued underground. The small band of Jesuits remaining secretly in China indeed found themselves in a tenuous position: they were both disavowed by the Pope in Rome and at the same time declared illegal by the emperor in China.

After several decades, the Jesuits regained their official status in the Roman Catholic Church in 1814. The Society of Jesus continues to be a significant force in the Roman Catholic Church to the present day. As of the 2010s, the Jesuits numbered over 16,000 members globally. In China, the underground Roman Catholic Church survived despite being declared illegal. In the early 1700s, there were about 200,000 Catholics. By the middle 1700s, the number had decreased to around 150,000 Catholics. And by the early 1800s, before Christianity was declared legal again, there were perhaps 200,000 Catholics once more.

Christianity survived, but the emperor never did convert to Christianity. Christianity was illegal when Robert Morrison arrived in 1807, but in the 1840s, Christianity was again declared legal. We turn to that story.

REFLECTION QUESTIONS

1. What is a society or culture? (Consider this definition: A society or culture is founded on a body of traditions accepted by all its members. These traditions become rooted in history, and they are an inherent part of social behavior, ways of thinking and feeling, and even language.)

2. What were the shared traditions in late Ming China? What were the shared traditions of the European missionaries? What would happen when these two traditions were brought into contact with one another?

3. What is the best strategy to convert a people group? To convert Chinese people? Is it better to first convert the emperor and the elite? Or should reaching the masses be prioritized?

4. When is the best time to reach a country—when the shared traditions are "working," or when the people perceive weakness in their traditions and culture?

SUGGESTED READING FOR CHAPTER 3

Batchelor, Robert K. *London: The Seldon Map and the Making of a Global City, 1549–1689*. Chicago: University of Chicago Press, 2014.

Brockey, Liam Matthew. *Journey to the East: The Jesuit Mission to China, 1579–1724*. Cambridge, MA: Belknap, 2007.

Ganss, George E., ed. *Ignatius of Loyola: The Spiritual Exercises and Selected Works*. New York: Paulist, 1991.

Mungello, D. E. *The Great Encounter of China and the West, 1500–1800*. New York: Rowman & Littlefield, 2009.

O'Mally, John W. *The First Jesuits*. Cambridge: Harvard University Press, 1993.

Ricci, Matteo. *On Friendship: One Hundred Maxims for a Chinese Prince*. Translated by Timothy Billings. New York: Columbia University Press, 2009.

———. *The True Meaning of the Lord of Heaven (T'ien-Chu Shih-I)*. Translated by Douglas Lancashire and Peter Kuo-chen Hu. St. Louis: Institute of Jesuit Sources, 1985.

Ross, Andrew. *A Vision Betrayed: The Jesuits in Japan and China, 1542–1742*. Maryknoll, NY: Orbis, 1994.

Spence, Jonathan D. *The Memory Palace of Matteo Ricci*. New York: Penguin, 1983.

PART TWO

Protestant Missions and Chinese Angst (1807–1900)

THE PACE OF CHINESE church history accelerated exponentially with the arrival of Robert Morrison in China in 1807. Within a one hundred year time span, despite political complications and seemingly insurmountable odds, the Protestant evangelical church had taken root in Chinese soil.

In 1800, the evangelical churches in Great Britain were experiencing red-hot revivals, and by 1900, just one hundred years later, those fires had been transported to China. Even as the fervor among evangelicals cooled in Great Britain after 1900, the zeal of the newly planted churches in China began to heat up.

Robert Morrison arrived alone in China; one man called by God determined to preach the gospel of Jesus. He did not land on the shores as part of a flotilla of military ships, nor did he command an organized movement of thousands of missionaries qualified to preach the gospel in a foreign culture. He did not know the language or the culture of China, and he probably did not comprehend the vastness of the land, but he knew God, and he believed the gospel could transform the empire.

Two stories should be told of nineteenth-century Christianity in China. The missionaries, on the one hand, constructed a massive infrastructure of churches, schools, and hospitals that transformed the landscape in China. During those same years, a delicate, small indigenous Chinese church was born. In many cases, the Chinese Christians participated in building the impressive Christian institutions, but the real story revolved around the spark of life implanted in the believers. That life, in the twentieth century, could not be extinguished by the violent Boxer uprising of 1900, the ardent

33

intellectual assaults during the anti-Christian movement of the 1920s, or the dismantling of the missionary infrastructure after 1949.

The dramatic, but mostly invisible, growth of indigenous Christianity in China between 1807 and 1900 might be likened to the first century of Christian history. The Holy Spirit arrived at Pentecost among a small group of Jewish people, an unremarkable ethnic and religious minority living on the outer fringe of the mighty Roman Empire. Within a few short years of the birth of the church, the Apostle Paul, arguing for Gentile acceptance into the church, noted that like the Jewish believers at Pentecost, the Gentiles had also received the Holy Spirit. The Holy Spirit did not recognize ethnic boundaries, but filled and empowered people who embraced the new birth in Jesus Christ. Within one hundred years, even as Christian growth stagnated among the Jews, the spiritual fires that filled and animated the apostles and the early Jewish believers had been transported to the Gentile church. Christianity was still largely unknown in the Roman Empire, and barely a concern of the emperor, but the church was established. In the same way, the fragile Western missionary presence in China had, by 1900, successfully planted an indigenous Chinese church.

Robert Morrison and the missionaries who followed him to China could not have overestimated the difficulty of the task that faced them. A relentless series of tumultuous episodes marked the nineteenth century in China. Beginning with the agonizing Opium Wars in the 1830s, continuing with the deadly Taiping Rebellion in the middle of the century, and culminating with the Boxer uprising of 1900, China underwent painful transformation. The story of missions and Christianity revolved around these swirling events.

Part Two, the years from 1807 to 1900, is subdivided into three time periods. For each period, I look first at the missionary efforts in the field, and then I examine a representative Chinese response. At each point, it seemed that the missionaries became more deeply entangled in the inexorable crises of China, and Christianity itself became more suspect by the majority of the Chinese people. The missionaries made extraordinary sacrifices and, by and large, exhibited unimpeachable personal piety. They achieved innumerable accomplishments in China, and yet most Chinese could not differentiate the acts of the missionaries from increasingly aggressive actions of Great Britain.

We can easily misunderstand the story of missions in China during the nineteenth century. In Chinese historiography, the missionaries have often been considered indistinguishable from the British imperialists, and in Western history they have been derided as flagrant examples of aggressive and malignant Western imperialism. In fact, however, a careful examination of the evidence suggests the missionaries bore a deep compassion for China, and they desired what was best for China's people. Unfortunately, they faced an unending series of impossible choices in nineteenth-century China. It might seem they chose wrongly in many cases, leading to innumerable misunderstandings and bad outcomes, but perhaps no better options existed. Nonetheless, throughout the drama of the nineteenth century, a small Chinese church continued to form on Chinese soil.

SUGGESTED READING FOR PART TWO

Laamann, Lars Peter. *Christian Heretics in Late Imperial China*. New York: Routledge, 2006.

Menegon, Eugenio. *Ancestors, Virgins, and Friars: Christianity as a Local Religion in Late Imperial China*. Cambridge: Harvard University Asia Center, 2009.

Mungello, D.E. *The Catholic Invasion of China: Remaking Chinese Christianity*. New York: Rowman & Littlefield, 2015.

4

Robert Morrison, the British, and Liang Fa

ROBERT MORRISON: FROM ENGLAND TO CHINA

ROBERT MORRISON WAS BORN in England in 1782, at a moment when the world was on the precipice of radical transformation. Robert Morrison was ten years old when William Carey, the "Father of Modern Missions," penned his classic missions volume prodding England into global missions. In this treatise, sometimes simply referred to as *An Inquiry*, William Carey pressed the case that if British imperialists and merchants could risk their lives to travel the world in pursuit of wealth, how much more should the disciples of Jesus Christ take the gospel to all places? After publishing this book in 1792, William Carey himself served as a missionary in India from 1794 to 1834. Carey profoundly impacted missions in India, but his utmost contribution lay in sparking Protestant missions from the English-speaking world to China and all peoples.

In the aftermath of the series of British revivals in the eighteenth century led by evangelists such as John Wesley and George Whitefield, many evangelical Christians responded to the missionary call of William Carey. By 1800, Britain was in the midst of an economic resurgence and on the verge of becoming the most powerful nation in the world. Robert Morrison responded to that call to missionary service. In 1798, at sixteen years old, he joined the Presbyterian Church, and in 1802 he began preparation for missionary work. He joined the London Missionary Society in 1804, and in 1807, at twenty-five years old, he was ordained for ministry and sailed for China.

Field Notes: On Appreciating the Cultural Gap

In class, I try to help students comprehend the immense gap in culture and understanding between the British missionaries and the Chinese people in the nineteenth century. One way to visualize the gap is to view photos from the time. For instance, one picture of Robert Morrison shows a man who looks traditionally British and self-confident. He is dressed sharply in a tailored, dark colored, Western suit with a high collar. A picture from the same era of the Jiaqing Emperor (嘉慶帝, 1760–1820) is dramatically different! In one portrait, the emperor is seen as a dignified ruler wearing long, flowing, ceremonial yellow robes. In other photos, common Chinese people of the period are pictured, dressed in long robes and traditional Chinese vests. On the one hand, we consider Robert Morrison, who was steeped in British culture and convinced he must preach the gospel to all peoples, and on the other, we consider the Chinese, who were a vast and powerful people with an enduring culture who felt little need for any message or support from the outside world. I ask students to consider the potential for misunderstanding among these various peoples, especially when they first make contact.

THE DECLINE OF THE QING DYNASTY

In 1800, Great Britain and China may have already been on an inevitable path towards a deadly clash. According to the British worldview, all nations were equal, and Great Britain grew determined to force open the door of China and to establish a system of trade. China, conversely, looked inward, and they only viewed the British as nothing more than one of the many insignificant tributary nations which it customarily treated with disdain. Furthermore, historians have noted that even when discounting the arrival of the British around 1800, China most likely faced a decline in the nineteenth century. Even as the Qing Dynasty reached its apex in 1800, dark clouds on the horizon included the instability caused by massive population growth, the increasing scarcity of farmland that could be cultivated, the lack of industrialization, and the subjugation of women (seen, for instance, in the common custom of foot binding). The early Protestant missionaries endeavored to plant Christian churches in the midst of these volatile political, economic, and social tensions.

Chinese culturalism, a chauvinism that rejected new and foreign ideas, further exacerbated these tensions. While England reinvented itself through the industrial revolution, China refused to change. The relationship became even more strained through the nineteenth century as the British showed themselves superior to the Chinese not only militarily, but in many other ways as well.

Throughout the century, the Han Chinese became increasingly suspicious of the Manchu rulers of the Qing Dynasty. The Han Chinese believed the Manchu rulers to be the reason for China's weakness, and more and more Han Chinese began to advocate the overthrow of the Qing. The British and the missionaries surely aggravated the problems, but it would appear that China and the Qing Dynasty, even without the challenge from Britain, were headed for tragedy.

Robert Morrison arrived at this transitional moment. In 1807, Britain was poised to become the most powerful nation in the world. By contrast, China faced the commencement of a century long descent. The missionaries had little or nothing to do with the trajectories of the two nations; nonetheless, the story of missions in China in the nineteenth century would unavoidably play out in the context of that drama.

ROBERT MORRISON AND
PROTESTANT MISSIONS IN CHINA

Many people are familiar with the story of Robert Morrison's arrival in China on September 4, 1807. As Morrison disembarked at the harbor in China, an American businessman looked at him with a smirk, and, with some contempt, asked him, "Now Mr. Morrison do you really expect that you will make an impression on the idolatry of the Chinese Empire?"
"No sir," said Morrison, "but I expect that God will."

Field Notes: On Hearing from a Chinese Christian

I had always loved this story, and I had heard it many times before, but I gained a new perspective on it several years ago. I heard the story from a Chinese Christian, and, coming from the lips of a Chinese believer in Jesus, it made Morrison's celebrated response all the more prophetic and

> *powerful. And indeed, while the American businessman is forgotten, God is making an impression on China through the Chinese Christians who continue to tell and re-tell this story today.*

Settling in Macau, a tiny Western outpost on the far southern outskirts of China, Robert Morrison considered what he might do first. His first steps would establish several patterns for nineteenth-century missions in China, and so they should be carefully examined and understood.

Christianity had been considered an illegal sect for decades. The East India Company, a dominant force in Macau, did not welcome missionaries, as the missionaries tended to interfere with their business interests. For this reason, Morrison had been unable to sail to China on a British ship; rather, he had been forced to journey first to America and then to China on an American ship. In sum, neither the Chinese nor the local foreign community welcomed Robert Morrison. In 1809, two pivotal events occurred, for Morrison personally and for the long-term missionary endeavor in China.

First, Morrison secured a job with the title "The Office of Chinese Translator to the English Factory at Canton" for the East India Company. This position allowed Morrison to remain long term in a "closed country," providing him with a "platform." With no other viable options, this job seemed to be an ideal opportunity for Morrison. However, Morrison's decision to become involved with the British and commercial interests created repercussions. Although this first step of aligning with the trading and imperialist interests seemed innocuous, unintended and undesired consequences may have resulted for future missionaries in the decades to come.

Second, in 1809, Robert Morrison married Mary Morton. The arrival of Protestant missionaries in China introduced a new dynamic into Christian missions. Matteo Ricci, the great Jesuit missionary, had been single. When Martin Luther, breaking with Catholic practices, married Katharina von Bora in 1525, he set the pattern for marriage among the Protestant clergy. This held true for Protestant missionaries arriving with their spouses and children into China at that time. Missionary wives and children certainly added benefits on the missions field, but their presence also exposed the distinct cost of additional suffering and sacrifice.

In early 1810, Mary gave birth to a son, but he died shortly after. In 1812, they welcomed a daughter and in 1814, they added another son. However, these pregnancies caused Mary's health, which had always been poor in China, to decline further. She was forced to return to Britain in 1815, while Robert remained in China. She returned to China in 1820, and she was soon pregnant again. Tragically, in 1821, she fell critically ill, and both she and her unborn baby died. At first Morrison kept the other children with him, but by the beginning of 1822, he sent them back to England. Morrison only reunited with his children in 1823 when he returned to England for a furlough that lasted until 1826. While in England, he met and married Eliza Armstrong. Many of the missionaries and their families in China paid a high price for their service.

Morrison's work for the East India Company distracted from his Bible translation, which sometimes frustrated him. Nevertheless, he completed the New Testament translation into Chinese in 1813. In 1817, as an official interpreter, he received an assignment to accompany a British diplomatic delegation to Beijing. The following year, while still unable to begin a mission station or a church in China, he did establish the Anglo-Chinese College in Malacca on the coast of Malaysia, along with fellow missionary William Milne. The college had two purposes: to train future missionaries to China and to provide Christian training for young Chinese boys.

When considering the strict restrictions placed on Morrison, and when keeping in mind the establishment of the college in Malacca, one may surmise the background of the early Chinese Christian converts. For instance, they would not be from the north. They would probably not be from the elite. They would be from the far south of China, and they would most likely be from families of limited means. They would be people who, for one reason or another, would be interested in pursuing an education from foreigners in a foreign country. And those first converts, from this very particular background, did become the foundation for the Chinese Protestant church.

Meanwhile, Morrison completed the translation of the complete Bible in 1823, in cooperation with William Milne. Another major landmark occurred in 1830 with the arrival of Elijah Coleman Bridgman, the first American missionary to China. His entrance marked the beginning the long and special relationship between China and the American churches. While India enjoyed a special relationship with Great Britain, I have always felt that China and America enjoyed a unique relationship. From 1830 to 1951, thousands of American missionaries arrived on Chinese soil.

Field Notes: On China and America's Relationship

When I try to explain the reason for this special relationship between America and China, I joke with my students that Americans are interested in China because, at the very least, it is a country with a long and illustrious history of 5,000 years, while American history is embarrassingly short. At the same time, I suspect Chinese are fascinated by America because of its exceptionally brief 400 years of history. I point out to my students that it does seem easier to become an expert in American history!

Robert Morrison sacrificed tremendously and served faithfully, and he is rightfully remembered as the "Father of Protestant Missions in China." He was a prodigious linguist, producing translations and grammars that assisted missionaries for years to come, and his tireless service proved inspirational. He put numerous missionary patterns into effect, some of which will be discussed below and in future chapters. Morrison died in 1834.

LIANG FA AND THE CHINESE CHURCHES

Liang Fa (梁發) was born in 1787 in the south, near Guangzhou, matching the modest profile of many of the first believers. He did not have much education, but he did learn woodblock cutting. That skill would be greatly prized by the highly literate missionaries translating the Christian bible and hoping to publish evangelistic tracts. In 1815, Liang Fa accompanied William Milne to the Anglo-Chinese College in Malacca. There, while in Malacca, he was converted, and Milne baptized him. Together they produced the *Monthly Chinese Magazine*, a periodical that was printed for seven years. Liang Fa returned to China in 1819 at the age of thirty-three.

At the time of his return, Christianity was still illegal, and China did not allow missionaries to enter. Only those Christians who were Chinese Christian converts could enter. Liang Fa courageously began to distribute gospel tracts, and, not surprisingly, he was arrested and suffered thirty blows with a bamboo cane.

Field Notes: On Missions Strategy and Ethics

At this delicate moment in Chinese church history, what should Robert Morrison have done?

This case study provides content for fruitful discussion of missions strategy and ethics. Liang Fa was almost certainly the most vital asset to the Protestant missionaries at that moment. While the missionaries were still not allowed into China, a Chinese Christian could travel freely. Chinese Christians could speak the language natively, even as the missionaries continued to struggle with language learning. As a Chinese convert himself, Liang Fa would most likely have been most effective in evangelism. He was irreplaceable. Beyond that, he was an intimate colleague and probably a close friend. If it was within the power of the missionaries to assist Liang Fa, what should they have done?

If the missionaries enjoyed the proper social and political connections to intervene with the Chinese government, should they have spoken up and asked for help for a persecuted Chinese brother? In conversation, I find most of my students agree that Morrison should have provided whatever assistance he could. However, I occasionally have perceptive students who recognize the implications of this intervention. They recognize that Morrison, as early as 1820, was stumbling into a new direction for missions in China, and for the Chinese churches.

I believe that morally and ethically Robert Morrison had no choice. If he could have spoken up and relieved the suffering of Liang Fa, then he should have, because Liang Fa was an effective minister of the gospel in China and because he was both a Christian brother and a friend. Nonetheless, if Robert Morrison intervened, he would, possibly irrevocably, tie Christian missions with politics and political power.

Morrison intervened through his connections with the East India Company, and fortunately Liang Fa was released. Unfortunately, the die was cast, and political power was tied to missions.

Liang Fa then returned to Malacca, and after several years, traveled back to China in 1823. His skills in wood block cutting proved valuable as he helped print the first Chinese bible. The London Missionary Society (LMS) appointed him as a native evangelist, and in 1827, Robert Morrison ordained him as the first Chinese Protestant pastor in China. During those early years, he wrote numerous tracts, including his most famous tract entitled, "Good Words to Admonish the World" (*Quanshi liangyan* 勸世良言).

Liang Fa traveled extensively in Guangdong province, and he passed out thousands of tracts. The triennial civil service exams in China provided an opportunity to distribute evangelistic materials, and he, sometimes together with missionaries, passed out the pamphlets during the exam. Through his ministry, a number of the candidates were converted, and some of them became fellow workers. One man who received a tract outside of the exam center was Hong Xiuquan, later the founder of the Taiping Rebellion, who would use the writing as one of the Rebellion's foundational documents.

Liang Fa paid a high price for his fearless and faithful service. The Imperial edict against conversion of Chinese and the printing and distribution of Christian tracts was still in full force. In 1834, authorities apprehended a number of Liang Fa's colleagues. One of them endured a severe beating, and another suffered death. Careful inquiries revealed that Liang Fa was the leader of the evangelistic activities, and he fled. Eventually, he escaped to Singapore.

In the midst of his lifelong suffering and persecution, like many saints who were part of the "great cloud of witnesses," he contributed a weighty quote to church history: "I call to mind that all who preach the Gospel of our Lord Jesus must suffer persecution; and though I cannot equal the patience of Paul or Job, I desire to imitate the ancient saints, and keep my heart in peace."[1]

In 1839, Liang Fa, only fifty-two years old, returned from exile to China, and he continued steadfastly to proclaim the gospel. He pastored a small church of about thirty believers, and he also served as an assistant at the LMS Hospital in Guangzhou beginning in 1848. By the time of his death in 1855, the modest Protestant Christian work among the Chinese had been firmly established.

Liang Fa could only serve in China from 1839 until his death in 1855 because of a dramatic political shift. Over one hundred years earlier in 1724, Christianity had been declared an illegal sect by an imperial decree of Emperor Yongzheng (雍正帝), but by 1840 that decree was significantly modified. The Chinese Emperor, however, did not initiate the new religious regulations in 1840; this time the British forced China to accept the new freedoms for Christian missions and the Chinese churches.

REFLECTION QUESTIONS

1. Was China destined to experience transformation after 1800 even if the British and Western imperial powers (and Protestant missionaries) did not arrive on its shores?

2. What was the attitude in China toward Christianity even before the arrival of Robert Morrison and the Protestant missionaries?

3. How might the Chinese perceive Robert Morrison when he arrived in China in 1807? How might they perceive Protestant converts to Christianity?

---

1. Sunquist et al., *Dictionary of Asian Christianity*, 482.

4. What were the cultural and religious influences that shaped Robert Morrison and the other Protestant missionaries? How might those factors shape the development of the Protestant churches in China?

SUGGESTED READING FOR CHAPTER 4

Cook, Richard R. "Overcoming Missions Guilt: Robert Morrison, Liang Fa, and the Opium Wars." In *After Imperialism: Christian Identity in China and the Global Evangelical Movement*, edited by Richard R. Cook and David W. Pao, 35–45. Studies in Chinese Christianity. Eugene, OR: Pickwick Publications, 2011.

Daily, Christopher A. *Robert Morrison and the Protestant Plan for China*. Hong Kong: Hong Kong University Press, 2013.

Hancock, Christopher. *Robert Morrison and the Birth of Chinese Protestantism*. New York: T. & T. Clark, 2008.

5

The Opium Wars, the Taipings,
and Hong Xiuquan

THE OPIUM WARS OPENED a new era in Protestant Christianity in China. At the advent of the wars, Christianity remained a persecuted religion and China excluded missionaries from entering the country. After the First Opium War, five port cities were opened to missionaries by the terms of the treaty and, by the end of the Second Opium War, Christianity was legalized, and missionaries were permitted to penetrate the Chinese heartland.

Field Notes: On Perspective

In my classes on Chinese Church History, I suspect my Chinese students are keen to hear the perspective of an American historian on this topic. Having discussed the Opium Wars with perhaps hundreds of Chinese students over the years, my sense is that the Chinese Christians continue to harbor deep-seated feelings related to this period of history. Those emotions are likely an odd mixture of resentment toward the British, shame as a Chinese, and guilt as a Christian. I am persuaded that an honest reckoning of the era could be healthy for China and the Chinese churches even now in the twenty-first century. (We will return briefly to this theme in Chapter 16, on the present and future of Chinese Christianity.)

The intent in this chapter is not to defend the British, nor to condemn them. The goal is to accurately portray the volatile context of missions in

China between 1835 and 1865 and address some of the seemingly insoluble issues the missionaries faced during those decades. For instance:

- Do we prefer the tentative and unpredictable ministry of Robert Morrison and Liang Fa, or do we hope to see a strong and sympathetic political power come to the aid of the fragile young Chinese churches?

- Why were the missionaries involved in the negotiations of the "unequal treaties"? Is there any possible explanation that might justify their participation?

- Might God have put the missionaries in place in China "for such a time as this"? That is, if we grieve the suffering of Liang Fa and the Chinese Christians, and we hope for their vindication and acceptance in China, then maybe we must be sympathetic to any efforts the missionaries made to address the persecution of Christianity.

THE OPIUM WARS

The Opium Wars exposed the harsh reality of the simultaneous decline of China and the rise of the British Empire in the nineteenth century. The missionaries in China could do nothing about the crisscrossing trajectories of these two nations, and they could only attempt, as best they could, to influence the rapid succession of events at the margins.

The British considered trade restrictions as the core issue. British trade had been expanding through the early nineteenth century, and they desired greater access to Chinese raw materials and markets. However, as some historians have noted, the Confucian Chinese officials considered commercial activities to be harmful for their society, so they restricted trade. Trade with China could only be carried out through government approved agencies (*hongs* 公行). These severe limitations increasingly frustrated the British; they believed these limitations led to corruption and the widespread practice of bribery, and so they demanded printed tariff rules.

The trade restrictions comprised only part of the broader diplomatic problem. While the British expanded their presence around the globe, the Chinese emperor remained largely ignorant of the European nations' customs. In the area of diplomacy, he defaulted to treating all countries as tributary nations. The account of Lord McCartney's diplomatic mission to China in 1793 is informative, even though many of the oft-repeated details of the account might be apocryphal. The Qing emperor required Lord McCartney to kowtow at his feet, or so the story goes. He refused, insisting that a representative of her Majesty the Queen of England would not bow before anybody. As the two nations engaged in more regular contact, small incidents inevitably became more common. For instance, British gunners accidentally killed Chinese bystanders in a cannon salute, and China demanded that the guilty sailors be released to them. The British agreed very reluctantly, and an Englishman was finally executed by the Chinese.

Chinese restrictions on trade limited the goods that the British could introduce into China. That limitation created a tremendous trade imbalance that favored China and forced Britain to find a product the Chinese would purchase. That product was opium. With the rapid growth of the opium trade in the opening decades of the nineteenth century, the balance of trade reversed, and by the late 1830s, the balance of payments favored Britain for the first time. The demand for opium continued to grow as the problem of addiction in China increased.

Field Notes: On The Opium Trade

The British, as far as I can tell, have been demonized in China since that time. The British did trade opium, but did they intentionally promote opium addiction? This question appears to be a very sensitive one in China. Further, did the Western missionaries play any role in the trade? Even if they did not actively promote the traffic in opium, did their presence in China facilitate it? And if they chose to remain silent, are they guilty for not speaking against the practice?

Many years ago, I came across the argument that the British did not understand the addictive and pernicious properties of opium at that time. The British, according to the argument, did not think that opium was any more dangerous than alcohol. They did not believe that opium was a good product to sell, but it was surely not more harmful to try to sell it than to sell alcohol. It was only later generations who would discover opium to be singularly addictive and repugnant.

Initially, I was not persuaded by the thesis, as it sounded like a British justification to evade their responsibility. However, I eventually did become curious about the missionary role in the opium trade as I wondered why the missionaries did not speak against such an evil practice. Were they protecting British financial interests? Were they afraid to speak? Did they disregard the potential harm to the Chinese people?

In actuality, the missionaries often delighted in criticizing their home government. They spoke regularly and vigorously about British abuses against indigenous peoples around the world. This type of vehement protest occurred, for example, when they led the charge against the slave trade. Why, then, didn't they campaign against opium? I believe, for the first several decades of the trade, they were mistaken about the nature of the drug. The missionaries finally did speak up in opposition to the opium trade, but, unfortunately, that happened several decades later.

After the Opium Wars, the missionaries gradually recognized the insidious nature of the drug, but the British commercial interests stubbornly ignored their concerns. As they had done decades earlier in opposition to the slave trade, the missionaries mobilized themselves to gather the concrete data necessary to demonstrate the evil nature of opium. In 1890, at the Shanghai Missionary Conference, the missionaries organized the Permanent Committee for the Promotion of Anti-Opium Societies. As with many social causes, the missionaries worked on the cutting edge of the issue.

The missionaries became an increasingly vocal voice, issuing another clear condemnation twenty years later from the Edinburgh Missionary Conference of 1910. Once they were aware of the significant dangers, the missionaries did (belatedly) assume responsibility for speaking out. Unfortunately, their opposition seems to have been largely forgotten in China, and not even known by the Chinese Christians, at least among the Chinese students in my Chinese church history classes.

The growth of the trade imbalance and the social problems surrounding addiction in the 1830s pushed the Daoguang Emperor (道光帝) (r. 1820–50) to respond. He outlawed the opium trade, and he dispatched Commander Lin (Lin Zexu 林則徐, 1785–1850) to Guangzhou to enforce the order. Commander Lin demanded that the British traders hand over their stock of opium. The British refused for several weeks but eventually relinquished the opium. In a dramatic and public demonstration of power and audacity, Commander Lin had the opium washed into the sea, provoking not only the British traders but also the British government. Britain, having grown reliant upon the income, had to respond.

The merchants turned to the British government and demanded a war against China to win trading concessions. The government dispatched a small fleet of ships, financed by the traders, which was able to capture several cities along the coast of China. The emperor was forced to capitulate.

The Treaty of Nanjing, signed in 1842, required China to adopt several concessions. The British forced China to open an additional four "treaty ports" for foreign trade, including Xiamen (Amoy), Fuzhou, and Shanghai, in addition to the one already located in Guangzhou. Foreigners, including missionaries, could reside in the treaty ports. The Qing government was forced to pay reparations that included the costs of the war. Finally, the government ceded Hong Kong Island to the British Queen "in perpetuity."

Perhaps most importantly, clauses in the Treaty of Nanjing opened the door to "extraterritoriality," which exempted British subjects from the jurisdiction of Chinese law, and the idea of "most favored nations," assuring that Britain would receive any gains negotiated by other foreign powers. Contentions festered over the following years, and the relationship between Britain and China continued to deteriorate.

The five-treaty port era of missions in China was relatively short-lived, continuing for the twenty-five-year period from 1840 to 1865, but long-lasting missionary principles and practices formed in that time. The missionaries generally adopted a three-pronged approach to their ministry, initially undertaken in the port cities, and then throughout the entire empire after 1860. Evangelism and church planting took priority in the work. Second, the missionaries established schools and, over time, institutions of higher education. And third, they became involved in medical missions, establishing not only local clinics, but eventually world-class hospitals and medical schools. (Each of these ministries were successful, but, as discussed in other chapters, created unintended consequences.)

Field Notes: On The Missionary Role in Negotiating Treaties

The role of the missionaries in the negotiation of the Opium War treaties is a sensitive topic, and their involvement seems to have tarnished their reputation. The missionaries were recruited to serve as translators, and they actively contributed ideas to the conversations. Should missionaries have abstained from participation?

I believe there is a historic context for the missionaries' participation in the negotiations. Indeed, Robert Morrison began serving as a translator for the East India Company in 1809, creating a pattern for missionary involvement in trade and government. In classroom discussions, students usually agree that it was appropriate for Morrison to take that position, as it served as a "platform" and allowed him to remain in China. By 1842, the year of the negotiation and signing of the Nanjing Treaty, Robert Morrison had already died (in 1834 at the age of fifty-two), but his son John Robert Morrison, whom I affectionately call, "Morrison, Jr. (小馬禮遜)" in class, was on the translation team. Other missionaries were also involved, most notably the prominent German churchman, Karl Gützlaff.

> *As I explain the situation to my students in Chinese church history, the missionaries were "sitting at the negotiating table" among the people who were writing policy and law for China. Given that opportunity, should the missionaries have attempted to speak up for the Chinese Christians? Robert Morrison had intervened on behalf of Liang Fa when he was arrested and beaten with a bamboo cane. If the defense of persecuted Chinese Christians was justified at that time, were not the missionaries in 1842 also justified as they served as translators? Christianity had been illegal, and Christians such as Liang Fa were persecuted, but now the missionaries could press the British government to impose toleration for Christianity. If the most ethical choice for Morrison was to use all means necessary to protect Liang Fa, then was it also the most ethical choice for the missionaries to attempt to protect the Chinese Christians later in 1842?*
>
> *In my classes, students agonize over this dilemma. On the one hand, they can see that the missionaries must speak up. Given the opportunity, the missionaries should have pressed for fair treatment of Christian converts and advocated for a change in the laws so Christianity could be legalized. They should have endeavored to open not only the treaty ports, but also the entire land of China to missionary and evangelistic activity. On the other hand, students see the danger. When the missionaries became involved in the negotiations, they also implicated themselves with the worst aspects of the treaties.*

Like Morrison before them, the missionaries did speak up. Within the two treaties, they helped carve out legal protections for missions, Chinese Christians, and the Chinese churches. Not surprisingly, when the missionaries found their way to the cities, towns, and villages all over China, the local people could not easily distinguish between the hated British imperialists and these white Christian missionaries.

THE TAIPING REBELLION

In February of 1847, when Christianity was illegal and the missionaries were confined to the five port cities, a Chinese man traveled to the port city of Guangzhou to seek out a white missionary. There he met Issachar Roberts (羅孝全), an American Baptist missionary, a man who undoubtedly considered himself called by God to preach the gospel to the unreached people in China. The young Chinese visitor announced boldly to Rev. Roberts that he had personally seen the Heavenly Father, that he himself was God's "Chinese son" and the younger brother of Jesus, and that he was called to overthrow the Qing Dynasty. He was going to establish the Taiping Heavenly Kingdom (太平天國). Hong Xiuquan explained to Issachar Roberts that he desired to be baptized.

Field Notes: On A Unique Encounter

With my students, I sometimes muse on the dramatic scene. As I imagine the American missionary called and anointed by God standing face to face with the stranger claiming to be "God's Chinese Son," I cannot help but wonder who should seek baptism from whom?

The Taiping Rebellion, led by Hong Xiuquan (洪秀全), proved to be a tight knot of paradoxes and contradictions. The Taipings, a growing collection of people seeking to establish their own kingdom, embodied a massive movement that almost toppled the Qing Dynasty. For ten years, they conquered and controlled the southern half of China, and they managed to establish a capital in Nanjing. The battles and the general chaos cost the lives of 20 to 30 million Chinese people, according to the best estimates.

But who were the Taipings? Were they an indigenous Chinese movement? Were they an anti-Qing movement? Were they an anti-Manchu movement? Were they peculiar to the ethnic minority Hakka? Were they a Western-inspired movement? Were they a Christian-inspired movement? Alas, it seemed that they were all these things, at least in part. Their success suggested that they tapped into anxieties deeply felt among the people in China in the 1840s and 1850s.

At the time of the rebellion, Christianity was still illegal in China and the missionaries were confined to the treaty ports. Thus, Hong Xiuquan received no foreign assistance as he rapidly mobilized his religious converts, and he might be construed as the leader of the first mass movement to Christianity in the country. If he had succeeded, he perhaps would be remembered as the "Constantine" of the Chinese Empire.

Hong Xiuquan (1813–1864) was a colorful and complex character. Born to a well-to-do Hakka farmer in the northern part of Guangzhou, he received a good education. In 1828, he made his first attempt to pass the exam for the lowest civil service degree. (Throughout Chinese history, the exam system provided a kind of release valve for the pent-up ambitions of capable young men. With the population explosion during the Qing

Dynasty there were many more exam candidates, but the government bureaucracy had not grown at the same pace. Because of the glut of qualified candidates seeking the same number of positions, the system became more competitive and more corrupt.) Hong failed the exam. If Hong had been successful, Chinese history might have looked quite different.

In 1836, he attempted the exam a second time. Although Christianity was still illegal, missionaries would occasionally slip into China to conduct evangelistic ministry. Leaving the examination hall in 1836, Hong Xiuquan encountered the American missionary Edwin Stevens, along with a Chinese interpreter, preaching the Christian gospel. Hong listened to them and dialogued with them, and on the second day of the exam he accepted a set of nine Christian tracts. The tracts, entitled "Good Words to Exhort the Age," were authored by none other than Liang Fa. Apparently, Hong only glanced at the booklets and then stored them at home on his bookshelf. He again failed the exam.

The following year, in 1837, Hong made his third attempt. He failed again, but this time the disappointment overwhelmed him, which led to a nervous breakdown, and he had to be carried home. He remained in his room for over a month, lashing out at demons and entering deep trances. He finally awoke with memories of visions where he ascended into heaven. While in heaven, mysterious surgeons replaced all of his internal organs, and he was then led into a throne room where an old man in a black robe and golden beard handed him a sword. The old man instructed him to slay demons. He also witnessed the black robed man scolding the image of Confucius, who was made to confess his guilt.

Hong Xiuquan believed he had received divine authority to overthrow the Qing Dynasty and to rule China. Associates around him testified that he swelled visibly in physical stature and spoke with a new authority, changing from compliance and insecurity into a fiercely self-confident leader.

Six years later, in 1843, Hong sat for the exam for a fourth and final time. After failing, Hong made an angry vow to overthrow the Manchus, whom he believed controlled the examination process. Later that year Hong's cousin noticed the set of tracts on Hong's bookshelf, and he encouraged Hong to read the books.

Hong Xiuquan became convinced that the pamphlets written by Liang Fa corroborated his dreams from years earlier. The black robed figure was God, his father, and Jesus Christ was his older brother. Hong was God's "Chinese Son." As the younger brother, Hong believed he was sent to earth with the sword to quell "demons," that is, the foreigners. While a first guess might suppose the "foreigners" to be the British, Hong believed that he was called to rid China of the non-Han Chinese Manchus who were ruling China. He claimed that once he rid China of these *yao* (demons), the Chinese people could recover their original religion. The Han Chinese could again enjoy an age of *taiping* (great peace), and a new age of universal harmony and brotherhood would arise.

Hong began to preach his new ideology in his hometown, and he took to smashing the local Confucian tablets. The elders opposed him and eventually forced him to flee. Having fled from his home, he began a search for a base for his rebellion against the Qing Dynasty, and he also continued to develop his theology as well as his ideology of revolution. Eventually, with the help of Feng Yunshan, an early convert, he settled in the relative safety of the Mt. Thistle area. In 1846, the two men established the *Bai Shangdi Hui* (拜上帝會), or "God Worshippers," and by 1847, after Hong returned from his visit to Issachar Roberts, the movement grew to number two thousand converts.

At the outset of the movement, they were considered bandits and outlaws, but they stabilized and grew in the remote hilly areas. Eventually, they gained control of some villages, and then larger cities, winning further converts. They procured money and arms as they progressed. They successfully conquered large swathes of territory in the south, and in 1851, they declared that the Taiping Heavenly Kingdom had arrived. Having secured legitimacy by capturing Nanjing in 1853, they set up a rival government to the Qing in Beijing. Although they were thwarted when they attempted to conquer the north, they successfully held Nanjing for eleven years.

CHARACTERISTICS OF THE TAIPING MOVEMENT

Field Notes: On Studying the Taiping Movement

Although Taiping theology was unorthodox, Christian church leaders and the missionaries might find valuable insight from the movement, as it could shed light on what a successful mass church growth movement might look like in China. The Taiping movement provides a fascinating case study.

The Taipings achieved stunning success, and several factors have been suggested in explanation. First, they faced a very weak central government in Beijing, as the Qing government declined throughout the nineteenth century. A second reason included their solemnity toward religion or ideology.

They seem to have been sincere in their Old Testament-type Christianity. At least at the start of the movement, they were zealous believers. Third, they proposed an attractive political vision: the overthrow of the Qing Dynasty. Many Han Chinese were becoming more and more resentful of Manchu rule. Fourth, they created a cohesive social vision. Some historians have argued they were forerunners of the communist movement in China.

The Taiping leaders rose from the bottom of society, and they spoke forcefully against using opium, gambling, drinking, and engaging in sexual immorality. They endorsed gender equality, and they opposed foot binding and the taking of concubines. They also favored a land law that gave land to the peasants from the landowners, a principle some observers have suggested was a kind of early communism. However, these reforms were never fully implemented as the control of the Taiping government was never absolute.

The Taiping Rebellion finally failed in 1864, and historians have also discussed the reasons for their collapse. Internally, the movement experienced several weaknesses. First, most likely they committed tactical errors, and the possible error most debated involved whether they should have marched first on Beijing. As the Taiping armies prepared to capture Nanjing in 1853, they also considered bypassing Nanjing and approaching Beijing directly instead. Historians note that if they had moved north in 1853, they probably would have done so unopposed. They could have marched effortlessly into Beijing and captured the Forbidden City. But as it was, by the 1860s, the emperor and Qing forces had re-established themselves and were able to quash the rebellion.

Second, by the 1860s the top echelon of the movement began to experience growing division. The initial strict adherence to rules of morality had grown lax, and some of the leaders displayed open corruption by taking harems and living in luxury in Nanjing. Since the founding of the movement, its followers' goals, policies, and practices were based on Hong Xiuquan's dreams and prophecies, and his ongoing visions were also considered authoritative. In addition to Hong's revelations, other key advisors also boasted of prophetic visions. The prophecies of various leaders sometimes conflicted, and shrewd management was required to control the movement. By the 1860s, Hong was losing his ability to impose command over his top advisers. He was also becoming increasingly irrational and unstable.

Third, the Taipings began to lose support among the peasants as the political and social reforms proved unsuccessful. The promise of land had attracted them, but when those reforms were not carried out, the peasants' disenchantment grew. Finally, with its rapid growth, the Taipings had been forced to absorb into its government and into the movement many individuals and groups who did not share their beliefs. Most notably, and perhaps most controversially, they worked together with the Triads (三合會), secret societies that were often considered criminal. This cooperation, of course, created further disillusionment among the true believers.

Beyond the internal reasons which led to failure, external factors also contributed. The influence of the West and the involvement of the missionaries also played a role. Initially, the missionaries delighted to learn of a mass movement toward Christianity in the inland. A former British naval officer who volunteered his services to the Taipings offered this optimistic view of the Taiping movement:

> Neither shall I ever forget the noble, enlightened, and patriotic designs, which absorbed them: to propagate the Bible, to destroy idols, to expel the Tartars (Manchus) from China, and establish one complete and undivided native empire; to become brothers with the Christian nations of the West, and introduce European sciences and manufactures—seemed always their principle wish and determination.[1]

The missionaries and the British quickly reversed their opinion, however, as additional information about the movement and their heretical doctrines became known. Certainly, Hong Xiuquan provided the missionaries and the British diplomats with cause to oppose him. His behavior was increasingly erratic, and his beliefs could not be considered orthodox. However, there arose more cynical reasons to oppose him. Most importantly, the unequal treaties, which included extraterritoriality and the most favored nations clauses, had been signed by the Qing emperor. If a new government were to be installed in Beijing, the British and the other Western powers would have to negotiate new agreements. The British threw their support behind the Qing emperor, and most famously, the mercenary Charles "Chinese" Gordon (aka "Flash Gordon") led foreign troops against the Taiping armies on behalf of the Emperor.

The most vital reason for the ultimate suppression of the Taiping government in Nanjing, however, came through the successful reforms carried out by the Qing government in Beijing. The Emperor Tongzhi (同治帝, (r. 1861–1875) initiated the Tongzhi Restoration (同治中興), a reform movement that allowed the Qing to survive an additional fifty years. A key figure in the government reforms, as well as in leading an army to defeat the Taipings, was Zeng Guofan (曾國藩, 1811–1872), the commander of the Xiang Army (湘軍, or Hunan Army). Zeng Guofan exemplified what some have called an ideal Confucian, a government official who exhibited good morals and showed himself to be a talented scholar. He developed a

1. Lindley, *The Project Gutenberg EBook*, 75.

local militia based in his home province of Hunan in 1852. That militia was incorporated into the Hunan Army, an army that would ultimately display loyalty not to the Qing emperor, but to Zeng himself. Thus, Zeng represented both the traditional ideal of a Confucian scholar, while at the same time he developed a modern military base of local power.

CHRISTIAN INFLUENCES ON HONG XIUQUAN

Multiple sources undoubtedly inspired Hong Xiuquan, and scholars have struggled to identify his guiding influence. Some scholars have argued that Hong's ideology was indigenous to China and not unlike other religious millenarian rebellions, which were often Buddhist, throughout Chinese history. Other scholars have emphasized the Christian influence on the ideology of Hong Xiuquan, however. The writings of Liang Fa ranked first among his Christian sources. Unfortunately, Liang Fa's pamphlets, "Good Words to Exhort the Age," were somewhat vague and open to misinterpretation, and they were not intended to be a theological treatise. They were intended to be evangelistic and should not have been considered a correct resource for comprehensive Christian doctrine. Furthermore, and more significantly, Hong only adopted the ideas from the books that he liked, feeling free to disregard other parts of the writing.

The second source of Christian influence on Hong arose from his mysterious visit to the American Baptist missionary Issachar Roberts in 1847. After two months of visiting with Roberts in Guangzhou, Hong asked Roberts to baptize him. It appears that he might also have asked for long-term financial support. Hong claimed that if he did not receive support, he would need to return home. Roberts may have been concerned with Hong's urgency, and he decided to consult some of the other Chinese around him.

Field Notes: On Financial Support

As an American professor teaching Chinese students, I enjoy relating this story about Roberts and Hong Xiuquan to my students. Of course, as I share this story, I am aware that many of our students in the seminary need financial assistance and can relate to Hong's problem. (I also needed significant financial assistance to get through seminary!) I ask them to consider what Issachar Roberts' Chinese associates and students might surmise about the brilliant, but probably peculiar, Christian seeker. Should he be provided financial support?

Apparently, Roberts' Chinese associates confirmed his suspicion of Hong, and he therefore decided not only to delay Hong's baptism, but also to reject Hong's request for financial support.

With no ability to stay in Guangzhou, Hong returned home in 1847, only months before launching the Taiping Rebellion. There is no way to know how history might have turned out differently if Hong had remained longer with Issachar Roberts. The two months in Guangzhou comprised the only formal Christian training that Hong Xiuquan ever received. Up until the closing years of the Taiping Heavenly Kingdom, Hong seems to have come across Western missionaries only two times, first when he heard the preaching and picked up the tracts outside the examination center in about 1833, and then again when he studied under Roberts for two months in 1847.

The bible, translated into Chinese, added a third source of Christian influence on Hong. The Taiping version of the bible was published in 1853 in separate volumes, one for the Old Testament and one for the New Testament. There was no title given for the bible as a whole, just "Old Testament" and "New Testament." An analysis of the content of the Taiping Bible shows it to be almost identical with the Gützlaff translation completed in the 1840s.

The publication of the Chinese translation of the bible independent of the missionaries raises significant questions. The early Roman Catholics did not publish translations of the bible, and in fact, the brilliant linguist Matteo Ricci did not produce a complete translation of the bible. Providing a translation of the bible was not a priority in his ministry, nor was it a priority within Roman Catholic doctrine or practice. Martin Luther, by contrast, insisted on translating the bible into vernacular German at the outset of the Protestant Reformation. His belief in the perspicuity of Scripture, that the bible could be read and interpreted by all believers, became a central and enduring tenet of Protestant Christianity and Protestant missions.

For the Roman Catholics, any study of the bible was reserved primarily for the church and the clergy. In China, Roman Catholics were long skeptical of the Protestant efforts at translation, and the events of the Taiping Rebellion, including 20 to 30 million deaths, validated their criticism. A Catholic book published in 1909 provided this searing denunciation of the Protestants' view of bible translation:

> There can be no doubt that the indiscriminate circulation of the Bible, aided by the "inalienable right of private interpretation" thereof, is capable of producing the most disastrous material results. Of such nature was the Taiping Rebellion . . . We also

see in this movement the effect of distribution in the country of Bibles and Christian tracts.[2]

Field Notes: On Proper Use of Bible Translation

I ask students to discuss this quote, and I believe it is healthy for Protestant Christians to wrestle with this criticism of bible translation. Protestant missionaries should probably take caution when pursuing bible translation, a view that was eventually adopted by Hudson Taylor and the CIM. However, I disagree that the Protestants grant an "inalienable right of private interpretation" when they encourage private study of the bible in one's own language. Rather, Protestants should consider themselves subject to the community of interpretation. I would also challenge the assumption, as implied in the quotation, that the Roman Catholic Church or the Pope can completely protect the church from "disastrous material results." As with Protestantism, Roman Catholicism has struggled with many heresies, abuses, and disasters within the church.

Regardless, Hong Xiuquan did not simply adopt the bible as an authoritative source, but he felt free to edit the bible as he saw fit. Hong Xiuquan's response to an 1861 letter sent to him in Nanjing from the missionary Joseph Edkins yielded an astonishing document. In the original letter, Edkins, in fluent classical Chinese and beautiful calligraphy, attempted to address some of the theological errors associated with the Taiping movement. He provided several relevant quotes directly from the Scripture to back up his points.

Field Notes: On An Encounter with History

As a student of Chinese language and a missionary, I was fascinated to come across a copy of this letter several years ago. I marveled at the fluency and beauty of the writing of Joseph Edkins, and I enjoy showing it to my students. The document is a testament to the learning, linguistic sophistication, and orthodoxy of the Western missionary. However, it was what Hong Xiuquan did with Edkins' letter that makes this one of my favorite documents from Chinese church history! Although almost unthinkable, Hong Xiuquan, in red ink, added his "corrections" to the bible. I cannot

---

2. Wolferstan, *Catholic Church in China*, 105.

help but smile when I imagine the picture of the Taiping Emperor, God's "Chinese son," wielding his red pen and offering his suggestions to God.[3]

Where Hong disagreed with Edkins, including in several sections where Edkins simply quoted directly from the bible, Hong audaciously added his own edits. For example, when Hong read a Scripture quote referring to God's "only Son," he took his red pen, and, with a flourish, he actually drew a red line through the word "only." Hong Xiuquan was convinced that God had at least two sons!

Hong Xiuquan's own dreams provided his fourth source of inspiration. He believed the dreams provided confirmation of the content of the tracts written by Liang Fa. At the same time, the tracts verified that his dreams were reliable by way of circular reasoning.
Hong wrote:

> These books . . . are certainly sent purposely by heaven to me, to confirm the truth of my former experiences; if I had received the books without having gone through the sickness, I should not have dared to believe in them, and on my own account to oppose the customs of the whole world; if I had merely been sick but not also received the books, I should have had no further evidence as to the truth of my visions, which might also have been considered as mere productions of a diseased imagination.[4]

Hong Xiuquan also claimed the calling he received to conquer China and to return China to the Father's Heavenly Kingdom, was from his visions. He wrote:

> Father had ordained the Heavenly Kingdom to be in China; since China was originally the home of the Heavenly Kingdom. It is therefore also the home of Father. Before Father descended to the earth, China belonged to Father, and yet the barbarian devils stole into Father's Heavenly Kingdom. This is the reason Father decreed that I should come to destroy them.[5]

Hong Xiuquan died in 1864 along with the fall of the Taiping government. China had yet again missed the opportunity for the first Christian emperor of China. Did the movement contain some orthodox followers of Jesus or were they all heretics? Their official doctrines were heretical, but

---

3. Spence, *God's Chinese Son*, front and back inside cover.
4. Jen, *Taiping Revolutionary Movement*, 21.
5. Wakeman, Jr., *Fall of Imperial China*, 144.

some of the followers, and maybe even one of the key leaders, most likely held more orthodox beliefs. While Chinese authorities confined the Western missionaries to the five treaty ports, this quasi-Christian movement scattered many biblical teachings over millions of Chinese people.

Meanwhile, the Qing government was successful to a limited degree in its reforms, and the government survived for another fifty years, until 1911. In 1860, at the close of the Second Opium War, the ratification of the Treaty of Tianjin marked the end of the five-port treaty era and offered the Chinese people freedom to believe in Christianity. The small and fragile Chinese church, which continued to grow, took permanent root in Chinese soil. This positive breakthrough, however, came at a cost. The perceived connection of the missionaries to both the Opium Wars and the Taiping Rebellion complicated the task of preaching the gospel even before the missionaries' arrival inland. Unfortunately, as discussed in the next two chapters, the missionaries soon found themselves embroiled in further controversy.

REFLECTION QUESTIONS

1. Why were the missionaries involved in the negotiation of the "unequal treaties"? Might God have put them in place for "such a time as this"?

2. Consider the Protestant missionary ministries that were launched during this initial opening of China: evangelism and church planting, education, and medicine. Were these wise ministries to adopt? Explain.

3. Hong Xiuquan contended that China had known the Heavenly Father. More recently other Chinse theologians have also tried to identify evidence of knowledge of Yahweh in ancient China. Why might Chinese Christians want to find this evidence?

4. Questions regarding the Taiping Heavenly Kingdom:

   - Why might the movement have grown so rapidly?
   - Was this an indigenous Chinese movement?
   - Was it an anti-Qing movement? Anti-Manchu movement?
   - Was it peculiar to the Hakka?
   - Was it a Western-inspired movement?
   - Was it a Christian-inspired movement?

SUGGESTED READING FOR CHAPTER 5[6]

Chouvy, Pierre-Arnaud. *Opium: Uncovering the Politics of the Poppy*. Cambridge: Harvard University Press, 2010.

Gützlaff, Karl F. A. *Journal of Three Voyages Along the Coast of China in 1831,1832, & 1833*: Elibron Classics, 2005. Facsimile of the first edition. London: Westley & Davis, 1834.

Lutz, Jessie G. *Opening China: Karl F. A. Gützlaff and Sino-Western Relations, 1827–1852*. Grand Rapids: Eerdmans, 2008.

Polachek, James. *The Inner Opium War*. Cambridge: Harvard University Asia Center, 1991.

Reilly, Thomas H. *The Taiping Heavenly Kingdom: Rebellion and the Blasphemy of Empire*. Seattle: University of Washington Press, 2004.

Spence, Jonathan D. *God's Chinese Son: The Taiping Heavenly Kingdom of Hong Xiuquan*. New York: Norton, 1996.

6. Although the movement only survived for a short period of time, its protagonists left an extensive amount of documentation from which we can learn. For any researcher who does not read Chinese, the full translation of the Taiping archives is a thorough and valuable resource (*The Taiping Rebellion* by Franz Michael).

6

Sowing the Seed

J. Hudson Taylor and the China Inland Mission

THE FLEDGLING CHRISTIAN MINISTRIES initially established in the five treaty ports quickly expanded to all parts of China after the Opium Wars. James Hudson Taylor founded the influential China Inland Mission in 1865 and it soon became the largest mission in China. This chapter focuses on Taylor and the CIM, only a small part of the growing missionary presence that began to establish churches, schools, and hospitals all over China.

In the aftermath of the Taiping Rebellion during the years between the 1860s and 1890s, China entered a season of modernization, hoping to keep pace with the advances occurring in Japan. The Qing government did successfully remain in power, and they achieved modest success in their reforms. The era thundered to a close, however, during the Sino-Japanese War of 1895. The Japanese thoroughly defeated the modernized Chinese Navy, leaving China defenseless against the foreign powers.

The people of China and the missionaries developed a complicated relationship during this period. They were loathed by some as part of the Western imperial complex, but at the same time also sought out as an abundant resource for Western learning and modernization. The missionaries succeeded in building their schools and hospitals, and China began the slow and often contested process of modernization. As more missionaries arrived, misunderstanding and conflicts became inevitable.

J. Hudson Taylor, as presented in this chapter, proved to be an exemplary missionary. The China Inland Mission perhaps represented the very best of the missionary movement in China, but like all missions organizations, it had to navigate the treacherous context of the late nineteenth century. After this chapter highlights the success and the tremendous sacrifice of the CIM missionaries, the next chapter will show the dark side of the Chinese response to the missionary movement. The missionaries, even the best of them, inadvertently triggered the violent Boxer uprising of 1900.

The paradox could not be more perplexing. In the face of hardship and opposition, Hudson Taylor and many Western missionaries regularly responded with patience and love. They buried countless family members in Chinese soil. And yet, they also aggravated the already adversarial relationship between China and the West. They found themselves entangled in a global drama that they did not cause and were powerless to remedy. The Chinese Christians were unhappily often caught in the middle, and yet the indigenous church continued to sink its roots ever deeper into the soil.

INLAND MISSIONS 1865–1911

A new era of missions began in the aftermath of the Second Opium War, and missionaries like J. Hudson Taylor began to form fresh strategies for the new context. The concessions in the Treaty of Tianjin, ratified by the Beijing government in 1860, included the right for Great Britain, France, Russia, and the United States to station diplomatic legations in Beijing. Previously, Beijing had been closed to outsiders. Eleven more Chinese ports opened for foreign trade, and China granted foreign vessels the right to navigate freely through the country on the Yangtze River. Additionally, foreigners were permitted in the interior regions for the purposes of travel, trade, or missionary activities. All Christians in China enjoyed the new right of religious liberty. Lastly, China was required to pay an indemnity to Great Britain and France, as well as compensation to British merchants.

The implications of the Treaty were profound and manifold. The Opium Wars have been referred to by the Chinese as a "humiliation," suggesting that even more than one hundred and fifty years after the events, they remain a scar in the shared Chinese memory. In my own observations, even many Christians who rejoice at the legalization of Christianity in China, and celebrate Hudson Taylor and the China Inland Mission, must navigate the complex emotions attached to the Opium Wars. Perhaps the wound has healed for Chinese Christians, but nevertheless, the scar remains as a reminder of the pain their nation had to endure at that point in history.

Field Notes: On Translation

Although the implications of the Treaty of Tianjin should be taken seriously, I cannot help but pause and have fun with my Chinese students in class concerning one unanticipated clause. Since I speak Chinese as a second language, I ask my students to help clarify the meaning of one Chinese character that is highlighted in the Treaty. In one amusing article, the British prohibit the Chinese government from referring to British officials with the Chinese character 夷 (yi), sometimes translated as "barbarian." Why, I ask, did the Chinese refer to the British as "barbarians," such an offensive word? My students usually insist, somewhat nervously, that I should not be offended by the word, and that yi *simply refers to people who are not Chinese, something similar to "Gentile" in the Bible. If that is true, I playfully press them, then why did the British put the prohibition in a formal treaty? The British were convinced the term meant "barbarian."*

Recently, I engaged in a more thorough and enlightening discussion concerning the word. I met a professional Chinese government translator, and I asked her, more seriously, what the word yi *meant. She suggested that the word had a broad semantic range, from an admittedly offensive word for "barbarian" all the way to a neutral and legal word for "foreigner." She helpfully added that traditionally, before the nineteenth century, Chinese government documents were not prepared for publication but were written for the eyes of the emperor only. The reference to non-Chinese people using the character* yi, *therefore, would not cause offense to anybody as it would only be seen by the emperor. The treaties imposed by Great Britain, and the open publication of those treaties in the nineteenth century, brought a new era in Chinese diplomacy.*

After the ratification of the Treaty, missionaries began to enter inland China, and the China Inland Mission soon grew to be the largest mission organization in China. The patterns of ministry developed in the original five-treaty ports were expanded across the country. The ministries they undertook were standard:

- The missionaries were extensively occupied in literature work, including the production of grammars, dictionaries, Bibles, booklets, and tracts.

- They practiced evangelism and planted churches among both the Han Chinese and many minority groups.

- They were involved in education at all levels, from elementary school to the university level. They provided medical training as well as theological education.
- They participated in a myriad of missions of mercy, including establishing orphanages, medical clinics, and hospitals.
- They provided vocal opposition to numerous social evils including foot binding, infanticide, and opium use.

This list includes much to be admired, yet all those ministries, one by one, produced mixed outcomes. The missionaries fanned out from the treaty ports, successfully planting small Christian communities across the land and establishing innumerable charitable outreaches. Unfortunately, those same ministries often unintentionally undermined the gospel message the missionaries desired to preach. The negative outcomes did not necessarily result from "bad" missionaries or misguided mission strategies; rather, the negative outcomes resulted from the complex realities of the post-Opium Wars era. In fact, this chapter examines the exemplary life and ministry of Hudson Taylor and the CIM in order to highlight the incongruity of how excellent missionaries and sound practices could still inadvertently cause harm to the name of Christ and the indigenous churches. (Chapter 8 on "Missionary Compounds" contains additional discussion of the complex outcomes arising from the missionary methods.)

The numbers of missionaries grew significantly in the second half of the nineteenth century, leading the numerous missionary organizations to seek avenues for cooperation. Sadly, the missionaries stumbled into another misstep that alienated many Chinese people. With the best of intentions, they developed the principle of "comity." Noting the duplication of ministry in some areas, they naturally desired to distribute their efforts more efficiently, and in 1877, they successfully convened the first all-China Missionary Conference in Shanghai. In convening this conference, the missionaries also sought to alleviate another major concern: the confusion caused in Chinese minds by the different and sometimes competing mission societies and denominations. The missionaries were proud of their achievement as they realized a harmony across organizations and denominations that seemed impossible in their home countries.

These missionary efforts toward comity were initially unknown in a wider sense. As the Chinese people became more aware, they grew increasingly offended. These were foreign missionaries meeting on Chinese soil to discuss the most efficient distribution of the foreign missionary forces,

forces which were plotting to bring about the rapid conversion of the Chinese people.

Field Notes: On Massive Missionary Conferences

The stated reasoning behind holding the conferences was unimpeachable, and comity was an admirable Christian ideal. Not only could the missionaries distribute their resources more efficiently, but they could also establish a more unified Christian witness. In classes, students usually do not immediately identify the possibility that the conferences could be offensive to the indigenous people. Yet I remind them that this type of large conference of a foreign religion would probably not be welcome in any country.

There are legitimate reasons the Chinese intellectuals in the 1920s found the conferences offensive, but what else could the missionaries have done? They had to meet in Asia, as the missionaries' homes of origin were located in all parts of the world. They might have attempted to host the conference in a country nearby, but that solution would have been cumbersome and costly. The conferences may never have taken place. If comity was a worthwhile aim, as well as building fellowship and trust within the missions community, then holding conferences in China provided the only solution.

The missionaries held several of these all-China missionary meetings through the following decades, in fact, and resentment among the intellectuals exploded in ferocious Chinese opposition to a large Christian conference held in 1922 (which will be discussed in a later chapter). These meetings, sadly, added yet another layer of misunderstanding.

J. HUDSON TAYLOR AND
THE CHINA INLAND MISSION

Field Notes: On Hudson Taylor

Pictures of the mature Hudson Taylor are widely available. There are many pictures of him in Chinese garb, with his hair dyed black and combed into the distinctive queue, or braid, common in the Qing era. There are also pictures of him in formal Western dress, with a full beard. But I found a picture of Hudson Taylor with a fair complexion and wispy blond hair from when he was about twenty years old. The depiction is striking, and it is a challenge to young people today. At the time he posed for the portrait, his life accomplishments were all in his future. He was a young man who was willing to believe God and put everything on the line. And God used him.

Early Years

James Hudson Taylor was born in 1832 in Yorkshire, England. His father was a pharmacist and the local Methodist preacher. Only twenty-five years after the 1807 arrival of Robert Morrison in China, Mr. Taylor dedicated his son Hudson, his firstborn son, to China. Because of his poor health, Hudson remained mostly at home for his education, and he began learning Hebrew from his father at the tender age of four years old.

In 1849, at the age of seventeen, he had a transformative conversion experience, and he then set his heart on traveling to China. He dedicated himself to gathering as much information on China as possible, and he began to seek out ministry experience by working among the poor and the sick in England. He also assisted in evangelistic meetings. Knowing that he would journey to China where he would need to live by faith, he began to train himself at home. He donated two thirds of his small income to charity, learning to trust God for all his provisions. Additionally, he began medical studies at London Hospital in preparation for serving in China.

He traveled for the first time to China in 1854 with the China Evangelization Society, an organization that believed the Taiping Rebellion created an urgency for evangelism in China. He proved willing to interrupt his studies at London Hospital to begin his missionary career. In Shanghai, he studied Chinese until he could speak well enough to begin preaching in some of the nearby villages disguised in Chinese dress. In 1856, he moved to Ningbo and more importantly, he resigned from the China Evangelization Society. The society was poorly run, and it was a short-lived mission, but the experience helped him evaluate how a missionary organization could be more effective. He started an independent ministry.

In 1857, he married Maria Dyer, an orphan of missionary parents. Three years later, he returned to England to rest because of the threat of tuberculosis. He continued working on a version of the Bible in the colloquial Ningbo language, and he completed his medical studies at that time.

June 25, 1865 proved to be a key date in his personal life and a pivotal date for all of Chinese church history. On that day, he attended a church in England where he witnessed Christians worshiping in comfort. In his soul, he agonized as he remembered that millions of people in China were dying without Christ. He recommitted himself to the task of the conversion of those dying souls, and later that year, he disseminated his newfound fervor in his influential book *China: Its Spiritual Need and Claims*.

Unable to find a missions organization willing to accept him, he founded the China Inland Mission in 1865 (today it is known as the Overseas Missionary Fellowship). In the aftermath of the Treaty of Tianjin, he determined to take the gospel into inland China. Preaching to as many individuals as possible became his driving purpose. In 1866, sixteen missionaries set sail with Hudson Taylor and his family to China. The group included Hudson Taylor, his wife Maria, their four children, a married couple, five single men, and nine single women. During the long and dangerous journey, several of the crew on the ship were converted by the ministry of Taylor and the fledgling CIM family, thus displaying his deep commitment to evangelism in any situation.

This intrepid group was anxious to reach China, because, as Taylor often emphasized, there were "a million a month dying without God." Soon after their arrival, the first calamity struck as the Taylors lost one of their children. Maria was already intimately and sorrowfully familiar with the steep sacrifice needed to serve in China, as she herself had been a "missionary kid" who had been orphaned in China. The family would continue to suffer for the rest of their lives.

Missions Innovations

Hudson Taylor profoundly influenced missions in China and ministry in the Chinese churches, but his significance extended far beyond China. In the history of missions, he introduced enduring innovations in missions theory and practice.

Taylor launched the inland strategy. For centuries, missions had followed the trade routes and focused on the coastal cities around the globe. In 1865, missions had reached virtually every part of the world. What calling remained, in order to fulfill the Great Commission, was to take the gospel from the coastal areas into the inland. Shortly after the founding of the China Inland Mission, other mission agencies followed suit, such as the Africa Inland Mission and the Sudan Inland Mission. In alignment with Pauline strategy, Taylor's method focused on circling larger urban areas, preaching and distributing literature until the people had lost their fear of the missionaries. At that point, the missionaries then attempted to establish residence in the city.

In the CIM, Taylor introduced several additional influential innovations. Taylor knew that starting a new missions agency at the height of the "Great Century of Protestant Missions" might invite criticism, and he wanted to be sensitive to other missions organizations' concerns. Therefore, he determined to do his best not to compete with them. He did not primarily recruit missionaries with a theological degree as was common among the other agencies, but instead he welcomed candidates with less theological and bible training. He also did not wish to compete with the other agencies for missionary funding, and so he determined never to ask for money. One of his beloved sayings displayed this sensitivity and determination: "God's work done God's way will never lack God's provision."

His most significant contribution to missiology and missions history might be his introduction of the concept of a faith mission. Instead of determining an annual budget for the work each year and then hiring as many missionaries and workers as possible within that budget, he allowed anyone to join the China Inland Mission who would be willing to trust God fully for their finances. Today, faith missions, at least among evangelicals, are no longer regarded as innovative but considered the norm. However, CIM missionaries, unlike many faith missions today, were not permitted to ask for money. Taylor insisted that they should not solicit individuals or churches for money; instead, they should always take their needs before God. One of his favorite biblical expressions was *Jehovah-jireh*, the Lord will provide.

By the end of the nineteenth century, "civilizing mission" was becoming more prevalent, and some missionaries not only hoped to evangelize but also to Westernize indigenous peoples. Hudson Taylor intentionally contextualized his message and the mission, however. For instance, he prominently wore Chinese clothes, dyed his hair black, shaved the front of his head, and wore the typical Qing-era long braid in his hair, known as the queue. He focused specifically on the evangelization of China, not its westernization. Based on his experience with the China Evangelization Society, he determined that the headquarters of the mission should be on the field. He feared that if the leaders and decision-makers were located in London, they would not understand the issues on the ground in China. Even today, the Overseas Missionary Fellowship still adheres to these principles.

CIM Family Growing in China

Though the missionaries had prepared for a life of trial, they soon experienced more suffering than they may have anticipated. In 1868, while serving for only their second year in the field, the CIM missionaries were driven out of Yang-chow, a city north of Shanghai. Additionally, the funds for the CIM began to dry up. In less than five years, by the year 1870, Hudson Taylor had lost his wife Maria and three of their children. Maria had been the daughter of one of the first missionaries to China, and she was orphaned at only ten years old. She was a single missionary working in China when she married Hudson Taylor. Together, they brought seven children into the world: Grace, Herbert Hudson, Frederick Howard, Samuel, Maria, Charles Edward, and Noel. She conversed fluently in the Ningbo dialect, having lived in China since she was a young child, and she proved instrumental in helping Hudson with the Ningbo translation. The Taylors had been married for an eventful and rich twelve and a half years when Maria died of cholera in 1870 at thirty-three years old. Her death came only twenty-three years after her parents'. Hudson Taylor later recalled some of her last words. She told him, "I am so sorry, dear," but then clarified that she was not sorry to be dying, "Oh, no, it is not that; you know, darling there has not been a cloud between my soul and my Savior for ten years past; I cannot be sorry to go to Him. But I am sorry to leave you alone at this time."[1]

In 1871, Hudson married Jenny Faulding. They welcomed a son, Ernest, and a daughter, Amy, in 1875 and 1876 respectively. They also cared for the four surviving children from his previous marriage, and they adopted another daughter as well. Jenny served as a faithful spouse who cared for Hudson, through sickness and tragedy, until her death in 1904. She carried out a special ministry among Chinese women, and she also edited the China Inland Mission periodical, *China's Millions*. When their children were older, Jenny traveled with Hudson and became involved in speaking and writing, as well as the organizing work of the mission.

The mission grew quickly, and Hudson Taylor proved to be a tireless leader. In 1874, an injury forced him to return to London for recovery. Although he was required to endure a five-month bed rest in England, he continued to direct the mission from bed and even recruited eighteen additional missionaries. He was a man of tremendous faith, and when he prayed he believed God would listen. In 1881, he prayed specifically for seventy more recruits, and in 1886, he believed that God would send another one hundred missionaries. In 1890, he proposed the recruitment of 1,000

---

1. Doyle, "Maria Dyer Taylor," para. 24.

additional missionaries, to include all mission societies. He constantly kept in mind the millions of Chinese who were dying without Christ. By 1891, the CIM boasted around 640 workers. Taylor traveled to North America, Scandinavia, Australia, and New Zealand, and he inspired many people to consider and embark on worldwide missions. To this day, Hudson Taylor is known by Chinese Christians around the world, and he is widely loved and respected.

The Boxer uprising (which will be described in more detail in Chapter 7) occurred in 1900, when Hudson Taylor neared the end of his life. The China Inland Mission was the largest mission at the time, with the most missionaries located in the inland, and they suffered the largest number of casualties. The tragic toll on the China Inland Mission included seventy-nine CIM missionary colleagues and children killed.

The Price of China

Field Notes: On A Personal Note

When I discuss the Boxer uprising, I feel an obligation to express to my utmost ability the high price the missionaries paid for their service in China. As a historian, I try to understand the context of missions in China and present a fair and honest narrative. But as a missionary, I sense there is something deeper that the historian cannot grasp. I sense there is a pathos, a deep emotion. There is a tie that binds the missionaries to China, a special attachment to the land and the people. Missionaries gladly sacrificed everything, even their own lives and the lives of their families, in order to bring the gospel to China. Before considering (in the next chapter) the angst-filled story of the Chinese response to the inland period of missions in China, I believe we must take stock of the immense price the missionaries paid.

The Overseas Missionary Fellowship published a book in the year 2009 to commemorate the 110-year anniversary of the Boxer uprising, printing some of the most powerful quotations arising from the work of the CIM in 1900. These haunting expressions of devotion and love are worth a moment or two of careful meditation. Each of these individuals were martyred in 1900. Fully aware of the extreme dangers which faced them, they wrote these words in letters to be sent home shortly before their deaths.
Miss Susan Rowena Bird wrote:

"If you never see me again, remember I am not sorry I came to China."[2]

Mrs. Elizabeth G. Atwater wrote:

"I do not regret coming to China, but I am sorry I have done so little."[3]

Rev. Carl L. Lundberg wrote:

"We live and die for the Lord in China."[4]

Rev. Thomas Wellesley Pigott took the long view. He did not consider only the Chinese churches in 1900, but he looked forward one hundred years to the year 2000. He wondered whether those living in 2000 would believe that the high price seemed worth it, in hindsight.

Rev. Pigott asked shortly before he was murdered during the Boxer uprising:

"How shall we look on the investment of our lives and labor here, even from the near standpoint of 100 years hence?"[5]

I will finish this section with a personal story that I think illustrates the relentless persistence of the missionaries in China even in the face of deadly obstacles. (Furthermore, I believe the story depicts the occasional moments of glory for a scholar doing research in the archives.)

During my PhD studies, I was working on a research paper in the library. My research required that I read through the large annual volumes of the China Mission Yearbook, published for decades by the Christian Literature Society in Shanghai. I remember I had a tall stack of these large volumes on the long heavy wooden table in front of me. I was working through them, year by year, and I finally came to the late 1890s. I was tired and frustrated, and I certainly was not experiencing any of the "glory" of a scholar! I felt like quitting, but I did not want to come back, so I determined to finish all the volumes.

Each book was very dry and primarily provided simple facts and figures. For instance, for each city, the book listed how many missionaries lived there, how many missionaries arrived, how many missionaries departed, how many missionary children were born (*An aside: I often laugh with my students at how many children were born to missionary couples in China!*), how many Chinese Christians were baptized, etc. Each volume, representing

---

2. Wong, *In Remembrance of Martyrs*, 3.

3. Wong, *In Remembrance of Martyrs*, 2.

4. Wong, *In Remembrance of Martyrs*, 11.

5. Wong, *In Remembrance of Martyrs*, 15.

a single year, seemed numbingly similar. Precious little stood out, and no interesting drama livened any of the long chapters.

Haphazardly, I flipped open the volume for 1900. I was not paying attention to which particular volume I held in my hands. But then I read something unexpected. In the list of one city, two or three missionaries were listed as having been killed. The list provided their names but gave no other details. I continued reading. The next city also listed two or three more names. They were also martyred. In my stupor after hours of sitting and reading in a library, my mind swirled as it tried to grasp what I was reading. I continued reading, and the next entry provided the names of more people listed who had died. City after city. I quickly realized that I held the volume for 1900 in my hands, the volume that covered the year of the Boxer uprising.

I tried to focus my thinking, and I searched for perspective from the authors of the lists. I longed to find a description, even if only a short paragraph, explaining how the missionaries felt about their losses. But I could not find any personal accounts; I only found extensive lists of the martyrs and the other losses. In addition to the numerous deaths, many missionaries had to flee their homes. Still stunned, I turned to the next volume, the Yearbook for 1901. I thought, after a year had passed, the next volume might provide some description and context for the previous year. I was anxious to read what the missionaries in the following year of 1901 might have said about the tragic losses and senseless killing. But again, the Yearbook of 1901 followed the same format; it provided names and statistics. And for city after city, the book simply listed the number of people who had fled from the area in 1900, and how many now, in 1901, had returned. There was no complaint, there was no explanation; there was simply a meticulous statistical record of the missionaries' unshakable determination to continue the work to which they had been called.

Hudson Taylor's Final Years

In the summer of 1900, the elderly Hudson Taylor was in Switzerland convalescing from an illness. His heart broke with the news coming out of China. When the CIM leadership around Taylor learned of the high casualty rate within the mission, they were concerned about the effect of this news on his health. Rather than reveal the situation all at once, they devised a plan to tell him only small pieces of the story at a time, and then only on days when he was feeling a little stronger.

His cherished China missionaries, his co-laborers in the field, were being slaughtered by his beloved Chinese. I cannot imagine a more heartbreaking image of the elderly James Hudson Taylor. With deep compassion, in response, he encouraged the CIM to show the Chinese the meekness and gentleness of Christ.

Sadly, but predictably, the already tense relationship between China and the Western missionaries grew more contentious at the end of the Boxer uprising. The Western powers that had suppressed the Boxer uprising now required the Qing government to provide substantial sums for reparations, a debt that would take decades to repay. Many mission organizations were eligible for these funds.

The China Inland Mission, particularly hard hit by the Boxer uprising, was eligible for significant reparations. However, Hudson Taylor famously refused the funds. His decision on behalf of the China Inland Mission is highly respected in China and in missions history. He turned all their losses and needs over to God. *Jehovah-jireh*, the Lord will provide. The Lord was good to Hudson Taylor and the CIM, as the Boxer uprising issued into an era of openness and receptivity, a period when the seeds of the gospel were broadly scattered, and the fragile indigenous churches sank down roots that would nourish the growth to come.

In 1905, Hudson Taylor traveled to China for his eleventh and final visit. He took the opportunity to preach to Chinese Christians in Changsha in Hunan, and he died shortly thereafter. Taylor was buried in his beloved China, in Jiangsu province, next to his wife Maria and four of their children.

REFLECTION QUESTIONS

1. What political factors allowed J. Hudson Taylor to enter the inland of China in 1865?

2. What cultural and religious currents in England produced missionaries such as J. Hudson Taylor? Did the Chinese churches take on any characteristics from the churches in England?

3. Look at the list of ministries implemented by the missionaries in China (literature, evangelism, education, medical, etc.). Which ministry might be most effective in church planting? Which ministry might lead to the greatest tension and misunderstanding among the local people? Why?

4. How might an inland rural Chinese peasant perceive the arrival of a missionary from the China Inland Mission into his village? Might an impoverished and uneducated peasant take a different view than the educated village elite?

SUGGESTED READING FOR CHAPTER 6

Broomhall, A. J. *Hudson Taylor and China's Open Century.* 7 vols. London: Hodder & Stoughton, 1985.

Girardot, Norman J. *The Victorian Translation of China: James Legge's Oriental Pilgrimage.* Berkeley: University of California Press, 2002.

Wigram, Christopher E. M. *The Bible and Mission in Faith Perspective: J. Hudson Taylor and the Early China Inland Mission.* Missiological Research in the Netherlands 42. Zoetermeer: Boekencentrum, 2007.

7

Reaping the Whirlwind

Boxer Uprising

THE PROTESTANT MISSIONARIES SUCCESSFULLY planted the Chinese church in the nineteenth century, but they also amassed a growing collection of enemies. The Big Swords, a local group of landed gentry in Shandong, became vehemently anti-Christian in the 1890s. They represented just one of many segments of Chinese society that rejected the missionaries and their message, but their story is especially illuminating. A case study focused on the Big Swords uncovers how the missionaries inadvertently antagonized the local Chinese, and the study also reveals a central piece of the larger drama of the Boxer uprising.

In fact, that intense drama of the summer of 1900 has provided material for both riveting literature and thrilling movies featuring the events.

THE BOXER UPRISING

During the summer of 1900, newspaper readers around the world anxiously devoured reports from Beijing. The Chinese Court stunned the world when it declared war on an alliance of the eight most powerful nations in the world, and it did so standing alone. In the Sino-Japanese War of 1895 only five years earlier, China had mobilized its updated military forces against Japan's modernized military. These forces had been in development during the thirty years after the humiliation in the Opium Wars, but the Chinese Navy had been overwhelmed and summarily sunk to the bottom of the ocean. In 1900, Japan's military was clearly superior to China's decimated forces, and yet Japan acted as only a relatively minor partner in the eight nation alliance comprised of the global superpowers, including Great Britain, France, Germany, and the United States.

The Court declared a war that it was powerless to win because it was trapped between two inexorable forces. On the one side loomed the Western powers and the indomitable might of the Eight Nation Army, and on the other side stood a massive popular uprising of Chinese peasants, known as the Boxers. The Boxers consisted of an ever-growing mob of illiterate Chinese peasants protesting the growth of Western influence in China throughout the 1890s.

Originating in Shandong province along the eastern coast of China, the Boxer soldiers gained adherents as they moved from village to village, traveling northwest and finally arriving in Beijing in the summer of 1900. They pledged allegiance to the Qing Dynasty, and they advocated for the killing of the foreigners and Chinese Christians. As the Boxers advanced on Beijing, determined to eradicate the foreign residents in the spring of 1900, the terrified Westerners in China called on the Emperor to intervene and quell the unrest.

The Boxers' disdain for the foreigners was shared by many segments of society, as shown by a statement from one minor official in Beijing. He supported the uneducated, peasant Boxers and praised their goal to kill the foreigners and Chinese Christians. He wrote:

> Tens of thousands of Boxers have come from all parts the past few days. Most seem to be simple country folk . . . They have neither leaders directing them nor potent weapons . . . Seeking neither fame nor fortune, they fight without regard for their own lives . . . They wish only to kill foreigners and Christians and do no harm to the common people. From this perspective, it seems that they are fighting for righteousness.[1]

The uprising incited violence around the country, but mainly in the north in the areas around Beijing. In Zhili, the province surrounding Beijing, thousands of Chinese Christians were killed. Almost all of the missionaries in China were touched in some way by the tragedy, and many of them had to evacuate their missions stations, sometimes in the face of hostilities, and often protected by Chinese and Christian friends. The highest death toll among the missionaries was in Shanxi province.

The most dramatic event, at least from the perspective of the foreigners, occurred in Shanxi, on July 9, 1900. The governor Yu-xian (毓賢) set

---

1. Esherick, *Origins of the Boxer Uprising*, 291.

a deadly trap for the Western community. He was familiar with the Boxers' conflict with the foreigners as he had been governor in Shandong before being relocated to Shanxi, and he carried to his new post the animosity he had developed toward the missionaries while in Shandong. At the height of the unrest, he offered to protect the foreign community. Instead, when they arrived, he provided personal oversight for the murders of forty-four foreign men, women, and children. In Shanxi, a total of 130 foreigners were killed, along with 2,000 Chinese Christians.

The Beijing government found itself in an impossible situation when the Western powers demanded the suppression of the Boxers. The government could placate the Western powers and send troops to destroy the Boxers, but if it did that, it would lose the emperor's final shred of credibility in China. As China stumbled through the nineteenth century, many Han Chinese blamed the Manchu-led Qing government and Manchu emperor. The emperor simply could not ally himself with the Western powers, turn his guns on Han Chinese citizens, and still maintain his support among the Chinese people. And yet, the all-powerful Western nations were not going to sit by and allow young Chinese rabble-rousers to attack them and their interests in China. If the emperor would not act, they proclaimed, they would act on their own behalf. They would mobilize their own armies to enter the Chinese capital.

With no good choices available, the Court then declared war on the alliance. Throughout the summer of 1900, the world watched as the Eight Nation Army, seemingly in slow motion, advanced from the coast towards the Chinese capital for its inevitable encounter with the Boxers. In Beijing, the foreigners had been forced throughout the summer to seek safety behind the walls of the foreign legations. Many missionaries from the inland, as well as many Chinese Christians, joined the foreign communities seeking safety in the legations. As the Boxers' rampage through the city dragged on for weeks, the anxious Westerners watched and waited throughout the hot summer months for relief.

The Eight Nation Army began its march from Tianjin, the coastal city several hundred miles outside of Beijing, and slowly advanced on the capital. In August, the Army finally arrived and initiated the long-awaited confrontation. The vastly superior international force quickly dispensed with the Boxers, and the "Siege of Beijing" was lifted. The Western soldiers proceeded to ransack the capital. The emperor was forced to flee Beijing, and the foreign soldiers helped themselves to priceless relics in the Forbidden City and the Summer Palace. Some of those artifacts can still be seen today in the British Museum.

The intense drama of the summer of 1900 had ended, but the world was never the same. The missionaries and the Chinese Christians found themselves in the middle of it all, and the missionaries, even if unintentionally, had played a significant role.

THE ORIGINS OF THE BOXER UPRISING

The Boxer uprising has traditionally been known as the Boxer Rebellion. In a groundbreaking book published in 1987, *The Origins of the Boxer Uprising*, Joseph Esherick challenged several essential interpretations of the event. He even offered a fundamental reinterpretation of the common nomenclature, "Boxer Rebellion." First, he demonstrated that the Boxers were not simply a "martial arts" movement, or "boxers," but they also exhibited a spiritual dimension. He clearly described their practices of mass shamanism and spirit possession, as well as their widespread use of magical techniques. Because there were also "Boxers" in Chinese history who simply practiced martial arts ("boxing"), Esherick referred to the Boxers of 1900 as "Spirit Boxers."

Second, he persuasively argued that it was not a "rebellion." The Western powers actually created the fictitious notion of a "Boxer Rebellion." With the arrival of the Eight Nation Army and the defeat of the Boxers, the emperor had fled the capital. The occupiers were not prepared to rule China, and therefore they needed the emperor to return. They needed someone to take control of the government. Even though the emperor had declared war on the foreign powers, the story which circulated claimed that the Court had invited them into Beijing to help the emperor quell the "rebellion." Most importantly, having adopted this fiction, the occupying powers did not need to punish the emperor or the Qing Court for declaring war. Thus, the emperor was free to return to Beijing. Esherick helped dispel the idea that a "Boxer Rebellion" arose in China in 1900, and many scholars now prefer the term "Boxer uprising." The focus of *The Origins of the Boxer Uprising* is not on the uprising in 1900 in Beijing, but the causes behind the rise of the Spirit Boxers in the 1890s in Shandong province.

Field Notes: On Secular Scholarship and Missions History

This book may have been my favorite among the hundreds of academic books I read during my PhD studies. I believe that although Esherick is a secular scholar, he recognized the possibility that there was a deeply spiritual dimension to the chaos surrounding the events of 1900. Most significant for Chinese church history, he spells out why the missionaries, and the foreigners in general, were the target of the Boxers. In a spell-binding story, chapter by chapter, he builds the case for why the Chinese peasants and local leaders in Shandong became increasingly anti-foreign. The book is not about missions or missionaries, but I find it an exemplary work of exquisite scholarship which starkly portrays the context in which the missionaries found themselves in the late nineteenth century. As I read the book, I tried to imagine a young missionary family arriving at a village in Shandong in the 1890s. As described in the paragraphs below, Shandong was a minefield, and they could not have guessed the menacing peril. The missionaries had walked into a local, national, and international storm.

Esherick, in this study which focused almost exclusively on Shandong, also effectively confirmed the significance of regional and local studies in China. As a nation, China is vast and varied. Peculiar factors in one region such as Shandong might not be universal or present in another region. Church growth, in the same way, is likely to occur unevenly because of regional variations.

Background in Shandong Province

The Boxer uprising began in Shandong, a region of China with unique characteristics and history. This combination of factors formed a distinctive set of conditions which then facilitated the emergence of the Boxers. The Yellow River runs through the province located on a floodplain. In the 1890s, it was mainly a rough frontier area that experienced regular natural disasters, and there was a long history of floods and droughts in the territory. Shandong was densely populated, primarily by peasants who accounted for 90 to 95 percent of its people. Thick silt makes the river yellow and also contributes to the unusually flat topography of Shandong. It is so flat, in fact, that the Yellow River has radically changed its course several times over the centuries following major flood periods.

The province abuts the Pacific Ocean in the northeast part of China. On the east side of the province lies the Pacific coast, and on the west, the province borders the Grand Canal (京杭大運河). The Grand Canal, which connected trade between the southern parts of China and Beijing in the north, allowed economic activity in some of the towns and villages along the Canal in the western border areas of Shandong. However, most of the province remained impoverished. This difference created economic disparity between the relatively wealthy areas of trade in far western Shandong and the poverty-stricken majority in the rest of the province. By the 1890s, the growing discrepancy between rich and poor spawned banditry, as people who were unable to feed their families realized that some of their neighbors had plenty. The bandits united in order to survive, and as one could suspect, unrest festered at the intersection of desperation and wealth.

For centuries, the Chinese peasants had been vulnerable to crises. An English historian and social critic penned an apt and memorable image of the position of the peasantry as "that of a man standing permanently up to the neck in water, so that even a ripple is sufficient to drown him."[2] By the 1890s in Shandong, the ripples had not just turned to waves, but enormous swells which engulfed the ill-fated peasants.

The geographical characteristics, along with the proclivity for natural calamities, produced a specific popular culture in Shandong. Shandong province was known for giving rise to numerous heterodox sects and sectarian rebellions, particularly Buddhist millenarian movements. These sects boomed in the tumultuous 1890s, along with martial arts and boxing groups that became integrated in village life. These boxing groups were sometimes employed to protect wealthy landowners from theft, and, on some occasions, pitted the employed boxing youth against the jobless bandits.

Temple operas and story tellers were also ubiquitous in the province, and for centuries they provided a sense of community and extolled common virtues. The operas popular in north China included stories of spirit possession, chants, spells, and magic. In the 1890s, those operas inspired the Boxers, and some of the gods and heroes of the Shandong temple operas became part of the folklore of the Boxer movement.

Arrival of Foreigners in Shandong

Into this potent mix already primed to produce an uprising marched the Western powers. The First Opium War opened only five treaty port cities and did not greatly influence Shandong. However, the Second Opium War opened up a port in Yantai (Chefoo) on the east coast of the Shandong province. Because of its position as a coastal province, Shandong was particularly aware of the humiliation of the Qing Army in the Sino-Japanese War of 1895. With the increasing Western presence, resentment of foreign incursions intensified. In addition to the Western traders, missionaries also arrived in Yantai and moved into the inland.

2. Tawney, *Land and Labor*, 77.

As the missionaries moved into various cities and villages, they slowly established a young and fragile Chinese church. Tension between the Chinese Christians and their neighbors may have been inevitable, and animosity sometimes flared into the open. The small minority of Christians were vulnerable, and, when they suffered abuse, they sometimes turned to the missionaries for assistance. Like Robert Morrison who intervened on behalf of Liang Fa, the foreign missionaries often leveraged their influence to protect the Christians from persecution.

Indeed, the missionaries, with their well-placed and well-connected Western compatriots in cities all around China, could provide considerable help to Chinese Christians. While most disputes among neighbors were resolved at the local level, the missionaries made it possible for the local Chinese Christians to request aid from authorities above the local level. If the local leaders ruled against the Chinese Christians, the missionaries could then plead their case to a district or provincial authority. The local elders naturally resented the missionaries who enjoyed quick and easy access to the provincial governor.

Missionaries, if necessary, could even appeal a small local case all the way to the emperor in Beijing, a privilege even more offensive to the local leaders. When the provincial governor did not rule in favor of the local Christians and missionaries, the missionaries could contact their embassy in Beijing, claim the Chinese Christians were being illegally persecuted, and request further assistance.

With an appeal to their own Western government stationed in Beijing, the local missionaries could summon the emperor of China to rule against the provincial governor and the village elders. In many cases, due to China's weakness, the emperor was essentially obligated to acquiesce to the foreign ambassadors. Regardless of whether the Chinese Christians were in the right or in the wrong, that kind of access and power infuriated and humiliated the local village elite. In some senses, by bypassing the traditional political structures, the missionaries were fashioning a rival structure of political power in China.

Field Notes: On Antimissionary Bias in Academia

In his book, Esherick provided a convincing argument that the missionaries interfered in local Chinese affairs, and his case studies suggested that the missionaries were part of the imperialistic establishment that raised the ire of the Chinese. He generally painted the missionaries with a single, unflattering brush, but he did provide nuance on one point, however, and allowed that some missionaries took greater advantage of their political power in Beijing than others. Further research might attempt to tease out the difference among the Protestant denominations and various missions organizations.

Unfortunately, for the most part, Esherick did not engage with the negative stereotypes of missions found in much scholarship, but simply adopted the conventional view. In his otherwise thoroughly researched and groundbreaking study, Esherick even signaled his disinterest in treating the missionaries fairly by his choice of one chapter title: "Imperialism, For Christ's Sake." (It might be a clever pun, but it broke from the serious academic tone of the book, and, as far as I can tell, it was the only satire or humor in the entire volume.) While the other chapters include exemplary original research and the meticulous use of diverse first-hand sources, he uncharacteristically relied almost completely on secondary sources for this chapter, Chapter 3. I am disappointed that he did not apply himself fully to the chapter on missionaries. The haphazard way he treated missions does, however, highlight the important role Christian scholars of missions can play in challenging conventional historiography and scholarship.

The most offensive and imperialistic missionaries in China, according to Esherick, were those who were more forceful in their protection of their Christian converts. For instance, he asserted that the Protestants generally protected Christians in a less belligerent manner than the Roman Catholics. Among the Roman Catholics, he argued that the German Roman Catholic missionaries aggressively protected their converts, thus making these missionaries the most imperialistic. The German Roman Catholics mounted a more vigorous defense than the French and the Italian Roman Catholic missionaries, for instance. And the worst among the German Roman Catholic missionaries were those associated with the Society of the Divine Word. Finally, the two missionaries with the worst reputation within the Society of the Divine Word happened to be the two men stationed in Shandong province.

Shandong province was indeed a powder keg ready to explode in the 1890s.

The Big Swords

Within this context, the Big Swords (大刀會) evolved into an anti-Christian group. The development of the story was remarkable. As landowners, the

Big Swords grew weary of bandits pillaging their land. By the 1890s in Shandong, the central government had proven to be exceedingly weak and could not provide protection. At the same time, the jobless peasants, increasingly desperate and aggressive, organized into bandit gangs.

The landowners, naturally, determined to defend themselves. Without an effective police force, the gentry needed to protect their own land, and so they hired watchmen. Those landowners, who lived in the area that eventually produced the Boxers, banded together and called themselves the Big Sword Society. Their hired watchmen eventually organized into an armed militia.

Tension grew among these three groups—the frustrated Big Swords, the determined bandits, and the aggressive missionaries. The Big Swords were particularly troubled by specific missionaries in their area, the two imperialistic German Roman Catholic missionaries of the Society of the Divine Word. The bandits had learned that when they angered the Big Swords, they could flee to the missionaries for protection.

For instance, when the bandits were discovered in the act of stealing, they would flee, and the militia of the Big Sword Society would chase after them. In an almost comical scene, the bandits would race to the front gate of the mission church, and, with the militia in hot pursuit, they would bang on the door for entrance. When the missionaries met them at the gate, the bandits quickly claimed they desired baptism. When the Big Swords arrived and demanded the missionaries turn over the bandits for punishment, the missionaries would not allow the "converts" to be persecuted.

Not surprisingly, these types of shenanigans caused the Big Swords to adopt an anti-Christian view. When the Big Swords turned to the local authorities for assistance, the missionaries turned to the provincial governor. If the governor could not or did not provide satisfaction for the missionaries, the missionaries could appeal, through the German legation in Beijing, all the way to the emperor of China. Exasperated, the Big Swords ended up in a direct conflict with the missionaries and the foreign powers.

Field Notes: On Identifying False Converts

In his book, Esherick seems to imply that these bandits were false converts. However, it seems reasonable to believe that at least some of the conversions might have been authentic. Nonetheless, regardless of the authenticity of the conversions, the Big Swords were rightfully furious. At the same time, the missionaries also faced a very real dilemma. The missionaries did not necessarily harbor malevolent intentions. Admittedly, in some cases missionaries may have simply desired to exert raw political power, but in most cases, it seems plausible to believe the missionaries were attempting to do the right thing. Esherick does not investigate the motivations of the missionaries in Shandong, but other literature, such as Brian Stanley's book, The Bible and the Flag, *has examined missionary motivations. Brian Stanley concluded that missionaries were animated by spiritual concerns, not political and imperialistic ambitions. In many of the cases in Shandong, the missionaries may have been doing the best they could in a difficult situation.*

It is possible that the missionaries were well aware that some of the baptismal candidates were not authentic converts. One might wonder why a missionary would offer protection to a false convert, but, in truth, many Chinese churches today in the West face a similar dilemma. In the United States, for example, some Chinese visitors have asked Chinese churches and pastors to baptize them. In cases like these, the pastor may suspect that the real purpose for baptism centers around the applicant's intent to apply for asylum and remain in the US under rules protecting religious minorities. The pastor may have difficulty discerning the sincerity of the applicant's request. Even if the pastor is persuaded that the individual is not truly converted, some churches believe that providing baptism might help move the person towards true faith in Christ. These are difficult scenarios, and good people of good faith might disagree as to how to handle each one.

Regardless of the motives of the "converts" in Shandong, the German missionaries with the Society of Divine Word did aggressively protect them. Frustrated by the interference from the missionaries, the Big Swords sent petitions of complaint to the central government. The missionaries also sent their own letters of complaint. The dispute between the Big Swords and the missionaries occasionally turned violent. The Qing government in Beijing faced an insoluble problem regarding how to deal with the tense situation. If they sided with the missionaries, they would alienate the local gentry in the provinces. If they supported the local gentry, they would infuriate the Western governments in the capital.

After wavering, the Beijing government finally disbanded the Big Sword Society, providing the impression that the Qing Court was acting on behalf of the foreigners against the interests of the local Chinese in Shandong. By the late 1890s, it would only take a spark to ignite a widespread violent movement.

Local Missions and Global Geopolitics

A spark then lit. The Juye incident, the spark, set off a chain of events that altered the course of Chinese history. The incident itself was local and relatively insignificant, but the world felt its repercussions. On November 1, 1897, three German missionaries from the Society of Divine Word gathered at a missionary residence in Juye County in Shandong. In the middle of the night, a band of twenty to thirty armed men rushed into the missionary quarters and killed two of the missionaries. The Christian villagers heard the commotion too late, but they arrived in time to chase off the attackers, thus saving the third missionary. The band of attackers disappeared into the darkness.

The event was certainly tragic, but not unusual throughout missions history. In this case, however, the reverberations echoed globally. The murders provoked numerous superpowers to mobilize massive forces in Asia and Africa, and, on the ground in Shandong, the incident sparked the Boxer uprising. Rivalries among the world powers inflamed this otherwise unremarkable local story of the murder of two foreign missionaries.

In 1897, Germany had only recently unified and therefore fell significantly behind the other Western powers in the global contest for imperial and colonial domination. The Germans wanted to flex their international muscle, and by the 1890s, they were searching for an opportunity to catch up with the other Western Imperial powers. They were particularly interested in taking control of Jiaozhou Bay (Qingdao) in Shandong province. Kaiser Wilhelm II of Germany was waiting for a pretext to take the area, and he seized on the Juye incident.

Missionaries have often been charged with complicity in imperialistic endeavors, but many reasons exist to either qualify or reject that accusation. However, this case seems to provide an actual example of that supposed complicity. The German Bishop in China seemed to be deeply and personally committed to the German imperial ambitions in China. Referring to the Juye incident in 1897, the German Bishop of Shandong dashed off this note to the Kaiser:

> It is the last chance for Germany to get a possession anywhere in Asia and to firm up our prestige which has dropped. . . . [N]o matter what it costs, we must not under any circumstances give up Kiaochow (Qingdao). It has a future for economic development as well as industry, a future which will be greater and more meaningful than Shanghai is today.[3]

---

3. Esherick, *Origins of the Boxer Uprising*, 128.

Powerless to resist German aggression in Shandong, the Chinese turned to the Russians for help. At that time, Russia had an agreement with China to use the warm water port of Jiaozhou (Qingdao) during the winter, a deal that would be forfeited if Germany took control of the port. China pleaded with Russia to rebuff the Germans. The Germans, however, managed to persuade Russia not to fight with them over Jiaozhou, but rather to seize her own ports. Russia agreed with the Germans and proceeded to take control of Port Arthur (旅順口) and Dalian. This turnover initiated a "scramble for concessions" among all the powers in China, each one trying to carve out their own sphere of influence. Like a giant chessboard, each move in China also profoundly impacted the relationships of the global superpowers not only within China, but also in other parts of the world, to include Africa, where the scramble for colonial possessions intensified in 1898.

Conflict in a Local Village

In Shandong, yet another conflict arose. This incident occurred in a mid-sized village of about 300 families in Western Shandong. A sizable segment of the population had become Christian. They began building a church in the village on previously unused ground. Local villagers protested the construction, stormed the property, and used the building materials gathered by the Christians to build a temple. Initially, these events put the Christians in conflict with the local gentry, but later some young unemployed riffraff took up the dispute with the Christians. Finally, the young riffraff invited the Plum Flower Boxers to help in the prolonged dispute with the Christians over the grounds for the church. The situation was escalating.

The missionaries intervened on behalf of the Chinese Christians, insisting that the central government protect the Christians. The government vacillated, and it made decisions that sometimes favored the Christians, and then completely reversed those decisions. While this dispute dragged on, the Juye incident occurred. The Qing government was then compelled by the foreign powers to decide all outstanding cases in favor of the Christians. The Christian villagers in Shandong thus achieved a complete victory in the conflict over the grounds in the center of the village.

From this conflict emerged a new group, the Boxers United in Righteousness (*Yihe quan* 義和拳). This was the first use of the name "Boxers," but this group was primarily focused on the martial arts; they were not yet incorporating the spiritual dimension of the Spirit Boxers. In 1898, they adopted the slogan, "Support the Qing, Destroy the Foreigners!" The Boxers consistently maintained that slogan throughout the summer of 1900, thus substantiating Esherick's thesis that the Boxers were never a "rebellion," but instead originally organized themselves in support of the Qing.

The final tipping point that pressed Shandong into the violent Boxer uprising was an historic flood of the Yellow River in 1898, a flood so massive that it rerouted the river. The Qing government, again, proved powerless to provide essential assistance to the region, and even more tragically, a severe drought followed the flood.

Popular Anti-Christian Sentiments

The people of the region relied once again on a convenient scapegoat to explain the flooding and the drought, as they had with other natural disasters in the late nineteenth century: the presence of the Christians. By the 1890s, anti-Christian resentment reached new heights and proved widespread and popular. The fever pitch of the anti-Christian mood could be seen in a picture book, published in 1891, that contained revolting graphic drawings. When the book was published, the missionaries called for the punishment of the author, but the Chinese Foreign Ministry showed reluctance to crack down because it knew that arresting the author would further inflame public opinion. Missionary Griffith John (楊格非, 1831–1912) saw the images in the book and, overcome with shock, he wrote this description:

> Anything more horribly beastly and disgusting than these painted representations it would be impossible to imagine. Here you have, depicted in brilliant colours, the licentious worship of the Crucified Hog (Jesus), the extracting of the foetus, the cutting off of the nipples, the gouging of children's eyes, the emasculating of boys, the slaying of the goats (foreigners), the offering in sacrifice to ancestors of the dead Hog (Jesus) and the dead goat (foreigner), etc., etc., etc. I have not seen anything, during my long sojourn in this land, that has made me feel so sick at heart.[4]

The Christians, who were accused of disrupting the social fabric, became the obvious target to blame for the devastating flood of 1898 and the deadly drought of 1899 and 1900. The growing chorus of vitriolic voices called for the repression of the Chinese Christians and the expulsion of the Western missionaries. A missionary recorded this placard from 1900 which was "posted everywhere in North China, including cities, villages,

---

4. Perdue, "Introduction," para. 16.

and towns." The notice mentioned the rise of millions of "spiritual soldiers" who would rid China of the missionaries.

The placard read:

> On account of the Protestant and Catholic religions the Buddhist gods are oppressed, and the sages thrust to the background. The law of Buddha is no longer respected and the Five Relationships (of Confucianism) are disregarded. The anger of Heaven and Earth has been aroused and the timely rain has consequently been withheld from us. But Heaven is now sending down eight million spiritual soldiers to extirpate these foreign religions, and when this has been done there will be timely rain.[5]

The Spirit Boxers

Right around 1900, during this troubled time, a new group formed. The group adopted the name of the Boxers United in Righteousness, but Esherick contended that they were an original group. They were the "spiritual soldiers." In addition to incorporating the older elements of the earlier Boxers and the Big Sword Society, such as "boxing" and their anti-Christian and anti-foreign positions, this group added a spiritual dimension: the involvement of spirit possession and magical practices. The gods they chose were naturally from the pantheon of gods in the popular culture celebrated in the temple operas in Shandong.

The government quickly recognized the danger of these Boxers, but they proved hard to suppress. Leaders had arisen from the earlier Boxer groups, but those men had been arrested and dealt with summarily. These new Boxers, the Spirit Boxers, presented a different challenge. They did not recognize any central leader, and many of them were destitute. The spirit practices could be easily learned, and the practices spread quickly from village to village. Originally, a recruit, a new spirit soldier, could be trained in just a few weeks. As the movement grew ever faster, leaders claimed that the training in spirit-possession could be completed in a week. Eventually, a Spirit Boxer only needed one day of training. Spreading at that speed, the Spirit Boxers were difficult to stop.

As these Spirit Boxers moved rapidly from village to village, the Western powers put increasing pressure on the Qing government to suppress them. As Beijing hesitated in their commitment to suppress the Boxers, the Boxers' popularity among the people continued to grow. The Qing Court

---

5. Esherick, *Origins of the Boxer Uprising*, 282.

ultimately chose to declare war against the foreign powers. As we have already seen, the Eight Nation Army suppressed the Boxer peasants' siege of Beijing in August of 1900.

CONCLUSION

The Boxer uprising exposed several truths. First, the frailty and ineffectiveness of the Qing dynasty became obvious, and the dynasty crumbled in 1911. Second, nationalism was a growing sentiment among the people, and it emerged as a key issue the missionaries needed to deal with through the twentieth century. Finally, the uprising revealed a revolutionary power residing in the peasants. That power would lie dormant for several decades, but in 1937, Mao Zedong began his famous journey to Hunan province to investigate some peasant unrest there. He discovered that if properly directed, the peasants could provide a great storm that could sweep over China.

Field Notes: On One Family's Story during the Uprising

I take a deep interest in the Boxer uprising because of the light of hope that I see for Chinese Christianity at the end of the conflict. During the summer of 1900, a Chinese Christian named Dr. Wang took refuge in the foreign legation in Beijing, together with his pregnant wife and two-year-old daughter. At the height of the Boxers' strength in Beijing, he climbed the legation wall and looked over the city. Evidently, he feared that he would have to watch the murder of his expecting wife and his daughter before his own death, and so he decided to take action first. He committed suicide.

Dr. Wang had grossly misjudged the situation. Only weeks after his death, the Eight Nation Army subdued the siege of the city. And in late July of 1900, Mrs. Wang gave birth to their fatherless son, yet another victim of the violent clash between China and the West. Born during the chaos of the Boxer uprising, their son, Wang Mingdao, would grow up in the twentieth century determined to break away from the missionaries and establish an independent Chinese Christian church. We turn now to the fast-paced developments of the early twentieth century, as the roots of independent Chinese Christianity begin to sink deep.

REFLECTION QUESTIONS

1. How did the Big Swords (gentry) in the 1890s become anti-Christian? Are you sympathetic with their opposition to missionary interference? How might the missionaries justify their willingness to baptize bandits?

2. Why were the missionaries blamed for the floods and droughts of the late 1890s? How might a missionary respond to the accusation that they caused a natural disaster?

3. In 1900 the Boxers believed they were righteous defenders of tradition. By the 1920s, the modern scholars saw the Boxers as obsolete adherents of outdated Chinese superstitions. Why did the popular attitude towards the Boxers change in just twenty years? Which view do you prefer? Why?

SUGGESTED READING FOR CHAPTER 7

Clark, Anthony E. *Heaven in Conflict: Franciscans and the Boxer Uprising in Shanxi.* Seattle: University of Washington Press, 2015.

Cohen, Paul A. *History in Three Keys: The Boxers as Event, Experience, and Myth.* New York: Columbia University Press, 1997.

Esherick, Joseph W. *The Origins of the Boxer Uprising.* Berkeley: University of California Press, 1987.

Stanley, Brian. *The Bible and the Flag: Protestant Mission and British Imperialism in the 19th and 20th Centuries.* Trowbridge, UK: Apollos, 1990.

8

Missions Compounds
An Excursus

The most famous sign in China during the twentieth century blatantly declared, "No dogs and no Chinese allowed." This offensive sign, supposedly posted at a park in Shanghai around 1940, signified much that was wrong with the Western presence in China. This chapter, deviating slightly from the chronological flow of the book, seeks to examine the important topic of missionary attitudes between 1807 and 1949. What were the motives of the missionaries when establishing a presence, and why did they build Western-style enclaves within China?

The Western community in China had developed numerous institutions, and several nations even developed competing "spheres of influence" in Chinese territory. The missionaries grew into an essential part of the Western communities in China, often participating in the fields of publishing, education, and medicine. These Westerners published and distributed influential journals and newspapers, established beautiful grassy university campuses, and built sprawling modern medical centers. These institutions, with vast resources and extensive personnel, attracted restaurants, grocery stores, department stores, and other industries to service the growing communities. Some missionaries ended up residing in these foreign enclaves, and therefore experienced limited opportunity to live or work among the Chinese people. In Shanghai, the foreign community became so large and powerful it could keep the local Chinese people out of major city parks.

The idea of "incarnational ministry" teaches that missionaries should live among the people. They should "incarnate," that is, live in the same way as the local people. But by the 1940s in China, many of the missionaries appeared to share the exclusionary attitude of others in the Western community. The missionaries, even in smaller cities and towns, built missionary compounds that replicated the larger foreign-controlled enclaves in the large cities. The walls built around these missions compounds, seen through an outsider's perspective, isolated the missionaries and indicated that the Chinese people were not welcome.

Field Notes: On The Limitations of a Missionary

Originally, as a student of missions, I was reflexively critical of the "ethnocentric" nineteenth-century Euro-American missionaries. I was incensed that the missionaries had created their own enclaves, or "compounds," in some cases actually surrounded by walls, all over China. I was convinced they should have "incarnated" into the towns and villages, living among the people, and I could not imagine any excuse for walls.

While I was still a student, I visited an impoverished district of a developing country when my oldest son (at the time my only child) was one year old. As I left the train station, I observed extreme poverty and block after block of unwashed homeless people living on the trash-covered sidewalks. I noticed one family with a small son, who appeared to be the same age as my son. I grieved for these people, for their suffering, poverty, and probable disease, and especially for this family I encountered. I prayed that God would send Christian missionaries to serve them. I even wondered if God might send me to those people. Suddenly, I felt guilty because I realized that I might not easily be willing to "incarnate" among such desperate people.

In class, I like to ask my mission students to answer honestly the questions of whether they would be able to move their family and live among the poorest of the poor. I saw again in my mind's eye that young boy, with his tattered clothes, oily hair, and his dripping nose, and I thought of my own son. I realized that if I brought my family into this context, I would want to create a safe place for them. I began to sense that missionaries surely have emotional and physical limitations, and there are situations which take them beyond their capacity to cope. Reevaluating my uncritical acceptance of so-called "incarnational ministry," I began to develop a more nuanced appreciation for missionary compounds. The principles of incarnational ministry offer valuable insights, but, I believe, depending on the time and the place, there is also wisdom in building missionary compounds.

Those nineteenth-century missionaries surely committed many errors, but I am convinced that extenuating circumstances influenced them within their peculiar context, and it is my hope to offer a more positive explanation for the existence of the missions compounds. The missions compounds do not seem to have been a specific mission strategy; rather, they grew naturally out of the three primary prongs of the missionary work in China: evangelism and church planting, education, and medical missions. In the conclusion, I will come back to that very famous sign in Shanghai.

THE CREATION OF MISSIONS COMPOUNDS

The missionaries left China after 1949, leaving behind a massive missionary infrastructure that had cost millions of dollars and countless hours to build. This chapter is not a case study of a particular mission compound, but rather a composite picture of how I believe the compounds came into existence, based on my years of reading about and my observation of missions in China. The following paragraphs provide a likely progression of events based on that knowledge of missions work in China. First, when a Protestant missionary family arrived at a new village, they would need to locate housing. In most cases, the family would find a residence among the local people, where they could live and minister among them.

EVANGELISM AND CHURCH PLANTING

I can imagine that the missionaries, once settled in their new home, would build new friendships and relationships with their neighbors. Natural bridges then formed for them to share the gospel as they busied themselves learning the local dialect and customs. As local people came to faith, the missionary family might start a small intimate worship service in their own home. Ample opportunities for discipleship would arise, and the new Christians could begin to bring their family and friends to the services.

The home fellowship would be sufficient for a while, but eventually the church would outgrow the living room of the missionary. They would need to secure an additional location for the fledgling group to worship together. Attendees might rent a room or a hall nearby, and the church could continue to grow.

EDUCATION

As the church was becoming established, the missionary family would also need to educate and care for the children. At first, schooling at home would make the most sense. In the nineteenth century, many of the missionary families had numerous children and so the burden of educating them all at home would be steep. As the church continued to grow, a second missionary family might be invited to help with the work. Once two or three missionary families settled in the same area, the team would likely decide on an appropriate division of labor. Perhaps one of the members of the missionary community offered to take charge of educating all the children.

At this point, the missionaries would face an interesting question. If they are running a small school for their own children, should they open the school to the children of the Chinese Christians? The school could provide valuable preparation for the next generation of Chinese church leaders. An unintended consequence of allowing this opportunity, however, might be that educating Chinese Christian children in their schools would arouse the jealousy of neighbors. In the nineteenth century, rural villagers did not have any other avenues to pursue education. By granting equal opportunity to all community members to attend the school, the missionaries could also open doors for friendship and evangelism.

I can imagine many of the missionaries would naturally gravitate toward opening their homes and their schools to both the Christians and the larger neighborhood. They would, of course, then need a larger location, and they would likely begin to recruit new missionaries who were professionally trained and gifted schoolteachers. As these teachers arrived, they, along with their families, would also need to locate living accommodations. Thus, the Western and missions community continued to grow.

In addition to bringing in new foreign faculty, the thriving and busy school would soon need to hire local people to staff the operations. In an impoverished village, an opportunity to work at the mission school would be a plum opportunity. The growing missions community would quickly attract many jobseekers, both to serve in the school as well as to provide domestic help in the home of the missionaries.

Hiring local staff could prove to be problematic. How much should they be compensated? To pay them at the same scale as the Western missionaries would be fair in some respects, but it would probably make them extraordinarily wealthy among their neighbors and peers. To pay the employees the average local wage for similar work opens the missionaries up to the charge of racism: why should Westerners make more money than Chinese? If they are doing the same work, it seems appropriate that they should receive the same pay. For some jobs, such as a position requiring fluency in Chinese, the Chinese might even deserve higher pay than the Westerners. Should these Chinese staff then receive higher pay? There were no good answers to these questions, and any critic of the missionary movement could find fault with whatever they did.

Most of the missionaries were welcomed into their communities, but they would also begin to elicit animosity eventually. Surely some of the neighbors would not welcome the missionary family, would not embrace their message, and would not view their schools in a positive light. Even as the missionary community grew and effectively reached out to the community, opposition would also deepen. In fact, the intensity of the opposition might correlate with the degree of success in ministry. With mounting opposition, would the missionaries be warranted to protect themselves and their families?

If local malcontents started throwing rocks at the church, or attempted to burn down their buildings, which happened occasionally around the world, what should the missionaries do? Would they be justified to build a wall?

Missionaries might determine in the face of danger that they can trust God and that God will protect them. Is that courageous conviction sufficient, however, when they must protect their children who did not choose to enter the mission field? What about the Chinese converts? Is it fair for the missionaries to ask these new Christians to put their lives and the lives of their families in jeopardy? Furthermore, the missions supporters at home gave sacrificially to build the ministry. Could a missionary in good conscience return home on furlough and inform the supporter that the entire ministry had been burned to the ground, especially when that missionary knew that the loss could have been prevented if proper security measures had been implemented?

Many observers found the barriers offensive, but perhaps the decision to build walls to protect life and ministry grew out of a proper justification and showed wisdom.

MEDICAL MISSIONS

Safely inside the compound, the ministry would continue to grow. As that growth happened, yet another issue would most likely emerge. The missionaries had brought with them some of the best medical supplies from the West. When their children or families were sick, they would rely on those resources. Furthermore, if the illness were severe, they would send the sick to another city for superior medical attention, or, if necessary, to Shanghai. In the worst cases, the missionaries could return home for recovery. In some ways, a pure form of "incarnational ministry" was impossible. The missionaries always enjoyed access to resources that were not available to the local people.

Field Notes: On "Incarnational Missions"

As I stated before, when I first learned about "incarnational missions," I was persuaded. Just as Jesus had condescended to become human, missionaries should also completely incarnate among their target people. However, after studying missions history and living as a missionary myself, I quickly recognized that exceptions must be made to the general principle of incarnation. Missionaries, for instance, occasionally need space from ministry, connection with family, and the consolation of comfort food. Intermittent visits to the grimy hamburger joint called Mary's Hamburgers in Taipei provided more than familiar food; it offered me space to unwind and recharge. If, while on the mission field, a missionary asserts that he follows "incarnational" principles, but he cannot live them out fully, I fear he will undermine his credibility.

In actuality, the incarnation of Jesus differed significantly from any experience a foreign missionary faced. For instance, unlike Jesus, the missionary is not born into the target culture and does not speak the language natively. Jesus did not have a family, and he did not need to acculturate children who could return to live in the home country. Jesus never interrupted his ministry, but missionaries must return home for furlough and support raising. Raised in a culture different from the adopted culture with its distinct attitudes, manners, and diet, any human missionary will be confined by emotional limits.

I now believe that the idea of incarnational ministry does offer valuable insight for the missionary because it reminds the missionary to live simply and humbly among the local people. At the same time, missionaries must attend to the needs of their family, and their own physical, emotional, and spiritual health, even if that means leaving the mission field or pulling away from the daily duties of ministry for a time. I find it unhelpful and inauthentic for a missionary to claim to practice "incarnational ministry."

Beyond utilizing the medical resources for personal needs, the missionaries could also extend medical assistance to their Chinese colleagues. The missionaries relied on the faithful assistance of indigenous workers, and so the foreign missionaries could justify using ministry funds for the workers' medical needs. However, providing medical assistance for those workers' families and children might be harder to rationalize as a ministry expense. Of course, as their Chinese colleagues were also close friends, the missionaries would surely provide any assistance possible. In fact, if the local missionaries could not handle the medical emergency, they might arrange to send the ailing person to a large city, or even to Shanghai.

Although providing the Chinese Christians this kind of care was admirable and understandable, their aid could also draw an unfavorable response from their non-Christian neighbors. From the neighbors' perspective, the missionaries were bestowing unearned and unfair benefits upon the Christians, benefits not available to others in the community. Inadvertently, the missionaries were creating tension and a feeling of inequality. Perhaps the non-Christian neighbors might suspect that the Chinese "Christians" had only joined the church to gain the benefits, or maliciously accuse their Christian neighbors of seeking baptism because their child needed Western medicine.

Field Notes: On Medical Missions

In class, as we discussed this material, one student eagerly interjected a proposal that would allow the missionaries both to provide medical assistance to the Christian community and to remain fair to the broader community. She inquired, "What if the missionaries were to administer medical services for everyone within the village?"

I responded, "That is an excellent observation, and that is precisely why some of the missionaries got involved in medical missions." While various critics have regarded medical missions in China as a distraction from evangelism and church planting, they developed as a natural extension of the evangelistic efforts and out of compassion for the people. The pioneer missionaries, those who opened new territories and planted churches in new villages, quickly recognized the need for talented colleagues with specialized medical training. The original missionaries would then seek to invite medical professionals to join the team in the growing missions station. They hoped that doctors and nurses who believed they were called by God to offer medical care in a missions context would heed the call.

Once established, a small medical clinic would begin to grow. If everyone would be welcome to use the clinic, then the staff would need additional help from overseas and from the local community. For the local people to be qualified to serve as medical staff, technicians, nurses, and doctors, they would need training in Western medicine. Thus, the schools needed to be expanded.

The clinics and hospitals relied on the medical colleges for a stream of qualified candidates, and the medical colleges, in turn, relied on the expanding network of preparatory and elementary schools. The missionaries were therefore called on to provide more than simple literacy training as they had in the past; they now offered an entire national educational system, eventually including sprawling green campuses that housed universities and graduate schools.

These sophisticated facilities and highly trained staff needed protection. The missionaries provoked antagonism from many segments of society, including the traditional local gentry who felt threatened by these new well-educated elites graduating from the Western-style universities.

OPPOSITION TO THE MISSIONARY COMPOUNDS

By receiving baptism, the new Christians could seek well-paying jobs in the missionaries' homes, in the churches, or in the other missionary-related institutions. They could learn English, place their children in the schools, and obtain Western medical assistance. In times of natural disaster, the Christians would be the first to receive Western relief supplies, such as water and rice.

In fact, in some ways, as we will discuss in chapters 9 and 10, the entire social fabric had been revolutionized by the missionaries. Access to education had been democratized, and the poor and women were offered equal opportunity. The traditional social and cultural elites often did not welcome the new challenges, and they frequently riled up opposition among the illiterate peasants. The missionaries found they needed higher and sturdier walls, and perhaps even occasional police protection, to protect the vast missionary infrastructure. Thus, the enemies of Christianity were even further provoked, and their desire to tear down the walls and destroy the institutions grew with time.

In addition to resistance from traditional enemies, a different voice of opposition to this Western missionary infrastructure arose in China in the early twentieth century. Many sincere Chinese Christian believers, surprisingly, also came to resent the missionary presence. These Chinese Christians worried that the numerous privileges offered by the Western missionaries attracted lukewarm or even false "believers" to the church. They suspected these people joined the church for a job, for an opportunity to go to school, or for medical assistance.

Those so-called Christians, who were not truly converted but drawn to the material benefits supplied by the missionaries, were commonly referred to as "rice Christians." Chinese pastors and church leaders, some who suffered persecution and paid a high price for their faith, did not appreciate being confused with these false believers. The pastors thought the false Christians polluted the church and hindered church growth. They believed the Chinese church could grow more rapidly without the Western influence. They longed for an independent Chinese church that could shed the complex infrastructure and simply preach the gospel.

CONCLUSION

The famous sign in a park in Shanghai, "No dogs and no Chinese allowed," has offended both Chinese and non-Chinese for decades. But it probably never existed.

Field Notes: On a Discussion of China Scholars

Several years ago, I was part of an academic email group of several hundred China specialists. One day I read an inquiry where the questioner stated that he was trying to locate a photograph of that famous sign. Many of the scholars participated over the next several days in an animated discussion. The conclusion, to my surprise, was that the sign probably never existed. That seemed to be the only way to explain why no one had ever seen a photo of the infamous sign. Nonetheless, the sentiment expressed by the nonexistent sign was probably accurate. That is, several scholars surmised that the park in Shanghai probably did not have a single sign, but it may well have had multiple signs. And one of the signs may have read, "No dogs," and another sign in another part of the park may have read, "No Chinese."

There may have been, in the same park, a sign that said, "No dogs," and another sign that said, "No Chinese," but happily there was no sign maker who had the audacity to sit down and paint a sign that read, "No dogs and no Chinese allowed." That truth, sadly, is a small consolation; the park in Shanghai did exclude both dogs and Chinese people. The chauvinism prevalent among many in the Western population in China poisoned Chinese perceptions of both the West and Christianity.

The schools and hospitals introduced untold blessings into China, and they were on the cutting edge of the modernization of China in the twentieth century. Yet these very institutions also sometimes served to undermine the gospel message and the witness of the indigenous churches. The Chinese churches would need to find a way to break away from the heavy baggage created by the Western missionaries and develop independent Chinese churches.

REFLECTION QUESTIONS

1. Consider the three-pronged approach to missions in China: Evangelism and church planting, Christian education, and medical ministry.

   - What is the value of each ministry? Were all three parts necessary for missions in China?

   - How might education and medical ministry aid the development of evangelism and church planting?

   - How might education and medical ministry distract from evangelism and church planting?

2. Should the Western missionaries have hired local people to serve in their households? How should their wages have been determined?

3. Would the local Chinese welcome a school established by the missionaries? Would the traditional gentry be open to allowing the poor and women to attend these schools? If they were opposed, should the missionaries have still opened the schools?

PART THREE

Independent Chinese Churches (1900–1949)

THE WORD "ANGST" DESCRIBES the general attitude in China as a nation following the Boxer uprising. The massive turmoil in the nation's capital and the unrelenting whirl of international events all undermined Chinese self-confidence. China's intellectuals were searching for a new direction for their country in light of recent events. Many of the prominent radical Chinese thinkers of the early twentieth century were inspired by the Enlightenment, the West, and Judeo-Christian traditions, but, ironically, they rejected both the missionaries and Christianity. Just at the moment the Chinese intellectuals looked to the West for inspiration, when the missionaries could have served as an ideal resource to help China move toward modernization, Christianity had become distasteful for many decision-makers. Additionally, the nature of the opposition toward Christianity was shifting. In 1900, the illiterate and irrational Boxer adherents had blamed Christianity for disrupting the mystical equilibrium of the people. By the 1920s, conversely, highly educated Chinese intellectuals denigrated Christianity for its illogical nature and equated the Christian belief system with the irrational superstition of the Boxers.

The Qing Dynasty fell in 1911, and the period of the Chinese Empire devolved into the period of the warlords. At a time when many Chinese people judged that Chinese culture and institutions did not work or serve them effectively, the era might have been ripe for rapid conversion to Christianity. Again, however, the Christian churches were not able to fully take advantage of the opportunity.

Surprisingly, two Christian presidents served in China between 1900 and 1950, and the number of foreign missionaries continued to grow. The ubiquitous Christian schools and hospitals were changing the landscape of the society. Because the mainstream intellectuals and the vast majority of the Chinese people rejected the missionaries and the Western-style Christian churches, Chinese Christians increasingly recognized the importance of breaking away from the missionaries and the missions-related institutions. They needed to forge an independent Chinese Christian church.

Part Three explores this era and the emergence of independent Chinese Christianity. The nineteenth-century missionary efforts, concluding with the Taiping Rebellion and the Boxer uprising, generated pressure to create an independent Chinese Christian church. First, Chapters 9 and 10 discuss the historical *canvas* of the era. Chapter 9 examines the closing years of Qing Dynasty, and the following chapter highlights the May Fourth era. Second, Chapter 11 studies the *currents* washing over China during this period. These tidal waves of nationalism, fundamentalism, and global Christianity dramatically influenced the direction and growth of the Independent Chinese churches. Chapter 12, thirdly, introduces the *constraints* on independent Christian growth resulting from imperialism. Imperialism was an unavoidable obstacle impeding and distorting the growth of Chinese Christianity.

Finally, the fourth chapter, Chapter 13, considers two of the *characters* from that era. The chapters on the *canvas*, *currents*, and *constraints* provide the multi-textured backdrop for the spellbinding story of the emergence of independent Chinese Christianity during the first half of the twentieth century. Rather than trying to recount the entire, overarching narrative of this story, I will relate instead the stories of two Chinese Christians in Chapter 13. These Christians are examples of the *characters* who brought independent Chinese Christianity to life, and their lives are intertwined with the tumultuous events of their era.

SUGGESTED READING FOR PART THREE

Harrison, Henrietta. *The Missionary's Curse and Other Tales from a Chinese Catholic Village.* Berkeley: University of California Press, 2013.

Hunter, Jane. *The Gospel of Gentility: American Women Missionaries in Turn-of-the-Century China.* New Haven: Yale University Press, 1984.

Kessler, Lawrence D. *The Jiangyin Mission Station: An American Missionary Community in China, 1895–1951.* Chapel Hill: University of North Carolina Press, 1996.

Yeh, Wen-hsin, ed. *Becoming Chinese: Passages to Modernity and Beyond.* Berkeley: University of California Press, 2000.

9

New China

A Christian Civilization . . . without Christ?

CHINA MOVED RAPIDLY TOWARD modernization and westernization after 1900. Part Three considers the two strands of Chinese church history. Following one strand shows us that China increasingly adopted the modernizations introduced by the Western missionaries and their extensive institutions. Those who adopted these modernizations did not embrace the Christian faith, but they gradually welcomed the ideals that grew out of Western Christian civilization and the Enlightenment. At the same time, a second strand of Chinese church history emerges as the small community of authentic Christian believers born in the nineteenth century became the foundation of indigenous Christianity in China.

In a short period of about ten years, from 1900 to 1911, the China that the missionaries had known and experienced disappeared. The Qing Dynasty declined at breakneck speed, and it appeared that the entire imperial system itself might collapse. Chinese leaders eagerly explored Western ideas in search of a way forward for China into the twentieth century, and they took particular interest in the concepts resulting from the European Enlightenment of the seventeenth and eighteenth centuries. The missionaries, including the evangelicals, were well-equipped and well-placed to play a significant role in the modernization of China. Despite the willingness of the Chinese political and intellectual leaders to embrace many of the trappings of a "Christian civilization," at the same time, they rejected Christ himself.

The decade began with the turmoil of the Boxer uprising. Puyi, the last emperor in China, was born in 1906, and he began his short reign as a young boy in 1908. Not only did the Manchu Qing Dynasty fall, but the entire imperial system dissolved in 1911. And in its place, promising a new democratic and prosperous future, arose the leader of the Revolution, a Christian medical doctor named Sun Yat-sen.

This chapter paints the canvas to the era in the years from 1900 to 1911 and highlights first the existential threat faced by the Qing government. The second section covers the desperate reform attempts made by the Qing court to save the Dynasty. The political reforms failed, but the third part reveals that the intellectuals successfully thrust China into the modern global era. Fourth, the chapter touches on the social transformations which rocked Chinese civilization. Finally, a brief description of the political revolution that successfully toppled the Qing Dynasty will close the chapter. Sadly, the new government failed to establish a lasting administration, and by the mid-1910s China dissolved into the warlord era.

BACKGROUND ON 1900–1911

In 1900, the Western powers invited the Qing court to return to Beijing to rule China, but they also imposed the Boxer protocol, which imposed huge financial burdens on the collapsing Qing Dynasty. With the treasury in disarray, China also faced new international pressure when the Russians moved into Manchuria and the Japanese moved into Korea. In 1904–5, the Japanese defeated the Russians in war, a battle that was waged on the Korean-Manchurian border. Thus, China suffered the humiliation of two foreign powers staging warfare on Chinese soil. The victorious Japanese gained the rights to the southern third of Manchuria.

GOVERNMENT ATTEMPTS AT REFORM

The need for reform became glaringly obvious. Post-1900 China saw the introduction of the New Policies (庚子後新政). These reforms marked several dramatic breaks from Chinese tradition and history, introducing transformations to the educational system, the military, and the government. The proposals for educational reforms were of particular significance to the missionaries, as the future of many of their schools was at stake.

Education Reforms

Missionaries were deeply involved in all levels of education by the year 1900, and they supported many of the reforms being discussed. Education through the missionary network had become contentious, as numerous dilemmas had arisen in the nineteenth century. The government desired to resolve some of those issues and reassert control over the system.

When the missionaries first arrived in China, offering education and establishing schools was a natural development. Among literate people living in the cities, the missionaries introduced Western sciences and Western ideas, for example. Among the vast impoverished and uneducated masses, they introduced a literacy-based and rudimentary education plan, offering classes for both boys and girls. Not surprisingly, the village elite sometimes feared that the missionaries were challenging their unique privilege in society. Education can be revolutionary, and the political leaders wanted to guide the future expansion.

The content of the missionary education was also problematic. For centuries, the Chinese imperial exam system, which was the mechanism by which one entered the civil bureaucracy, focused on the Confucian classics. The Chinese education system at the time, only available to the highly privileged, heavily emphasized memorization and recitation of facts from literature and history. When the missionaries opened schools, they were not prepared or qualified to offer this kind of classical education. Naturally, the missionaries gravitated towards teaching Western subjects, with the goal of helping China globalize and modernize.

English and Western Literature

One subject which became increasingly popular after 1900 was English as a language. Students learned rudimentary conversation and would occasionally advance to reading English literature and the Western classics. Perhaps the missionaries underestimated the close connection between language and culture. The world was globalizing, and the missionaries were convinced that learning English would be a useful tool for the modernization of China. However, they might not have fully appreciated the challenge Western education introduced into Chinese society. For instance, by simply opening their schools to the poor, they were challenging the privileges of the wealthy. When they allowed girls to learn alongside boys, they were introducing new notions of gender equality.

Even among the educated elite, the missionaries provoked new questions and conflicts. For instance, traditional Chinese scholars received an education in the Confucian classics and in subjects such as Chinese calligraphy, but the missionary-educated academics learned English and specialized in Western science and classics. Could a person whose education was not steeped in the Confucian classics and Chinese subjects be denationalized, or even considered less "Chinese"?

A scathing but all too common criticism of the Chinese Christians emerged: "one more Christian, one less Chinese."

Science and Mathematics

Even when the missionaries focused on science and mathematics, subjects that might be considered less controversial and less tied to culture, they might still be undermining Chinese culture. Many critics of Western training in China argued that even science and math were Western subjects and built on presuppositions that were Western rather than universal.

Bible and Christianity

Ultimately, the missionaries wanted to teach reading and writing so that Chinese people could read the Bible. Their highest goal was to convert them to Christianity. The critics of missions contended that conversion to Christianity undermined Chinese culture and weakened the Chinese character of the individual. Therefore, the government proposed reforms that would eliminate the mandatory teaching of the bible and Christianity in the schools. (The issue of Christianity supplanting Chinese culture and character will arise again in future chapters.)

New Policies to Reform Education

The New Policies after 1900 attempted to address some of these challenges from the missionaries in the field of education. They abolished the Imperial examination system in 1905, a tradition that stretched back to the Han Dynasty and had been the major path into the bureaucracy since the time of the Tang Dynasty. At the time the exams were abolished, they were criticized for testing only knowledge of the Chinese classics and literary style and not evaluating any technical or professional expertise.

The government, as part of the reforms, zealously started new schools to counteract the plethora of missionary schools. By 1909, they had established about 50,000 schools around China. By this measure alone, it appears evident that missionaries profoundly shaped China. Unfortunately, many of the government schools proved ineffective as old teachers, apparently unqualified to teach modern topics, staffed them. The missionaries, by contrast, were often highly trained and qualified.

Ti-Yong

As with the missionary schools, the new schools needed to determine the content of the curriculum. What subjects should be taught? During this period, Zhang Zhidong (張之洞, 1837–1909) promoted a provocative suggestion of combining the learning of the East and the West. Although the idea was not unique to him, he advocated the *ti-yong* principal, which is "Chinese learning for essence (*ti*), Western learning for application (*yong*) (中學為體，西學為用). This proposal brought into focus a critical question. Was it possible to adopt Western science and mathematics, but not adopt the deeper Judeo-Christian and enlightenment ideas undergirding them? Further, what exactly was the "Chinese essence," and why should it be preserved? These questions were of intense interest not only for the Chinese intellectuals, but also for the missionaries and the missionary educators.

China determined to respond to the educational infrastructure developed by the missionaries by developing their own nationalistic system. However, with the fall of the Qing in 1911, followed by the rise of the warlords, the educational reforms ceased for a time. The next chapter, on the May Fourth movement, returns to missionary education and the nationalistic response in the 1920s.

Military Reforms

In addition to its attempt to reform education, the government also pursued reform in the military and within the government administration. The Qing government employed many foreign military advisors, and these specialists introduced new ideas. Some of the new modern schools were military academies designed to train future political and military leaders in modern thinking and modern warfare. The military became increasingly staffed with career military men who were well-paid, well-trained, and well-armed. Yuan Shikai (袁世凱, 1859–1916), who took over as president from Sun Yat-sen in the middle 1910s, rose from the ranks of the military. His career was indicative of a new path to power in China. Chiang Kai-shek would also receive his primary education and training in the military academies, and his rise to power came through the military.

Government Administration Reforms

Finally, the government attempted to reform itself. It endeavored to rid its infrastructure of useless posts, and it established numerous new ministries. Perhaps its most important reform involved the establishment of a government ministry for foreign affairs. No longer were the foreign powers to be treated as tributary nations, but rather as international counterparts to be engaged. Thus, the Qing government finally officially elevated the status of foreign diplomats in China.

The government also discussed the idea of a constitutional monarchy, possibly based on the model in Meiji Japan. The first provincial assemblies formed, making way for the eventual devolution of power from the central government to the provinces. Missionaries again had the opportunity to serve as key consultants. Alas, these reforms never had time to develop as the government fell in 1911.

RAPID INTELLECTUAL TRANSFORMATION

The intellectual revolution caused more profound and long-lasting change than these government reforms. This intellectual transformation from the turn of the twentieth century still affects the Chinese worldview today. Numerous Chinese philosophers and social reformers, proposing deep and radical changes, altered China permanently during this era. Their ideas, when considered carefully, sometimes correlate with Christian teaching. The modern intellectuals, scholars who were most active from about 1895 to 1920, are sometimes classified as the "first generation," while the "second-generation" are those who came of age in the 1920s. This chapter discusses the first generation and the next chapter the second generation.

Field Notes: On Thinking as a Christian
about Philosophy and Culture

These intellectuals are well-known in China even today, and in my history classes they are familiar to my Chinese seminarians. Nonetheless, I find that some of my students have never thought to analyze the proposals of these thinkers from a Christian perspective. I challenge them to look carefully at Yan Fu and Liang Qichao, for example, and discern how their ideas do or do not conform to Christian teaching.

This section will consider two transformational Chinese intellectuals from the first generation, Yan Fu and Liang Qichao. Significantly, the opportunity to emerge as a popular, public intellectual owed some debt to the missionary movement. Many of these intellectuals were trained in or influenced by Christian schools. With growing numbers of literate people, the missionaries also cultivated a vibrant market for newspapers and magazines in China. In the 1850s, some of the foreign residents began to launch newspapers and magazines in China. By 1895, there were nineteen Chinese language periodicals, and by 1912, there were 500 journals and periodicals, with perhaps 2 to 4 million readers. New ideas, therefore, could be disseminated quickly to a wider audience by the early twentieth century. These newspapers and magazines profoundly affected the first-generation intellectuals, and the next chapter will discuss how the second generation derived even more profound impact.

Intellectuals at the turn-of-the-century experienced massive transformations during their lifetime; they were born in the old Imperial China and then led the way toward a new, modern democratic China. Yan Fu (嚴復, 1854–1921) is a prime result of the myriad of new opportunities available in the late Qing. Yan Fu was born in 1854 to a poor family, but, because of the changes already occurring at the time, he was able to get an education at the Fuzhou arsenal (福州造船廠) and afterward studied in England. With his expertise in English, he began to translate Western literature into elegant Chinese, giving Western ideas more appeal in China. He translated the works of Charles Darwin and Adam Smith, for instance, and also included an introduction and commentary. His unlikely career culminated with his selection as the first president of the modernized Peking University in 1912.

Among his many ideas, Yan Fu examined two concepts that cut to the heart of the existential challenges China was facing. First, Yan Fu discussed social Darwinism. Second, related to social Darwinism, he stressed that history progresses, and that nations must go forward or they die out. Rather than presuming a continuous rise and fall of Imperial dynasties, Yan Fu suggested the possibility that China might die. As China faltered under Qing rule in the late nineteenth century, the suggestion that China might "die," or completely cease to exist, seemed plausible and was therefore terrifying.

Liang Qichao (梁啟超, 1873–1929), nineteen years younger than Yan Fu, built on the former intellectual's ideas. Liang Qichao was a prodigy and a genius, passing the first imperial exam at just 11 years old. As he grew into adulthood, he became interested in politics. Because of his radical political positions, in 1898 he was forced to escape to Japan where he continued to pen numerous articles. He promoted the importance of newspapers, education, and representative government, stressing that the survival of the nation was at stake. Among his contributions, Liang Qichao stressed two themes that deserve special attention: "social cohesion" (社會團結) and "new people" (新百姓). The notion of a "new people," the young modern youth making a clear break from the old ideas and traditions, was a radical idea in a Confucian society that values age and continuity.

The primary and most fundamental challenge from Yan Fu and Liang Qichao might not have been immediately obvious. They suggested a new conception of China by introducing the idea that China could be considered a "nation." Historians noted that the Chinese had traditionally identified themselves as the "land under heaven," or *Tianxia* (天下), and therefore to conceive of China as a "nation" would have been revolutionary. *Tianxia* can be difficult to translate; it might be translated "realm," or "the whole of China," but it literally translates as "all under heaven." The Chinese perceived themselves as "all under heaven," and everyone else was uncivilized. As a concept, it was quite contrary to the modern West and the idea of nation-states.

Within Western Europe, each nation developed in the sixteenth and seventeenth centuries with often equally powerful neighbors, and thus each emerging nation developed a strong sense of nationalism. While these nations may have presumed their own superiority, they also recognized the legitimacy and the equality of the other nations around them for the most part. China, perhaps for thousands of years, never had an equal competitor in its own neighborhood. They never developed a sense of the equality of nations, but only the sense of "us" (*Tianxia*) and "everybody else."

Field Notes: On Language Learning and the Meaning of Tianxia

I enjoy dialoguing with students concerning the meaning of Tianxia, *as this idea is puzzling to me as an American and I find Chinese students also struggle to explain it clearly. My simple understanding of the term is that it means that China (and the Chinese people) comprises all that is under Heaven, and that everything else is thereby peripheral. Any other people or "nations" are lesser, tributary nations, expected to offer tribute*

> to the Chinese Son of Heaven. (*More bluntly, I suspect* Tianxia *implies that Chinese people traditionally believe that China is civilized, and everything else is barbarian.*)

If indeed the term *Tianxia* represented a xenophobic and chauvinistic view, then it was radical for Yan Fu and Liang Qichao to suggest that China was a "nation," and just one of many nations. They introduced a new worldview, a world where China comprised only one of many equal peoples. Further, if China were simply a nation, then social Darwinism suggested it was a nation that could become extinct. In recognition of this possibility, the two intellectuals promoted the need for "new people," breaking from and challenging ancient tradition, to ensure the survival of the Chinese nation. As these ideas gained currency, it should have created tremendous openings for the gospel in China. The next generation of intellectuals, the "second-generation," grabbed hold of these proposals and further developed them (see the next chapter).

RAPID SOCIAL TRANSFORMATION

In addition to the promotion of government and intellectual reforms, radical social transformation arrived next on the agenda for change. Many of the promoted ideas paralleled the thoughts of the missionaries, such as the push for modern schools and industry and the championing of equality.

In a society that had historically valued the virtuous Confucian scholar above all, the pursuit of commerce, profit, and money became more acceptable. For instance, some individuals from the gentry began to pursue modern business. Zhang Jian (張謇, 1853–1926) started his career before 1900 by pursuing entrance into the civil bureaucracy, and in 1894, he successfully passed the *jinshi* exam (進士). After 1900, however, he became an advocate for modern business and education. He founded over 20 companies and over 370 schools. His slogan announced, "Enterprise as Father, Education as Mother."

Social changes during this time allowed for better education and extended more opportunities for women. The well-known struggles and successes of Qiu Jin (秋瑾, 1875–1907), an anti-Manchu feminist revolutionary, would have been unthinkable in past years. She came from a wealthy background, but she fled from an arranged marriage, and she eventually traveled to Japan to study. She returned to China and started a school for girls. She launched an unsuccessful uprising against the Qing, and she was executed in 1907. As China experienced this radical social transformation, the missionaries witnessed it and, to some degree, advanced the changes.

POLITICAL REVOLUTION AND SUN YAT-SEN

Optimism persisted in some quarters at the time that China might be on the brink of revitalization (waking the "sleeping dragon"), and that China, perhaps under a constitutional monarchy, could reemerge as an important part of the global community. Nonetheless, at the same time, revolutionaries continued to push for the overthrow of the Qing. They believed that China could not transform itself under Qing leadership.

Most famous among the revolutionaries was Sun Yat-sen (孫逸仙, 1866–1925). Sun Yat-sen, as leader of the 1911 Revolution, is remembered positively in modern history, but his role in Chinese church history is perplexing. He identified as a Christian, one who became president of China. In some ways, he embodied the answer to the prayers of both Western and Chinese Christians for a Christian breakthrough in China, but the story proved more convoluted.

Sun Yat-sen was part of a large contingent of overseas Chinese. By the early twentieth century, ten million Chinese people lived overseas, mostly from Guangzhou and Fujian. He moved to Japan from Guangzhou when he was thirteen years old, and he became Christian during three years of study at a Christian school. He moved next to Hong Kong, then a British colony, where he earned his MD degree. In 1895, he applied for a job in the Qing government but was turned down, a rejection which apparently opened his eyes to the necessity of deposing the Qing.

He gathered a revolutionary group, and in 1895, they attempted to overthrow the Qing government. While other leaders of the attempt were executed, he escaped to England. Then, through a dramatic episode in England, he became world-famous. The Qing legation kidnapped him and held him prisoner in the Chinese embassy. Despite his confinement, he was able to secret a letter to the outside world, and the British heroically rescued him. His book, *Kidnapped in London*, turned him into an instant international celebrity revolutionary. He traveled the world raising money and recruiting Chinese followers, especially in Japan and Hawaii. He launched over a dozen attempts at revolution, but each time they failed.

Sun Yat-sen wrote out his ideology for government, the "Three Principles of the People" (三民主義). The three principles identified were: Nationalism, Democracy, and People's livelihood (or socialism). Based on influences from the United States, he proposed a five branch system of government. Although his principles were inspirational, he did not develop them carefully. His critics suggested that he did not provide a concrete program, but merely slogans. Nonetheless, although he might not have been a thoughtful political theorist, he proved to be very tenacious. He continued to wage a revolution.

The final fall of the Qing Dynasty, and with it thousands of years of Chinese imperial rule, was rather anti-climactic. After a series of political crises that left the Qing government vulnerable to overthrow, in October 1911, some local revolutionaries in central China exploded a bomb by accident. The investigating police in the city found a list with names of the revolutionaries, so the revolutionaries were forced into action. They had to launch their revolution before they were arrested. Somewhat unexpectedly, the revolutionaries enjoyed immediate success. They hastily forced the provincial governor and military general to flee, and the new governor called on the other provinces to join them and declare independence from the Qing. By mid-November of 1911, in little more a month's time, all but three provinces had joined the revolution in a war with very little fighting. Sun Yat-sen, the world-renowned celebrity revolutionary, was not in China at the time of the revolution. Rather, he was in Denver, busy raising financial support. With news of the revolution, Sun first traveled to England to assure its neutrality in the war.

Sun Yat-sen was elected provisional president in the new Nanjing government upon his return to China. Optimism remained high. Numerous China observers in the West felt the overthrow of the Qing Dynasty would lift the shackles holding China back. They believed a democratic China could blossom, and many missionaries shared their optimism.

But the hope of a new democratic China never materialized. After his election as provisional president, Sun Yat-sen faced one remaining obstacle: the emperor still ruled in Beijing, and the three adjacent provinces in the north remained loyal to him. Yuan Shikai, the military leader, negotiated an end to the standoff. Yuan persuaded each side, both of whom feared massive bloodshed and the destruction of China, to stand down. The boy emperor Puyi agreed to abdicate the throne, Sun Yat-sen agreed to resign as president, and the clever Yuan Shikai installed himself as the new president of China. Sadly, China quickly descended into chaos, and Yuan Shikai himself died in 1916.

In the aftermath of the fall of the Qing Dynasty and the failure of the new democratic government, China descended into the warlord period. The warlord period, beginning in the mid-1910s, left China with only a figurehead central government, as real power devolved to local strongmen who controlled weapons and militia. The size of their military fiefdoms ranged from very small, maybe only a city or two, to quite large, perhaps two or three provinces. The brief warlord period was characterized by militarization throughout China, exploitation of the people, increased opium abuse, and extreme disruption. While tragic, the warlord era created new opportunities for the missionaries, and it featured some extremely colorful characters. Some of the warlords were known by snappy monikers, such as the "Confucian Warlord," the "Philosopher General," and the "Dogmeat General."

Field Notes: On The "Christian Warlord"

Personally, my favorite warlord was the "Christian Warlord," Feng Yuxiang (馮玉祥, 1882–1948). He was known to baptize his soldiers before they went into battle by lining them up in formation and drenching them with a firehose!

CONCLUSION

China needed radical reform. The failure of the Revolution acutely emphasized the need for change. Revolutionary political leaders and radical intellectuals vigorously debated a wide range of concepts and philosophies that could impact their homeland. The missionaries should have been particularly well-positioned and qualified to participate in these varied and many discussions. However, the missionaries were increasingly shut out. The Chinese Christians were also spurned, even though many of them were highly educated in the missionary schools and in universities overseas. Even worse, the Chinese Christians themselves were deemed part of the problem. As we will see in the next chapter, they were not even welcome to join the deliberation to find a solution. The fast-paced events in China, yet again, inexplicably seemed to conspire together to marginalize the Chinese Christians and exclude them from the broader society. The Christians responded by further distancing themselves from the missionaries and through establishing indigenous Chinese churches.

REFLECTION QUESTIONS

1. How would the formative experiences of a person born in China in 1900 differ from a person born in 1870 (just one generation earlier)?

2. In what ways did the radical new ideas discussed in the 1910s and 1920s reflect biblical values? How were the ideas contrary to biblical values?

3. Could Western ideas have been be incorporated selectively into China without the wholesale adoption of Western culture, philosophy, and worldview? Was the Western worldview necessarily Christian? Could China have embraced ideas like science, equality, and democracy without first adopting Christianity?

4. How did the warlord period (1910s–1927) offer unprecedented opportunity for Christian missions and Christianity?

SUGGESTED READING FOR CHAPTER 9

Duara, Prasenjit. *Rescuing History from the Nation: Questioning Narratives of Modern China*. Chicago: University of Chicago Press, 1995.

Dunch, Ryan. *Fuzhou Protestants and the Making of Modern China, 1857–1927*. New Haven: Yale University Press, 2001.

Tang, Xiaobing. *Global Space and Nationalist Discourse of Modernity: The Historical Thinking of Liang Qichao*. Stanford: Stanford University Press, 1996.

10

New Enemies of Christianity
The May Fourth Era

THE WARLORD ERA OF the 1910s and 1920s produced a flood of intellectual activity and literary productivity in China. Modern China was born during this highly charged era of political chaos. The fall of the Qing Dynasty and the rise of the warlord era temporarily lifted the rigid ideological and philosophical shackles that the central government had traditionally imposed. With no one exercising control in Beijing, intellectuals enjoyed unprecedented academic freedom. In practical terms, that meant intellectuals did not need to fear arrest. If they offended a local leader or warlord, they could simply relocate to the jurisdiction of another warlord. And even if all the warlords rejected the ideas of a particular intellectual, that individual could always flee to Shanghai for the protection provided by the British. With almost complete freedom, the intellectuals eagerly challenged Chinese traditions and culture.

The author Lu Xun composed and published a popular short story in 1918 to emphasize the need for change in China. In the story, Lu offered a scathing satirical critique of Chinese culture and tradition. He portrayed Chinese culture as cannibalistic, a society that revered the powerful and cared little for its weaker members, a culture where people ate one another. The central character in the story was a madman who became convinced everyone wanted to eat him. In his psychotic state, he wrote out his paranoid observations in a diary. For instance, in one diary entry, he talked about his well-intentioned older brother. His brother brought a doctor to the house, but the madman became convinced the doctor was an executioner in disguise. When the doctor felt his pulse, the madman was sure the doctor was inspecting his flesh to determine his amount of fat. The doctor told him to rest for a few days, and the madman presumed the sinister doctor was just waiting until he had grown fatter so there would be more flesh to eat. Soon, the madman suspected his own brother was also involved in the plot to eat him with his mother collaborating.

One night when the madman could not fall asleep, he read through the Chinese classics on "virtue and morality." But written on each page, between the lines, he saw the words "eat people." Near the end of the story, the madman chillingly came to realize that he himself may have unwittingly been involved in eating his own dead sister's flesh. In desperation, with an understanding of the full complicity of everyone within his society, including himself, the madman desperately cried out, "Save the children!"

This groundbreaking and influential short story by Lu Xun (魯迅, 1881–1936) is called *Diary of a Madman* (狂人日記). With powerful symbolism and the use of easy-to-understand Chinese, Lu skewered four thousand years of Chinese history and culture, a culture where, according to the madman, everyone became an unwitting participant in eating the flesh of others. Lu took an axe to the very root of Chinese civilization by having the madman read the classics on "virtue and morality," where the madman saw the words "eat people" between the lines. The imagery revealed that the problems in China did not just manifest during the period of the warlords, but that even the very best of Chinese culture, the revered classics, produced wickedness within Chinese society. The famous final words of the story established a watchword for the New Culture Movement of the 1910s: "Save the children." Chinese culture was ripe for revolution, and the intellectuals were anxious to foment it.

The vigorous intellectual milieu of the 1920s might have offered the missionaries and Chinese Christians an unprecedented opening to interact with Chinese intellectuals and Chinese culture. Instead, at this precise and most inopportune moment, the schism between the Protestant modernists and the fundamentalists ruptured the Christian community. The internecine church dispute that had been gaining momentum for decades in the West, especially in the United States, spilled into China in the 1920s. On one side, the modernists believed Christian doctrines could be harmonized with modern developments, particularly in the scientific fields, and the missionaries aligned with this view were convinced that the survival of the Chinese churches was at stake. Christianity in China could only survive, they contended, if the tenets of the church could be modernized to match the spirit of the May Fourth movement. The fundamentalist missionaries agreed that the survival of the Chinese churches was at stake, but they insisted, in contrast, that only faithful adherence to the fundamental and historic doctrines of the church could save the churches in China.

This chapter opens with a description of the intellectual breakthroughs of the New Culture Movement of the 1910s and the May Fourth Movement of the 1920s. But the Chinese intelligentsia did not only target Chinese tradition for criticism; they also took devastating aim at Christianity. The second part of the chapter, then, examines the venomous Anti-Christian Movement of the 1920s. Finally, the chapter briefly considers the dilemma that divided the missionaries. What was their message in the modern world, in the midst of the May Fourth movement? Should they present the answers found in the ancient apostolic faith, or should they offer solutions provided by modern science and philosophy? In short time, these questions also deeply divided the Chinese Christians.

THE MAY FOURTH MOVEMENT

On May 4, 1919, one of the best-known dates in twentieth-century Chinese history, college students flooded Tiananmen Square protesting the Versailles Peace Treaty. Their actions ignited the radical era of intellectual upheaval known as the May Fourth Movement.

Field Notes: On Christian Participation in Student Demonstrations

When I think of the May Fourth Movement, I like to look at it through the perspective of Wang Mingdao, who was a young Chinese student at the time in Beijing. Wang, as mentioned, was born in late July of 1900 in Beijing, during the Boxer uprising. He was just short of his nineteenth birthday as many young students stormed the square in 1919.

In Chinese church history classes, I often ask my students, "Where was Wang Mingdao on May 4, 1919? Where was he as his classmates and friends in Beijing demonstrated in Tiananmen Square?" Although Wang is almost universally known and respected among Evangelical Chinese seminarians, I have yet to find one student who knows the answer, but my question makes them very curious. Their ignorance of Wang's whereabouts that momentous day suggests to me that they are not yet connecting even the most explosive moments in Chinese history together with the development of the Chinese churches and the biographies of important Chinese Christians. As I will try to show in Chapter 13 when I cover his story, I believe Wang Mingdao was profoundly shaped by these events.

(*And, as I also tell my students in class, I won't answer the question of whether or not Wang participated in the demonstrations until then!*)

Background

The 1911 revolution was a failure, and the Republic fell into the warlord period. Foreign encroachments continued, and China keenly perceived its own weakness in relation to the Western powers. At the time, the Western nations were colonizing Africa, and numerous Chinese intellectuals feared that China would also be colonized, or, as some scholars put it, "carved up like a melon." At that moment, in 1914, World War I broke out.

Near the outset of the war, Japan joined the Allies, declaring war on Germany. The Chinese also joined with the Allies, and in the aftermath of the war, the Chinese expected the German concession in Shandong, the area that had been grabbed in 1898 in the build-up to the Boxer uprising, to be returned to Chinese sovereignty. However, as it was discovered after the war, the Japanese had negotiated an agreement with the Allied powers of Britain, France, and Italy. This agreement instead promised the German concession of Shandong to the Japanese. When this secret agreement became public at the Versailles Peace Conference in 1919, the Chinese were furious.

The United States had not been party to the secret pact, and President Woodrow Wilson opposed the plan. However, Wilson prioritized his hope to launch the League of Nations, and so he did not defend the Chinese territorial rights. Rather, he agreed that if the other powers would support the League of Nations, he was willing to acquiesce and allow Japan to take control of the German concessions in Shandong. Sadly, for China, the fragmented government of the warlords could not resist the foregone conclusion. The Chinese people felt humiliated and were further incensed.

This cauldron of emotion erupted when three thousand Chinese students protesting the Treaty demonstrated in Tiananmen Square on May 4, 1919, inaugurating a tradition of protest in the capital that continues today. They carried anti-Japanese posters, and they marched on the home of a cabinet member and burned down his house. When they approached the foreign legation, they were turned away and some thirty protesters were thrown in jail. Sympathy strikes arose across Beijing and in two hundred other cities. China never signed the Versailles Peace Treaty.

The May Fourth Movement grew out of the events of May 4, 1919, and it had its roots in the New Culture Movement of the 1910s. The 1920s saw the blossoming of a myriad of new ideas. Hundreds of new newspapers and magazines were published. Revolutionaries dared to challenge Confucian family ethics, as sons revolted against their fathers. Women unbound their feet and insisted on receiving an education. Foreign influence grew, more books were translated, and many scholars, such as John Dewey and Bertrand Russell, were invited to China. China was challenging its traditions and looking outward.

The New Culture Movement

One of the most important scholars of the era, the "second generation," was Chen Duxiu (陳獨秀, 1879–1940). In 1915, he founded *New Youth Magazine* (新青年雜誌) in order to promote "Mr. S" and "Mr. D" (Science and Democracy) (德先生和賽先生). The magazine was originally called *Youth Magazine*, but Chen changed the name one year later to *New Youth* when he realized many young people were slipping into old patterns of thought. In a traditional Confucian Chinese context, even the title of the magazine was radical. Chen, in this 1916 article, called on the new youth to step forward:

> Precious and beloved youth, if you consider yourselves twentieth-century people, you must get rid of old attitudes. Rid yourselves of the reactionary and corrupt old thinking about officialdom and wealth and develop a new faith. . . . Precious and beloved youth, forsake this narrow, selfish mentality and develop the characteristics of new youth. Bury the old youth whose narrow-mindedness led to conservatism and corruption. Be different![1]

These concepts churned among the intellectuals and exhorted them to change, and Christians also needed to interact with the new youth who held modern ideas.

Another significant, pivotal scholar was Hu Shi (胡適, 1891–1962). Perhaps the most far-reaching and enduring transformation of the May Fourth era was the "*baihua*" movement (vernacular movement) (白話運動), a movement popularized by Hu Shi in two articles published in *New Youth*. The articles, issued in 1917 and 1918, advanced ideas from the earlier generation. The revolutionary significance of moving away from classical Chinese toward the adoption of vernacular Chinese was captured in 1898 by the scholar Qiu Tingliang (裘廷梁) who wrote, "honor *baihua*, discard *wenyan*" (崇白話而廢文言). Qiu argued:

---

1. Schwarcz, *Chinese Enlightenment*, 61.

> *Wenyan* [literary language] is the matchless vehicle for keeping
> the nation in ignorance. *Baihua* [vernacular language] is the
> matchless vehicle for giving knowledge to the nation. . . . To sum
> up: if *wenyan* flourishes, learning will perish; if *baihua* expands,
> learning will thrive. If learning does not thrive, there will be no
> nation.[2]

Hu Shi adopted and popularized those ideas, and the success of the vernacular movement of the 1920s did serve to democratize literacy and learning in China in the twentieth century.

Field Notes: On Using Popular Language

Christians in China also needed to engage with these ideas. I will suggest later that, at the same time Hu Shi was popularizing the vernacular, Wang Mingdao became a master of using vernacular Chinese (baihua) to promote the gospel.

May Fourth and the Enlightenment

The 1920s in China has been referred to as the "Chinese Enlightenment," and ideas such as rationalism and equality became prominent. However, even as China moved towards ideals championed in the West, Christianity did not benefit from that transformation. Even worse, Christianity gained new enemies in China. In a speech delivered in 1925, Hu Shi noted that in 1900, it was the superstitious Boxers who opposed Christianity, but just twenty-five years later, it was the enlightened intellectuals who rejected Christianity as superstitious. The intellectuals of his generation were convinced that modernism and rationalism would save China, and they were willing, in varying degrees, to clear away centuries of Chinese tradition and civilization. They had scant interest in Christianity and its antiquated beliefs and traditions.

The May Fourth Movement ended in 1927, when Chiang Kai-shek and the KMT (Nationalist Party) succeeded in ending the warlord era and nominally reunifying the country. The academics lost some of their autonomy as they were again brought under the ideological control of the central government, at least in part. Furthermore, by 1927, some of the scholastic leaders had fallen under the influence of Marxism and the fledgling Chinese

---

2. Goldman, *Modern Chinese Literature*, 22.

Communist Party, which had been founded by Chen Duxiu in 1921. Finally, many intellectuals abandoned the pursuit of Enlightenment ideals, fearing that endless discussion of those ideals would lead to the death of China. Instead, they coalesced around conversation focused on the task of saving the nation. National salvation, not building a new culture or civilization, became their unifying goal. Later in life, Hu Shi regretted the move away from pursuing Enlightenment ideals, lamenting that nationalism was a "blow from which the New Culture Movement never fully recovered."[3]

THE ANTI-CHRISTIAN MOVEMENT

In 1919, the Young China Association debated the role of religious faith in new China. China faced a slew of problems. Rampant corruption abounded, and widespread suffering multiplied from the chaos caused by the warlords. Many people experienced grinding poverty. The Western powers threatened to "carve up" China as they had Africa. And yet, astonishingly, the young Chinese intellectuals were convinced the Christians could not contribute anything of value to the discourse. Hu Shi, Chen Duxiu, Cai Yuanpei, and many other intellectuals opposed all religions as superstitious, unscientific, and a hindrance to social progress.

This rejection of the Christian faith forms the backdrop of the anti-Christian movement of the 1920s. The anti-Christian movement played out in three phases.

Phase 1: Anti-Christian Protests, 1922

The first phase of the Anti-Christian Movement saw massive protests in 1922, demonstrations sparked by three significant developments in 1922 which occurred in rapid succession.

The publication by the missionaries of a massive tome on the state of missions and Christianity served as the first cause of the demonstrations. The oversized volume represented a staggering accomplishment. It carefully examined each part of China, identifying the names of cities and villages, as well as cataloguing the religious makeup of each area. Temple, mosque, and church locations were all mapped out, along with detailed statistics. The missionaries compiled the volume to help them efficiently serve the Chinese people and reach them with the gospel, but perhaps they did not

---

3. Grieder, *Hu Shih and the Chinese Renaissance*, 176–77.

anticipate how thoroughly offensive the book was to the Chinese people. To the Chinese observer, it was a massive Western project dedicated to spreading a foreign religion, and thus undermined China and Chinese civilization. While the volume itself was offensive, the title was worse. The unfortunate title of the book was *The Christian Occupation of China.*

The second event that sparked the anti-Christian protests of 1922 involved the publication of a book on Christian education. The work focused attention on the enormous influence of the education complex that the missionaries had built over many decades. The third and final trigger in 1922 was an international YMCA conference scheduled to be held in China, called the World Student Christian Federation (WSCF) Conference.

In response to the WSCF conference, students organized the Anti-Christian Student Federation to lead the anti-Christian demonstrations. The new Federation may have been influenced by the Socialist Youth Corps, as their literature contained some Marxist terminology and rhetoric. One proclamation from the Anti-Christian Student Federation from 1922 read:

> The capitalists from various countries have established churches in China, for the sole purpose of cajoling the Chinese people to welcome capitalism; they have also established the YMCA in China, for the sole purpose of bringing up docile and faithful walking dogs for themselves. In short, their aim is to suck dry the blood of the Chinese people. Therefore, we are opposed to capitalism; and at the same time we must be opposed to the current Christian religion and its churches which support capitalism while cheating the ordinary people.[4]

The missionaries and the Chinese churches faced fierce criticism, and the anti-Christian temperature continued to rise after 1922.

Phase 2: Educational Rights Recovery Movement, 1924

The second phase of the anti-Christian movement emerged about two years later in 1924. This phase comprised a move to restore education in China to Chinese sovereignty. The Educational Rights Recovery Movement was a determined effort to complete the process of nationalizing education that had begun during the final years of the Qing Dynasty. Because Christianity was considered a tool of Western imperialism which undermined Chinese civilization, the elimination of religious teaching from the schools became a

---

4. Kessler, *Jiangyin Mission Station*, 69.

priority. The quotation below effectively communicates a common Chinese critique of the foreign-controlled schools:

> Foreign-controlled schools undermined the state's prerogative to educate its own citizens as it saw fit. The students attending such schools became denationalized, losing their identity as Chinese, and often were poorly trained in the Chinese language, literature, and culture. The Chinese staff in these institutions were subordinated to their foreign superiors and given insufficient responsibility in the administration of the school. The subjects the schools taught and the values they imparted were "foreign" and unsuited to China's needs. In addition, many opposed the schools because they taught a religion they considered superstitious and irrational.[5]

The new regulations decreed that:

- The president or vice president of all the schools must be a Chinese person.
- The Board of Directors must have a majority of Chinese people.
- The schools were not allowed to spread religion, and they were not allowed to require religious classes.
- The curriculum must conform to Ministry of Education guidelines.

At the time, the missionaries were generally willing to comply. They particularly recognized the need for Chinese people to take over the positions of leadership in the schools. However, the restrictions on religious classes created more tension. Most of the missionaries had come to China with the desire to teach Christianity. Although China was still divided under the warlords, the reforms were adopted by the government in Beijing in 1925, and the KMT adopted the regulations for the entire country in 1928.

Gradually, the rules did effectively bring education back under the control of Chinese leaders. Finally, in 1949, when all the Christian schools were transferred to government control or closed, the era of missionary education ended.

Field Notes: On Bringing Missionaries Back to China Today

In China today, a fascinating debate has arisen concerning the old missionary schools. A number of years ago I met a retired government official

---

5. Kessler, *Jiangyin Mission Station*, 84.

who was an alumnus of St. John's University in Shanghai. St. John's was founded in 1879 by missionaries, and in the 1890s they began to use English as the language of instruction. It became possibly the most prestigious university in China, sometimes considered the "Harvard" of China. The man I met had graduated in the 1940s, before the school was closed by the Communist government in 1952. I learned from the man that a group of alumni in the 1990s hoped to reopen the school. There was one critical issue the alumni were debating. Some of them were committed to making the new St. John's a thoroughly Chinese school, rejecting the Western imperialism reflected at St. John's before 1949. However, the man I met was part of an opposing faction. This group maintained that a thoroughly Chinese school could not be "St. John's University." For instance, without the Western teachers and white missionaries roaming the campus, the University would not be the same. It would not be the school that they remembered. An interesting conundrum indeed.

Phase 3: May Thirtieth Movement, 1925

The third and most violent phase of the Anti-Christian Movement began in 1925, called the May Thirtieth Movement. These events, summarized only briefly here, had profound impact on the missionaries. First, Chinese workers went on strike in a Japanese textile mill, and on May 15, an eight-man delegation was sent to negotiate. The Japanese guard opened fire on the Chinese workers, killing one and wounding eight. The Shanghai Municipal Council, which was mostly British, did not arrest the Japanese guard, but instead arrested a number of the Chinese workers.

One week later on May 22, many more Chinese people were arrested at a memorial service for the dead Chinese worker. On May 30, 3,000 students protested the arrests in Shanghai, and the British police fired shots into the crowd, killing eleven people, wounding many others, and arresting many as well. There were then strikes, protests, and boycotts held around China. In December of 1925, the British attempted to diffuse the situation by dismissing the British police officials involved.

The tensions remained extremely high through 1926, and in March of 1927, the "Nanjing Incident" occurred (not to be confused with the better known "Nanjing Massacre" of 1937). In 1927, the KMT attempted to seize control from the warlords and to reunify China under KMT rule. Within that already volatile environment, an American educator and five foreigners in Nanjing were killed by soldiers, and property was also destroyed. In the aftermath of the killing, Chinese soldiers and civilians rioted against foreign interests, burning houses and attacking the British and American consulates. Then, on March 24, foreign warships bombarded the city, defending the foreign residents against the rioting and looting. By March 26, the KMT commander restored order in Nanjing. But thousands of alarmed missionaries were sent fleeing from their missions stations.

The Nanjing Incident of 1927 effectively marked the end of the Anti-Christian Movement, as the KMT successfully wrested control of the country from the warlords and as many missionaries withdrew from the country. Of the 8,000 missionaries in China at the beginning of 1927, 5,000 had left China by 1928. Another 1,500 took refuge in Shanghai, and 1,000 took refuge in other coastal cities. Only 500 missionaries, at least for the time, remained in the interior. The missionaries did return, but this incident only reinforced the need for an independent Chinese Christian church.

THE MISSIONARY RESPONSE

The missionaries fought two cruel battles in the 1920s. On one front, in China, they faced the Anti-Christian Movement, which included both intellectual challenges and physical assaults. Second, on the home front, especially in the United States, a deep schism had developed between the fundamentalists and the modernists. The split severed churches, denominations, and seminaries, and it threatened to leave missionaries without support. In China, both sides prepared to battle for the hearts and minds of the Chinese people, hoping to win over the growing indigenous churches.

Modernist–Fundamentalist Debate

The modernist–fundamentalist schism may have been most pronounced in the United States, but it also became intensely felt in China. Surprisingly, the issues that divided the American churches carried particular relevance in China. In fact, the division might have become even more pronounced in China than in the United States.

The two key issues of Darwinism and "higher" biblical criticism had split the churches in America. These issues both cut to the heart of biblical Christianity. Darwinism provided a natural explanation for the origins of the universe and humanity, while higher biblical criticism provided a natural explanation for the origins of Scripture. In China, during the "Chinese Enlightenment" of the 1920s, these issues also resonated.

In America in the 1920s, as intellectuals were moving away from an uncritical belief in creation and the authority of the bible, the churches needed to respond. The modernists believed that biblical scholars and theologians should keep pace with the modern intellectuals, and they should adapt to the profound developments in modern science. They were convinced there was nothing to fear from any truth that might be found in modern science. On the other side, the fundamentalists were determined to defend the ancient Christian beliefs, regardless of any novel philosophical developments or fresh scientific discoveries. They feared an embrace of modernism and science could lead the church away from the fundamental truths revealed in the bible.

In sum, both sides were fighting for the very survival of the churches in the modern world.

Modernists and Fundamentalists in China

Significantly, both the modernists and the fundamentalists feared for the young churches on the mission fields. While the mature churches in America could possibly withstand extended debate about the fine points of theology and science, the young churches in China might not survive the controversy. This controversy could explode into more than just an academic argument to become a life-or-death fight for the very survival of the churches. The debates among the missionaries grew strident and were quickly echoed by Chinese church leaders.

Why was the modernist–fundamentalist debate so readily transported to China? The young May Fourth intellectuals like Hu Shi and Chen Duxiu were drinking deeply of modern Western philosophy and science, and many of the modernist missionaries and modernist Chinese Christian intellectuals believed strongly that the Chinese churches needed to embrace modern ideology. If theology could not adapt, they reasoned, the young Chinese churches would surely die.

On the other side, fundamentalist missionaries believed just as strongly that the Chinese churches needed to hold tightly to their traditional beliefs in order to survive. Quickly, many of the Chinese Christians embraced fundamentalist theology, particularly those Christians who were not associated with the universities. Wang Mingdao was one of the Chinese Christians who readily joined the debate, and in an article from the 1920s he listed the "five points of fundamentalism." He numbered them from one through five, as they were being debated in America, and he insisted that true Christians must maintain these fundamental doctrines of the church. He was a staunch defender of fundamentalist Christianity, believing the life of the church was at stake. (Wang Mingdao and his colorful debate with the modernists will be discussed in the next chapter.)

Declining Significance of the Missionaries?

In the midst of this controversy, the missionaries found themselves in a peculiar situation. The modernist missionaries were engaged in a critical theological debate, both at home and on the mission field in China. Simultaneously, the Anti-Christian Student Federation wanted to disqualify all Christians from the contemporary cultural and political discussions, and their anti-Christian rhetoric, sometimes inspired by Marxism, opposed all religion. The modernist missionaries aspired, therefore, to interact academically with the Chinese intellectuals. They hoped to demonstrate that Christianity could be forward-looking and could act as a key dialogue partner of the emerging modern China. But they were not welcome in the debate.

The fundamentalist missionaries stood on the opposite extreme, insisting that the message should not be changed. The message of the ancient church and the apostles contained the same message that was needed in China in the 1920s. They understood the desperate situation in China, and they trusted traditional biblical Christianity could provide the greatest hope for China.

The modernists and fundamentalists held different concepts of the bible, the gospel, and China, and their understanding of these concepts became increasingly different with time. They simply could not agree on the meaning of the gospel for China. Frank Rawlinson, the longtime editor of the Chinese missionary journal, the *Chinese Recorder*, wrote an editorial during the 1920s that cleverly summarized the missionary quandary. Rawlinson wrote:

> The present China missionary mind is a Kaleidoscope. Trying to describe it is like trying to foretell the next arrangement of colors in a kaleidoscope. The missionary mind is made up of a hundred or more different and practically discordant thought-colors . . . the missionary mind has, so to speak, lost its cue . . . The missionary mind is uncertain as to whether first or twentieth century Christianity is to be the model for China . . . Looked

at in the large the Christian Movement appears messageless. A messageless movement must rediscover itself.[6]

After a little more than one hundred years of the Protestant missionary movement in China, a dark picture could be painted. The missionaries' message was still largely rejected by the majority of the Chinese people, and they could not agree, as a whole, on the fundamental tenets of the gospel. Even their highly successful schools were increasingly targeted for severe criticism. And, as in 1900 with the Boxer uprising and in 1927 with the Nanjing Incident, the missionaries occasionally became the target of violent attacks.

And yet, year after year, the missionaries continued to live out their calling, to show the patience and the love of Christ. And the Chinese Christians persevered in finding their footing as they toiled to cultivate an indigenous Chinese church.

REFLECTION QUESTIONS

1. Should a Chinese Christian have participated in the demonstrations on Tiananmen Square on May 4, 1919? Why or why not?

2. The Chinese intellectuals of the May Fourth period criticized Christianity for not being modern.

   - How did the modernists respond?

   - How did the fundamentalists respond?

   - How would you respond to the charge that Christianity was out of date and not relevant to the problems today?

3. Discuss the primary concerns of the Educational Rights Recovery Movement.

   - Should Christians have supported the movement?

   - In what areas would Christians have generally agreed with the goals of the movement?

   - In what ways would Christians have generally disagreed with the goals of the movement?

---

6. Cook, "Fundamentalism and Modern Culture," 83.

4. Can Christianity truly offer a path to a new culture or national salvation? In a setting as dire as China in the 1920s, do we as Christians have complete confidence that Christianity and the church could have offered a solution?

SUGGESTED READING FOR CHAPTER 10

Gilmartin, Christina Kelley. *Engendering the Chinese Revolution: Radical Women, Communist Politics, and Mass Movements in the 1920s.* Berkeley: University of California Press, 1995.

Goldman, Merle, ed. *Modern Chinese Literature in the May Fourth Era.* Cambridge: Harvard University Press, 1977.

Kwok, Pui-lan. *Chinese Women and Christianity, 1860–1927.* American Academy of Religion Academy Series 75. Atlanta: Scholars, 1992.

Lu, Xun. *Diary of a Madman and Other Stories.* Translated by William A. Lyell. Honolulu: University of Hawaii Press, 1990.

Rahav, Shakhar. *The Rise of Political Intellectuals in Modern China: May Fourth Societies and the Roots of Mass-Party Politics.* Oxford: Oxford University Press, 2015.

Schwarcz, Vera. *The Chinese Enlightenment: Intellectuals and the Legacy of the May Fourth Movement of 1919.* Berkeley: University of California Press, 1986.

Sheridan, James E. *Chinese Warlord: The Career of Feng Yu-Hsiang.* Stanford: Stanford University Press, 1966.

11

Cross Currents
Nationalism, Fundamentalism, and Global Christianity

THE INDIGENOUS CHINESE CHURCHES that emerged in the first half of the twentieth century did so among innumerable, swirling, socio-political currents, both globally and in China. This chapter will examine nationalism, fundamentalism, and global Christianity, and the next chapter will discuss imperialism.[1]

Nationalism, and nation building, became a global phenomenon throughout the twentieth century, and China experienced the potency of the movement particularly keenly. Protestant Fundamentalism, originating at that time from the United States, brought unfortunate division and thorny challenges to the young, non-Western missionary churches around the world, with the churches in China certainly included in that number. Global Christianity was only beginning to take root between 1900 and 1950, but the exponential expansion of Christianity in Asia, Africa, and Latin America throughout the twentieth century created a significant portion of the context of the development of indigenous Christianity in China. The growth of indigenous Christianity in China cannot be understood in a

---

1. My narrative thus far has focused on the "evangelicals," but from about 1920–1950, the historic evangelical movement split, and two new labels emerged: modernist and fundamentalist. The modernists generally evolved into the mainline Protestants identified with the ecumenical movement in the second half of the twentieth century, and many of the fundamentalists into the "neo-evangelical" movement. Although I properly use the term "fundamentalist" to describe people like Wang Mingdao, in current terminology he might be considered "neo-evangelical" or, more simply, "evangelical."

vacuum; it was buffeted by these three currents, and imperialism (discussed in the next chapter) most likely acted as the strongest current.

CHINESE NATIONALISM

An all-encompassing charge against the Chinese Christians that had become prevalent by the 1920s declared, "One more Christian, one less Chinese." In a Confucian culture which prized group cohesion and social harmony, this charge was a stinging attack. This once ubiquitous accusation, well-known into the 1980s, has become less common after 2000, but it is still worth considering why critics of Christianity would have uttered such an indictment. Amid the nation building in the first half of the twentieth century, critics asserted that Chinese Christians were de-culturalized, de-nationalized, and cajoled into dependence on the West.

De-culturalization

The charge that Christians were de-culturalized may have partially arisen from the missionary methods practiced in the nineteenth and twentieth centuries. Ideally, according to church growth theory, multiple members of a single family would join a church at the same time, and, even more desirably, that family would constitute part of a larger mass movement to Christianity. The conversion of entire communities would then facilitate cultural adaptation to the new faith. In China, missionaries endeavored to fulfill this plan - to win families to Christ, and then communities, but they were not always successful. Instead, baptism was often administered to individuals, which sometimes alienated those people from their families. Missions critics refer to this as "extraction," the process of isolating Christian individuals from their families or separating small Christian family units from their neighboring community. Once divided from their family and neighborhood, the Christians were often perceived as traitors to the community and the nation. There were a myriad of ways that the individual Christian could become suspicious to his peers, but a common problem centered around the refusal to participate in local community religious rituals. A Christian then exacerbated this refusal by also neglecting to provide regular financial support for the temple ceremonies.

In the home, individual Christians would also decline to participate in the customary family rituals. Because ancestor rites were at the center of family life, Christians were called on by non-Christian family members to participate in rituals to honor the dead. Even today, Chinese Christians in Taiwan, as well as in many communities around Asia, continue to struggle with this issue.

Field Notes: On Ancestor Rites

One Chinese friend in Taiwan told me this story. At his father's funeral, he was called on, as the eldest son, to lead the ceremony before his father's casket. At one point in the funeral, he was to lead the entire family before the casket and at his command, the family was to drop to the ground and kowtow to the father. (Kowtow is a word that entered the English language from Chinese, the word ketou 磕頭*. It means the same thing in English and Chinese—to knock one's forehead to the ground in reverence before a superior or a deity.) I am aware that Chinese Christians have many different opinions about how my friend should have responded to his family's request to lead the ceremony. My friend, after much prayer, decided that he could lead the family before the casket, but then when everyone else prostrated themselves, he would remain standing in silent and respectful prayer. As expected, his relatives were incensed. One uncle, the younger brother of his father, was animated in his denunciation of this shameful act. How dare the eldest son, the uncle raged, arrogantly stand with a stiff back before his deceased father? He took aim, and spit on my friend's shoes. Indeed, Christians can find themselves estranged from their families.*

Churches and Christian leaders today disagree about how to handle ancestor practices, and Christians from all cultures should be sensitive to the fact that religious adherents might resent the converts who betray the beliefs and rituals of the traditional family and community. Missiologists in recent decades have promoted the notion of dynamic equivalents with the hope that promoting the use of dynamic equivalents will help new Christians remain closely associated to their home culture.

Missiologists have suggested that indigenous Christians can be given substitutes for traditional practices. For instance, Chinese converts, sometimes with the encouragement of missionaries, have customarily destroyed the family altar in their home. The ceremony for the destruction of the altar and the idols was occasionally dramatic and usually performed in the open. A dynamic equivalent would be to create a similar family altar in the home. This new family altar would be Christianized and could serve as the center of Christian family worship. Not all Chinese Christians agree with this accommodation, however.

Field Notes: On My Ordination to the Ministry

I remember during my ordination examination, I was questioned about ancestor practices by several of the elderly Chinese pastors on my ordination committee. When I heard the question about the family altar, I was delighted because I felt I knew the answer, having learned about dynamic equivalents in seminary. I carefully explained my understanding of dynamic equivalents to the veteran Chinese pastors with many years of experience working with Chinese converts, and I almost failed the exam. Several of the pastors on my committee were unequivocal. They did not agree with "dynamic equivalents," and they were certain that all forms of idolatry must be entirely removed from the home of all Christians.

At the root of the dispute concerning ancestor practices, a debate which also raged among the Catholics throughout the Rites Controversy, lay a fundamental issue which needed to be addressed. Could a person be completely Chinese and yet reject basic Chinese cultural rituals and beliefs such as the ancestor practices? Was there merit, perhaps, to the contention that truly Chinese individuals could not be Christian?

Chinese Protestants continue in the struggle to reach a consensus on ancestor practices. While some Chinese Christians reject the rituals completely, others try to find accommodation. Many Chinese and many Christians disagree, but throughout Chinese church history, Christians have found creative ways to accommodate various aspects of Chinese culture.

De-nationalization

In the modern era, Christians around the world have debated the role of the church in the nation. An area of particular interest in China involved the Christian schools and the modern education available in the young, Western-style universities. Did a Western education undermine Chinese culture and Chinese nationalism? In the modern world, could a Chinese scholar be immersed in both the modern sciences and the Confucian classics? If a Chinese person pursued a Western education, was it inevitable that his affinity with Chinese literature and culture would be compromised? The missionaries, from the very start, established schools, and Liang Fa, for example, was removed from China as a young man and converted during his time at the Anglo-Chinese College in Malacca. Many of the Chinese who took advantage of the new educational institutions established by the missionaries converted to Christianity. The Chinese Christians might insist they were no less nationalist or less patriotic to China, but they did adopt an additional allegiance.

A more specific attack against the Chinese Christians emerged in the 1920s from the Chinese nationalist intellectuals. Wang Mingdao (who will be discussed more fully in chapter 13), for instance, was specifically criticized by the Chinese nationalists in the 1920s and later. Ironically, it was not Wang Mingdao who studied in the West, but many of the Chinese students such as Chen Duxiu, Zhou Enlai, and Deng Xiaoping, who learned about Marxism while they studied in Paris. Based on Marxist ideology, these Western-trained communists criticized the Chinese churches as antiquated and superstitious, unfit for the modern world. They accused the Chinese Christians of serving as the "running dogs" of Western capitalism, with much rhetorical bravado.

This harsh critique did not ring true for Wang Mingdao or many other independent Chinese Christians, who did not acquiesce to the West or serve the interests of imperialism. Wang, in fact, never set foot outside of China his entire life, and he remained doggedly true to Chinese culture and China. The entire life of Wang Mingdao, which spanned most of the twentieth century, and his stubbornly independent Chinese Christian church, provided an unambiguous response to the charge, "One more Christian, one less Chinese."

Field Notes: On Tomb-Sweeping

When I lived in Taiwan in the 1990s, I learned of a peculiar consequence of this history. On Qingming or Ching Ming Festival (or in English, "Tomb-Sweeping Day"), traditional Chinese families are expected to visit the gravesites of their ancestors and sweep the area and provide some basic upkeep of the grave. I remember expressing surprise that some of my Chinese Christian friends had participated in the ritual. They laughed and said, I am sure with some exaggeration, that it is only Christians who visit the gravesites. That is, they go because they know other Chinese criticize them for not participating in Chinese cultural activities. My friends told me that now, ironically, it is only the Christians who still participate in Tomb-Sweeping Day!

Participation in cultural practices such as Grave Sweeping Day might be commendable, showing Chinese Christian identity with Chinese culture, but overidentification is also a danger. Chinese Christians today, I suspect, have often reacted to the charge of anti-nationalism, and many have adopted overly nationalistic and patriotic positions. Christians should celebrate and champion the positive aspects of traditional culture, but they are also responsible to stand against cultural practices that are antithetical to biblical teaching. I suggest that Chinese Christians today may hesitate to offer timely prophetic critiques of Chinese culture, society, and politics because of the baggage from the first half of the twentieth century. For example, I fear that Chinese Christian "super-nationalists" might hesitate to speak out against government policies on abortion or abuses of minority people groups, and they might avoid critically assessing Chinese nationalist expansion and possible abuses into other parts of Asia, Africa, and the Latin America.

China suffered under Western imperialism and colonialism in the nineteenth century, but powerful people have subjected weaker peoples to abuse throughout history, prompting many Christian leaders to speak out against their own governments in the same way the Old Testament prophets spoke out against the corrupt rulers of Israel. Bartolomé de Las Casas, a Spanish Dominican missionary in the New World during the sixteenth century, wrote a scathing critique of the Spanish conquest of the Indies in a classic anticolonial pamphlet, providing an example of missionaries serving as "salt and light." John Wesley, the English churchman and revivalist, roundly denounced slavery in the eighteenth century. In the nineteenth century, the missionaries in China organized opposition to the opium trade, although they did so belatedly. This tradition of Christians and preachers offering biblical admonition from a fearless moral compass is necessary to all governments, including the government in China today.

Dependency

From the inauguration of the missionary movement in China, missionaries employed local helpers. Robert Morrison needed language assistants, and missionary families needed domestic help. On a small scale, utilizing the talent of locals most likely did not create problems, but as the missionary movement grew and the missionary infrastructure expanded and deepened across the country, the number of Chinese employees multiplied. In addition, the practice of hiring church workers proved more problematic than hiring domestic help. The young indigenous churches often could not afford to pay pastors, so the missionaries themselves would provide the salary for the workers as they recognized the effectiveness of indigenous church leaders. Initially, the arrangement seemed desirable, but like a spreading cancer which seems harmless at first, it grew into one of the greatest dilemmas for the Chinese churches.

Wang Mingdao expressed his sharp criticism of this practice in the 1920s and 1930s, observing that far too many Chinese feigned interest in Christianity in order to land a job. He feared that the foreign missionaries were not adept at identifying authentic Chinese Christians, and therefore they often engaged the wrong people, creating confusion and chaos in the churches. The critics of Christianity, in their complaints about the greed, selfishness, and sinfulness of the false Chinese church "pastors," were sometimes correct. Wang Mingdao desired a pure church, led by truly born-again and pious Christians, a church which was also thoroughly indigenous and Chinese. He believed that in order to achieve purity, an indigenous church must be self-supporting, and he scrupulously avoided receiving any foreign funds in his own church. Missiologists in the late twentieth century often decried the dependency that developed in the earlier missionary churches and advocated for the three-self church principles. However, the disproportionate wealth of the missionaries as compared to the indigenous Christians made dependency a difficult issue to avoid.

Field Notes: On Dependency, a Case Study from the 1990s

I met a Chinese church leader, Pastor Tan, in the early 1990s, and he disparaged the earlier generations of missionaries who created dependency. He echoed the arguments of Wang Mingdao and other Chinese leaders who insisted on financial autonomy. Pastor Tan, who was based in the United States, provided pastoral and biblical training to indigenous Christians in mainland China. After the revivals and rapid church growth of the 1980s, the churches sought that kind of training hungrily, and Pastor Tan determined to provide them with practical help to remain independent. He feared the Western missionaries would soon arrive again, offering large sums of money to build the Chinese churches and, perhaps unintentionally, seducing the churches into dependency.

When he would raise support in the United States and Taiwan for his training courses offered in China, he would passionately speak about his hope to prepare the Chinese Christians for the arrival of the coming wave of Western missionaries. He hoped to equip them with the spiritual maturity and discernment necessary to say "no" when the West offered them piles of money and a plethora of resources. He persuaded me that outside churches, including churches in Taiwan and Chinese churches in the United States, should be discouraged from offering direct financial support to the churches in China.

To my surprise, I noted that Pastor Tan, after several years of this ministry, was raising support not just for his US and Taiwan-based teachers, but also for the indigenous church leaders in mainland China. I found that odd, so I asked him why he was seeking those additional funds. His reply demonstrated the complexity and the subtlety of the issue.

He explained that the change had happened gradually. In the late 1980s, he and his colleagues initially provided two-week training sessions in rural areas where the students were very poor. Noting that some students could not attend the classes each time he visited, he discovered that many of the young and zealous Christians lacked bus fare. He realized that he could assure their participation in the valuable programs for just a few pennies. Other students, he soon observed, were leaving the sessions early to return to work their family farm. He asked them, "How much would it cost to hire somebody to do the labor on your field for the week or two you are in class?" Pastor Tan had already generously invested money, time, and resources into the courses, and he greatly desired their full participation. He realized that for a token cost, he could guarantee that the students could attend without distraction.

The wealthy Chinese churches in the United States and Taiwan were delighted to underwrite both the cost of administration of the courses and the nominal funds needed for the indigenous Christians to attend. Once the students graduated, they naturally became the most effective ministers in their home villages. They worked in unique and vital roles for the continued growth of the churches in rural China, performing ministry that could not be done by Western missionaries, or even by Chinese Christians from Taiwan or the United States.

Pastor Tan discussed sending long-term ethnic Chinese missionaries from Taiwan or the United States to China, but he realized those outside missionaries most likely could not withstand the brutal living conditions in rural China. The climate, the diet, the medical conditions, and myriad other factors made living among the rural people seem impossible. Even if the missionaries could survive, they would forever be outsiders. Therefore, he reiterated that the most effective ministers were going to be the graduates from the training seminars. Thus, in some cases, Pastor Tan continued to provide financial and other support for some of the graduates in special circumstances. For instance, when they were sick, he would

> *raise money to help the church workers seek medical assistance in a large city or provide small stipends so the children of the church workers could go to school. As I listened to his description of why he provided financial assistance for these indigenous leaders, I became far more sympathetic to the early missionaries in China. I can see that it is easy to criticize the missionaries for paying indigenous church workers, but it is much harder to find a viable alternative.*

Another form of dependency arose from the intense poverty afflicting China by the 1920s. The chaos of the warlord era provided an abundance of charitable opportunities for the missionaries and the Chinese churches. Desperate Chinese people, who could not rely on the fractured central government for basic assistance, found they could turn to the churches for help.

In many situations, especially during times of natural disasters, the churches served as a distribution point for flour and rice, welcoming both Christians and non-Christians to receive the charitable aid. Non-Christians sometimes chortled that they did not believe in Jesus, but they did go to church because they believed in "flour religion" (麵粉教).

The term "rice Christian" developed from this growing dependency. Originally, the term referenced the churches offering rice to the people during times of natural disasters and famine. Food and basic relief could be distributed effectively through the extensive infrastructure of missions organizations and Chinese churches. Over time, the term came to refer more generally to an unhealthy dependency, and by the 1920s, many Chinese Christians relied not just on free handouts, but on jobs in the churches and in the massive economy which developed around the mission stations, the Western schools, and the hospitals. Some people undoubtedly professed to be Christian just to gain work at the mission stations because they were charlatans taking personal advantage; some were otherwise honest people looking for a way to feed their families in a desperate situation. Nevertheless, the mixture of motivations among the church workers damaged the entire Christian witness to the community.

The Chinese Christians clearly needed to break away from the missionary movement. They needed a church that would not be perceived as subservient to the foreign missionaries, could provide a vibrant witness to the community, and would allow them to contextualize the Bible and the church to Chinese culture.

FUNDAMENTALISM

A second major current washed over Chinese Christianity and brought confusion with it: the deep split that emerged in the 1920s between the Protestant modernists and Protestant fundamentalists. Both groups adopted a different approach to the Chinese Enlightenment and the dilemmas facing China. The modernists embraced the social and political proposals of the intelligentsia, while the fundamentalists eschewed their ideas and maintained that the gospel remained the only solution to China's ills.

The Modernist Approach

On the one side, the modernists embraced the Social Gospel. They rejected, at least to some degree, the "other-worldly" solutions of the fundamentalists, in favor of advocating practical and concrete actions to improve politics and society. Ideologically, they wanted to emulate their intellectual contemporaries in areas such as science and politics, and they tended to advocate the same solutions, such as universal education and social programs to reduce poverty. They believed that Christians, in harmony with the social teachings of Jesus and the gospel of love, should reach out to the suffering and impoverished multitudes in China. Often adopting the language of the modern intellectuals of the era, their rhetoric occasionally harmonized with the Chinese Communists.

One of the colorful modernist Christians of the era was Dr. James Yen (晏陽初, 1893–1990). Jimmy Yen, a 1913 graduate of Yale University, faithfully supported the YMCA in China. Throughout his lifetime, he devotedly advocated for literacy and mass education for the people. During World War I, Dr. Yen first served the Chinese coolies working with the Allies in France, and, after returning to China, he organized the Mass Education and Rural Reconstruction Movement in 1923. (Decades later, in 1960, he would also organize the International Institute of Rural Reconstruction.) He believed literacy was a key to lift the *pingmin* (平民, common people) out of poverty in China. Everywhere he went, throughout his life, he tirelessly promoted mass education. His biographer, Charles Hayford, related a wonderful anecdote that underscored Yen's thoroughgoing commitment to this cause. Apparently, Jimmy Yen's friends teased him by claiming that when his children cried, they did not cry as ordinary children, but would cry "*ma . . . ma . . . sss . . . sss education!*"

While Jimmy Yen advocated education as the solution to China's problems, and other Protestant modernists promoted additional solutions,

Christian political leaders also encouraged change. Sun Yat-sen became the first provisional president of the Republic of China shortly after the revolution of 1912, but he quickly turned over leadership to Yuan Shikai and consequently possessed little opportunity to impact the direction of China's future. Chiang Kai-shek, who consolidated his power over most of China in 1927, served as president of China until 1949. It is difficult to gauge his Christian piety or the sincerity of his Christian faith, as (like Constantine, in some ways) he spent his adult life fighting a bloody battle for his own political survival.

Chiang and the KMT did achieve several significant political accomplishments during the Nanjing decade from 1927–1937, but the Sino-Japanese War and World War II add difficulty to any evaluation of the long-term effects of his presidency. As a Christian, he displayed ambiguity in his public witness during his presidency. He offered strong support to the missionaries, he was involved in Bible translation, he and his wife, Soong Mei-ling (Madame Chiang), had a personal impact on leading figures in the KMT, and his allegiance to Christianity was known publicly. At the same time, he demonstrated a cruel ruthlessness to his political foes, and even though he was president for many years, he did not have the kind of deep and lasting impact on Christianity that Constantine did.

The Fundamentalist Approach

The fundamentalists in China did not believe that the May 4th intellectuals, the Protestant modernists, or the Christian politicians could save China; instead, they trusted that China could only be saved by the gospel. They dedicated themselves to the preaching the Word, and they were convinced that the ancient Christian faith provided the only true hope that could save China. Wang Mingdao was a key voice for the fundamentalists, and he unabashedly rejected the possibility that reform to Chinese society could be instituted from the outside.

He was committed to a spiritual revival that would change Chinese individuals from the inside through a new birth into Christ. Because the intellectuals, the powerful, the wealthy, and even spiritual leaders were also all sinners, Wang rejected the possibility that they could rescue China. In 1927, when he was still only twenty-seven years old, Wang soberly warned his countrymen at the zenith of the May 4th euphoria:

> God finds many intellectuals, but in their eyes there is no God;
> God finds many with power, but they oppress the people; God
> finds many with wealth, but they are all selfish and self-serving;

> God finds many spiritual workers, but they are all contaminated
> by the world.[2]

And in another article, Wang took specific aim at the popular proposals of Hu Shi, Jimmy Yen, and others to educate the masses. He pointed out that much effort had already been expended in education, but there was no improvement in the national character. Perhaps Wang may have specifically alluded to Jimmy Yen's mass education efforts when in 1933 he wrote:

> Have we now clearly recognized the true face of mankind? All
> are sinners . . . There are people who want to use "universal
> education" to remedy the corruption . . . But what are the re-
> sults? The energy expended is great, and the results leave people
> profoundly disappointed. They say with surprise, "What hap-
> pened? We thought the power of education would improve the
> thought and actions of the people, how come we have yet to see
> any results? . . . How come we have now worked so tirelessly but
> society is still not any better than before?" . . . People are evil
> from the inside. If we start repairs from the outside, how can we
> hope for results?[3]

Both the modernists and the fundamentalists were starting independent churches by the 1920s, but, in Chapter 13, I suggest that Wang's fundamentalist Christianity was particularly well-suited for establishing an independent Chinese church. In fact, by the 1940s, he had formed the largest church in Beijing.

GLOBAL CHRISTIANITY

The third current which shaped the growth of indigenous Chinese Christianity came from global Christianity, an influence which appeared as early as in the 1920s but would not be made apparent until the dramatic church revivals of the 1980s and 1990s. Like China, many countries in Asia, Africa, and Latin America were deeply affected by Western imperialism and Western missions, but that shared experience manifested in different ways. Indigenous Christianity in China seems to have arisen independently, based on local and peculiar circumstances within that country, but it also certainly shared common factors with other parts of Asia, and Africa, and in Latin America.

2. Cook, "Fundamentalism and Modern Culture," 88.
3. Cook, "Fundamentalism and Modern Culture," 137–38.

The academic field of Global Christianity, or World Christianity, exploded after the year 2000, particularly after the publication of Philip Jenkins' groundbreaking book in 2002, *The Next Christendom: The Coming of Global Christianity*. Published by Oxford University Press, the book amplified knowledge that was already familiar in missions circles—that Christianity, although stagnating in the West, was not dying in the global South, but was being reborn and reinvigorated. The renewed interest in the growth of global Christianity made it possible to place the extraordinary growth of the indigenous churches in China into the broader global context.

Field Notes: On Creating a New Course in Global Christianity

In 2003, I was given the task to create a new seminary course on "Global Christianity in the Twentieth Century," but I had trouble finding sample courses from other seminaries or adequate textbooks covering the topic. I set out to create my own outline for the semester-long course, trying to identify common themes by reading extensively from the relevant literature on Asia, Africa, and Latin America. I divided the course into three historical periods, which I delineated by observing when Christians responded in a striking way to the activity of the Holy Spirit. (As an historian, I am trained to notice the patterns of people, but as a Christian I try to also note the activity of God.) I also adopt those three time periods in the discussion below.

Missions

First, the nineteenth century was marked by the Second Great Awakening in the English-speaking world and the explosion of the Evangelical missionary movement. Missionaries such as William Carey and Robert Morrison, inspired by evangelical zeal, traveled to all parts of the globe. The Holy Spirit seemed to be moving among these churches and these Christians for a missionary purpose. I identified this first historical period before 1900 as the "Missions" phase of twentieth-century global Christianity.

From Missions to Movements

The second period, "From Missions to Movements," was marked by the gradual ebbing of Western missionary enthusiasm and the growing evangelical excitement in Asia, Africa, and Latin America. The precise opening of this phase, around 1900, was difficult to establish, as was the closing date, circa 1920, but the key event which displayed the transition occurred in 1910. The Edinburgh Missionary Conference was an ecumenical council, primarily comprised of Western church leaders, dedicated to the evangelization of the world "in this generation." The conceit of the participants seemed to be the assumption that the Western missionary movement would be used by God to fulfill the Great Commission, and they overlooked the profound work of the Holy Spirit already occurring in Asia, Africa, and Latin America. The optimism of Edinburgh was soon dashed, however, first with the outbreak of World War I in 1914 interfering with the missionary efforts of the Western churches, and then after the war with the split of the churches into open schism between the Protestant modernists and fundamentalists.

In China, at this precise moment between 1900 and 1920, the seeds of the independent Chinese churches sprouted with the births of Wang Mingdao in 1900 and John Sung in 1901, men who were committed, among many others, to seeing an independent Chinese church rise out of the soil. In Africa, the seeds of Christianity were taking root and springing forth delicate new growth as well. William Wade Harris (1865–1929), for instance, served as an Episcopalian lay church leader in Liberia when he received a vision calling him to start an independent African evangelistic ministry in 1910. During a mission trip to the Ivory Coast between 1913 and 1914, Harris evangelized and baptized over one hundred thousand people. Similarly, Simon Kimbangu (1889–1951) started the Kimbanguist Church in the Belgian Congo in 1921 after a powerful faith healing ministry.

Movements: Thunder from Below

I called the third historical period "Thunder from Below," and it is distinguished by the filling of the Holy Spirit. Like the Jewish believers in Acts 2, and the new Gentile converts of Paul, these Christians bore the mark of authentic believers: the presence and indwelling of the Holy Spirit. The indigenous church movements in Asia, Africa, and Latin America became the animating force of the global Christian church in this era which started around 1920 and continues today.

World War II brought dramatic changes around the world: the disintegration of the British Empire, the birth of numerous independent states in Africa, and the rise of the Chinese Communist Party in China. The withdrawal of the Imperial powers from Africa caused many church leaders to fear that the African churches might not survive. They believed the fragile young churches relied on the extensive Western and missionary infrastructure of churches, schools, hospitals, and Western personnel for survival and growth, and they feared the churches might collapse with the removal of that infrastructure. In China, when the missionaries were forced to leave the country after 1949, Western church leaders also feared that the Chinese churches, like the African churches, would disappear.

The churches did not collapse, however. Instead, they experienced revivals and spiritual awakening that spread like wildfire between the 1950s and the 1980s. Whereas the Western leaders had imagined that the missionary infrastructure was *holding up* the young churches, it became apparent the extensive structures were actually *holding back* the churches, and Christianity became a defining characteristic of these peoples. Western Christian missionaries did not disappear, and they continued to provide strategic support to the indigenous churches, but they no longer played a dominating or leading role.

In his work on African Christianity, church historian Andrew Walls argued that to "know Africa," one must "know Christianity," and his corollary declared that to "know Christianity," one must "know Africa." Indeed, Christianity plays an integral part in Africa today, and African believers are an essential component of the mosaic of world Christianity. In the same way that Christianity has become an integral and indigenous faith in Africa, China has also been part of the global transformation of Christianity in the twentieth century. Today, to know China, one must know Christianity, and to know Christianity, one must know China.

Christianity is firmly established in China, and it is part of an extraordinary and breathtaking global transformation. Yet it still wrestles with the legacy of one persistently eroding current: imperialism.

REFLECTION QUESTIONS

1. Should Chinese Christians have broken away from the missions movement in China? In what ways can an indigenous church be "independent" from the missionaries?

2. Chinese nationalism matured after 1900 in an era of aggressive western and Japanese imperialism.
   - Should the Chinese Christians reject nationalism?
   - Should they embrace nationalism?
   - Why might many Chinese Christians after 1900 be tempted to adopt a super-nationalism?

3. What are practical ways Chinese Christians can provide a prophetic voice against any unbiblical ideas or practices in politics, society, and culture?

SUGGESTED READING FOR CHAPTER 11

Cook, Richard R. "Fundamentalism and Modern Culture in Republican China: The Popular Language of Wang Mingdao, 1900–1991." PhD diss., University of Iowa, 2003.

Hayford, Charles W. *To the People: James Yen and Village China*. New York: Columbia University Press, 1990.

Yao, Kevin Xiyi. *The Fundamentalist Movement among Protestant Missionaries in China, 1920–1937*. Dallas: University Press of America, 2003.

12

Rethinking Imperialism

THE DAMAGE OF IMPERIALISM has afflicted both the victims as well as the perpetrators. In the United States, both academia and popular culture in the second half of the twentieth century recoiled from Western imperialism, and, because they have linked imperialism to missions work, they have adopted anti-Christian and anti-missions biases. Like Christian converts in China, many Western evangelicals have had to confront the nineteenth-century legacy of imperialism and missions.

Field Notes: On Recovering from the Scars from Imperialism

In class, I have had many discussions with Chinese Christians concerning Western imperialism and the Opium Wars. I have observed a wide range of responses and attitudes, but some students, particularly those interested in history, still seem to harbor some lingering pain. One pupil recalled a lecture from high school in China on the Opium Wars: for the entire hour, the teacher recounted the events in tears. A year later, I shared that anecdote with another class, and they scoffed, dismissing the possibility of anybody feeling the pain so sharply even today. Although I still suspect the current Chinese churches have been partially shaped by the scars caused by the nineteenth-century events, I have found many individual Chinese Christians have developed a more nuanced and healthy view of the nineteenth-century missionary movement.

In fact, it was my friends in Taiwan who helped me deal with my own "trauma" from Western imperialism. In this chapter I reveal my background as a fervent anti-missionary partisan. Nonetheless, after my thorough conversion to Christ, I was called by God to missions. I hope my story of "recovery" from the scars of anti-missionary bias can be of value to others.

Growing up in the Midwest in 1960s and 1970s and before embracing a personal Christian faith, I had unconsciously absorbed an anti-missionary prejudice from my environment. At the moment of my decision to believe and follow Jesus in 1980, I vowed that I would not become a missionary, which proved ironic given my future missionary career. It was also an odd pledge because I was only seventeen years old, and I had no logical reason to reject missions. I had not grown up around Christian missionaries, nor had I read any Christian literature related to missions, either for or against missions. I seem to have absorbed uncritically the anti-imperialistic ethos of the age, arising in the 1960s, which included the assumption that missionaries perpetrated unmentionable harm on non-Western nations. Therefore, though willing to commit to following Jesus, I was unwilling to approve of or partake in foreign missions. The critique of missions during my formative years in the 1960s and 1970s had spread, I believe, far beyond the halls of academia and infiltrated popular culture through powerful media such as books and movies. For instance, James Michener's 1959 historical novel *Hawaii*, a book that I did not actually read until many years later, lampooned the missionaries in Hawaii with devastating satire. As a young Christian in the early 1980s, even as I began to grow in my Christian faith and desired to spread the gospel to all peoples, I continued to reject "missions."

When I first told friends that I wanted to go to China in 1983 to learn Chinese, I insisted that I was not going to become a missionary; rather, I was going to first learn Mandarin and then I would live in China to teach Chinese people the gospel and the bible. My friends told me that my plan indeed sounded like I wanted to be a "missionary," but I insisted that I only wanted to go to China and teach people the bible. I finally moved to Taiwan to learn Mandarin after I completed my undergraduate studies in 1984, and my new Chinese friends in my church in Taipei would ask me if I was learning Mandarin in order to become a missionary. I would patiently explain to them that I wasn't a missionary; I simply wanted "to learn Mandarin, and then teach Chinese people the gospel and the bible." To my surprise, many of these new Taiwanese friends commented, "That is too bad. I thought you wanted to be a missionary." In hindsight, I believe my uninformed anti-missionary bias was rather Euro-centric and not sympathetic to the perceptions of Chinese and Taiwanese Christians. I soon learned that my Taiwanese friends possessed a far more sophisticated understanding of missions than I did, and although they were aware of the anti-Christian bias aroused by the Western missionaries, they also were overwhelmingly appreciative of the tremendous sacrifice Western missionaries had made to bring the gospel to China.

I attended seminary in the late 1980s, earning an MDiv and a ThM in Missions, and in 1990, I began teaching at a Protestant seminary outside of Taipei. I still preferred to tell people that I was not a "missionary" but a seminary teacher. As a Christian, I believed that Christians were called on to bring the gospel to the whole world through missions, and I wholeheartedly embraced the missionary enterprise, but I was still uncomfortable with the legacy of the earlier generations of Protestant missionaries. In 1993, I returned to the United States and I started my PhD studies in Modern Chinese History, where I finally learned a more sophisticated and academic critique of the nineteenth-century missionary movement based on reading that included, for instance, the postcolonial study *Orientalism*, by Edward Said. In the university environment, where I suspected I was in the minority because the faculty and my classmates had little sympathy for missions, I began to search for a way to harmonize my calling to missions with my academic studies.

I discovered one helpful academic book in my search, *The Bible and the Flag*, written by Brian Stanley. Stanley scoured the missionary archives in Britain in an attempt to discern whether the earlier generations of British missionaries had, in fact, been motivated by imperialism. In an exhaustive and convincing study, he demonstrated that missionaries were motivated not by politics or a perception of British cultural superiority, but by spiritual impulses and a desire to share the gospel. I enthusiastically included a summary of Stanley's thesis on a paper I turned into one of my favorite professors, hoping he might soften his view of missions and the missionary endeavor. I was thoroughly disappointed, however, when he wrote on my paper that he was familiar with *The Bible and the Flag*, and he was friends with the author Brian Stanley, but he believed that Stanley had wasted years of his life researching the British missionary archives. My professor effectively dismissed Brian Stanley's entire thesis with a simple question posed to me on my paper: "Even if the missionaries were not motivated by imperialism and did not intend to support imperialism, did the missionaries still *function* as imperialists?" I found the question perplexing, as it seemed in many ways that the missionaries' presence on the mission field did facilitate the Western imperialistic project. Did this mean that even if the missionaries were called by God and motivated by a desire to bring the kingdom of

God to new people groups, that the missionaries nevertheless functioned as agents of Western imperialism?

Two books which I discovered about halfway through my PhD course work steered me toward a satisfactory solution. One of these books spoke from a more theological and biblical perspective and the other from a more philosophical and historical perspective. The first book, *Let the Nations Be Glad!* by John Piper, revolutionized my understanding of missions and the bible when it explained that missions, from start to finish, centered around worship. Missions work which included the goal of raising up more and more peoples to praise and worship God was not imperialistic, but marvelously pluralistic. God's design for missionaries expected them to call all peoples to know God and praise God, not to spread Western culture or even to "uplift" the various cultures of the world. I welcomed the insight of John Piper, but even if the Western Protestant missionaries set out with the intent of bringing all peoples to praise God, might they not have "functioned" as imperialists even so?

The second book electrified me by providing a theoretical foundation to address that question. Lamin Sanneh, formerly a professor at Yale, took a completely different track in addressing imperialism and missions in *Translating the Message: The Missionary Impact on Culture*. Rather than beginning with a study of missions and missionaries, Sanneh concentrated on the Christian message and the indigenous churches, that is, the actual Christian movements the message inspired on the ground. Sanneh studied Africa, but his thesis would apply to China and other parts of the world. Rather than asking if the missionaries were imperialists, he wanted to understand the nature of their message. His focus, therefore, was not on the messengers, but rather the message of the gospel. Sanneh observed that the Christian gospel was not imperialistic; on the contrary, it provided indigenous peoples with the tools they needed to ultimately resist and overthrow imperialism. He posited that it is the nature of the gospel and Christianity to empower and invigorate indigenous language and culture. Therefore, the predilections of the missionaries, whether they were imperialist or not, were irrelevant.

Lamin Sanneh observed that Christianity was *translatable*, containing a gospel and a message that could be translated into any language or culture. Something profound occurred the moment the missionary conceded that the truth of God could be expressed in the language and culture of the indigenous peoples: the missionary tacitly acknowledged the *relativity* of the source language and culture of the missionary, and he affirmed the adequacy of the target language and culture of the indigenous people to express the truths of God. Regardless of the missionaries, the gospel itself affirmed and empowered the target people. When Paul, in the early church, argued that the Gentiles did not need to first become Jewish in order to become Christians, he affirmed that Gentile languages and cultures were sufficient to express the Word of God.

Applying his thesis to Africa, Lamin Sanneh showed that when missionaries arrived at new areas within Africa, many of which were preliterate, the missionaries learned the indigenous languages and cultures. They worked to provide the people with a written language which then became a new tool allowing them to preserve their indigenous culture. As the people were enabled to read the Word of God in their own language, and to interpret the meaning for themselves, an organic Christian movement was born. The people involved in this new movement were then empowered to examine their own culture and determine which aspects of it could exist in harmony with truth and biblical teachings, and they became champions of those facets, working to preserve those cultural beliefs and practices. They could also speak out prophetically against any beliefs or practices within their own culture that were not scriptural. Both the embracing and denouncing of certain cultural aspects could be accomplished independently from the Christian missionaries. In fact, when they found the Western missionaries, or the Western imperial powers, acting against the interests of the local peoples or the indigenous churches, they could think biblically and independently and were thus empowered to oppose those outside pressures and promote their own indigenous interests.

The twentieth century brought an onslaught of Western modernity into Africa, but Lamin Sanneh has refuted the accepted thesis that Christian missionaries undermined African indigenous culture. He showed, contrary to common assumptions, that African indigenous culture was most successfully preserved in areas of intense missionary activity and translation. Sanneh further contended, based on his empirical research in Africa, that in locations that have fallen under Islamic influence, a religion with the untranslatable Arabic-language Koran, African traditional culture has not flourished, and thus it might be Islam which should be considered an "imperialistic" religion.

Lamin Sanneh noted that for decades scholars had maintained a Western and Euro-centric focus on the missionaries that blinded them, at least to some degree, to the remarkable work of God among the indigenous Christians around the world. The preeminent question should not revolve around the "intent" or the "function" of the missionaries, but the very nature of Christianity as it expands missionally to new people groups. God's intent, as noted by John Piper, is to raise up the nations to praise God, a distinctly pluralistic vision far from the (sometimes) narrow and imperialistic goals of the missionaries. If Lamin Sanneh's thesis about the translatability of Christianity into new cultures is correct, then Christianity can also be expected to translate or incarnate into Chinese culture, providing the indigenous Chinese church with the tools to evaluate all elements of Chinese culture, prophetically critiquing the aspects that transgress Christian Scripture, and advocating those aspects of culture that harmonize with Scripture.

For example, Chinese Christians might find much in the Hebrew Old Testament to affirm and validate Chinese filial piety, and therefore, even in the face of modernity and the accompanying pressures that might break down the family, the Chinese Christian church could become a champion of traditional Chinese family ties and filial piety. The Christians will not need to rely on the expertise of the foreign missionaries or follow their directions. Instead, as the Word of God is translated into their own language, they become agents capable of developing their own indigenous church and determining their own future course with the help of the Holy Spirit.

More recently, Robert Woodberry provided quantitative evidence for the rich contribution of the nineteenth-century missionaries. His work included a massive amount of data, ingenious research, and startling new statistics to build the overarching picture of such a contribution. Published in 2012, his seminal award-winning work, *The Missionary Roots of Liberal Democracy*, was inspired by a lecture he heard. During this lecture, a speaker surmised that a statistical link seemed to exist between liberal democracy and Protestantism around the world, and he suggested that someone should research that possible connection. Robert Woodberry, a sociologist specializing in the impact of religion on political development and economic change, was the perfect scholar to take on the task. Through exhaustive examination of historical data and careful mapping of earlier generations of Protestant missionaries, particularly locations where missionaries committed to the conversion of the indigenous peoples, Woodberry showed the "missionary roots" of liberal democracy around the world today.[1]

Because Woodberry's research and conclusion boldly refuted the decades of scholarship which suggested that earlier generations of missionaries advanced the cause of Western imperialism and undermined indigenous cultures, Woodberry felt compelled to redouble his efforts to provide indisputable statistical analysis. Today, slowly, scholars are acknowledging the power of Woodberry's thesis, and a new field of missionary analysis is emerging, accompanied by new research. I look forward to additional research which would apply Woodberry's profound insights specifically

---

1. For an excellent summary of Woodberry's contribution, see the January/February 2014 issue of *Christianity Today*. The cover reads: "The World the Missionaries Made. They've been called racist, imperialist proselytizers. They were also the greatest force for modern democracy."

to China, possibly leading to new interpretations and conclusions. I am indebted to Christian scholars and historians who have begun to rethink Western missions, removing the attention from imperialism, and putting the focus on the vibrant young churches that took root in Asia, Africa, and Latin America. In the next chapter, inspired by John Piper, Lamin Sanneh, and Robert Woodberry, I turn my attention to the story of Wang Mingdao, an indigenous Chinese Christian who carefully studied his bible and applied what he saw to the chaotic world of China in the first half of the twentieth century.

REFLECTION QUESTIONS

1. Is Christianity a "Western" religion? If not, why do so many Chinese people think so?

2. Is the nature of Christianity imperialistic? Is it a useful tool for an imperial power?

3. How does Christianity empower peoples and indigenous culture?

SUGGESTED READING FOR CHAPTER 12

Piper, John. *Let the Nations Be Glad! The Supremacy of God in Missions.* 3rd ed. Grand Rapids: Baker Academic, 2010.

Sanneh, Lamin. *Translating the Message: The Missionary Impact on Culture.* 2nd rev. and exp. ed. Maryknoll, NY: Orbis, 2009.

Walls, Andrew F. *The Missionary Movement in Christian History: Studies in the Transmission of Faith.* Maryknoll, NY: Orbis, 1996.

———. *The Cross-Cultural Process in Christian History.* Maryknoll, NY: Orbis, 2002.

13

Real Lives

Wang Mingdao and John Sung

WANG MINGDAO (王明道), born in 1900, grew up with all the tangible benefits of the missionary movement in China, but he set aside those benefits and forged his own path instead to establish his own independent Chinese Christian church. He never set foot outside of China, and his church accepted no assistance or funds from the missionaries, but his critics nonetheless ruthlessly accused him of being a tool of imperialism and the Western missionaries. John Sung, born in 1901, did study in the United States and received his PhD from The Ohio State University, but after a profound religious experience in 1926 while living in New York City, he returned to China and launched a powerful indigenous evangelistic ministry that crisscrossed China and East Asia. He combined a dramatic preaching style with a simple Christian message that was wildly popular around China. In different ways, both men put down the roots of an independent Chinese Christian church.

WANG MINGDAO

From the time of his birth in Beijing, the Chinese capital, until his death in 1991, Wang Mingdao's life was tightly interwoven with the events of the twentieth century. Wang Mingdao was born on July 28, 1900, just weeks before the suppression of the Boxer uprising, and thus, even before his birth, his life was turned upside down by the chaos in Beijing. His Christian father, apparently fearful that the Boxer armies would kill him and possibly first force him to witness the execution of his expectant wife and two-year-old daughter, committed suicide just weeks before the birth of his son Wang Mingdao.

Field Notes: On the Boxer Indemnity Funds

In the aftermath of the Boxer uprising, Hudson Taylor and the China Inland Mission famously turned down money for reparations out of the Boxer indemnity fund, recompense that was extracted by the British and the Eight Nation Army from the Qing government. The China Inland Mission made this decision even though it had suffered significant casualties and losses. Taylor instead said he desired to "demonstrate the meekness and gentleness of Christ to the Chinese." I had always been impressed by Taylor's decision, and I wondered why other mission organizations would have accepted the money, even doubting the integrity of their decision to accept the tainted funds. I thought that for years, until I became aware of the story of the mother of Wang Mingdao.

With the birth of Wang Mingdao, his young, widowed mother now needed to care for a two-year-old daughter and an infant baby boy. She could not work, and, in the grim world of post-Boxer Beijing in 1900, there was little reason to hope in any sort of a better future for her and her children. Fortunately, as a Christian family with ties to the Western missionary movement who had suffered from the Boxer uprising, her small family qualified for a nominal stipend from the Boxer indemnity funds. With that money, she wisely purchased a small family compound in Beijing. By dividing up the space and renting out rooms to boarders, the family was able to eke out a living. Wang, growing up without a father, described his childhood in bleak terms: a childhood in a harsh environment, surviving in the impoverished urban underbelly of the nation's capital, rubbing elbows with the constant turnover of unsavory and transient characters living in the rooms in his home. Although he experienced an undeniably difficult childhood, Wang and his family would have been utterly destitute without the benefit of the Boxer indemnity funds. From the beginning of his life, Wang and his family benefited from the Western missions presence in China.

As Chapter 8 described, Christian converts received many benefits from the Western missionary enterprise in China, and as part of a Christian family, Wang received an excellent missionary education in Beijing. Although his mother could not even afford the nominal tuition fee, Wang claimed to be first in his class at all levels, and so he earned a full tuition scholarship. Throughout Wang's formative years, China was transforming in ever-changing ways. These changes included the interruption of the centuries-old educational system through the abolition of the Imperial exam system in 1905 when he was five years old, as well as the fall of the Qing Dynasty in 1911 when he was eleven years old. With the rise of Sun Yat-sen after the Revolution of 1911, and by the time Wang was fourteen in the year 1914, he dreamed that he might one day become president, an aspiration that would have been unthinkable for a poor fatherless child in the Imperial world prior to the rise of the new world order of Republican China. He was inspired by Abraham Lincoln in the United States who, Wang noted, had also come from a poor family. Wang Mingdao was part of a unique generation that could dream of rising from the depths of poverty to the pinnacle of power in China.

Wang Mingdao continued to excel throughout high school, and upon graduation he intended to apply to the newly reorganized Peking University. However, apparently because of some disarray during the reorganization period, Wang's application was delayed for one year. During that interim year before matriculating at Peking University, Wang traveled a couple hours' distance outside of Beijing to the city of Baoding, where he worked as a schoolteacher at a missionary-run school. Again, Wang became a beneficiary of the extraordinary opportunities open to Chinese Christians because of the vast missionary enterprise in China.

In Baoding, the British missionary principal of the school quickly recognized the teenager's intellect and exceptional potential, and he promised to provide funding for Wang's studies at Peking University. He further added that if Wang continued to excel, the mission could also support him through seminary studies in China and, quite possibly, for doctoral studies in Great Britain. By 1918, all the doors of opportunity opened wide for the young Wang Mingdao. But his life would travel a different path.

In Baoding, Wang became confused when a young Chinese Christian friend suggested to him that baptism required a personal profession of faith and must be administered by immersion. Wang, who was at least a nominal Christian at the time, had been baptized by sprinkling as an infant. Perplexed, Wang set out to find the answer to this apparent discrepancy, turning initially to the British principal of his school. The missionary assured him that baptism by sprinkling was sufficient, but Wang decided he wanted to find his own solution to the issue, and thus he turned to the Chinese translation of the bible.

In that same year of 1919, the complete translation of the Chinese Union Version (和合本) Bible was published, the first full vernacular translation of Scripture. Previous translations had been published in classical

Chinese, but at this moment in history, following the recent push for a vernacular revolution in literature by Hu Shi and on the cusp of the modern May Fourth movement, Wang Mingdao was able to read his own bible, not in Greek, English, or even in classical Chinese, but in the vernacular language of the people. Because of the translatable nature of the Christian bible and the simple message of the gospel, Wang could scour the Scriptures for himself in his own language and develop his own conclusions. He became convinced that he should be baptized again by immersion.

The British principal of the school warned him not to be rebaptized, and he made clear that if Wang chose to be rebaptized by immersion he would be immediately dismissed from his teaching position in Baoding. Furthermore, the offer of support for university studies, seminary studies, and doctoral studies in Great Britain would be withdrawn. Fully aware of the gravity of his decision, Wang took several more days to search through the bible.

Wang emerged from his study convinced that, rather than submitting to the authority of the British missionaries, he had to follow his own understanding of the teaching of the bible. He had grown confident of the bible's teaching that baptism required a personal profession of faith and must be by immersion. He was immediately dismissed from his position at the school, and, in his autobiography, he described the dramatic scene that resulted. He led a small troop of five students who wanted to follow him in baptism by immersion out of the school grounds. They marched through the snow in the north China winter to the river in order to baptize one another by immersion, but, because the water was frozen, they had to continue walking until they found a rapidly moving portion of the river. Wang vividly described the moment when he emerged from the frigid baptismal waters, and his hair and baptismal robes immediately froze solid.

Perhaps Wang embellished the story a little, but the scene offered a powerful image of how Christianity and the translated bible empowered indigenous Christian movements. When he emerged from the baptismal waters, he was transformed. Up to that pivotal point in his life, he had been one of many beneficiaries of the Western missionary movement in China. He had received promises that might have helped him join the elite ranks of modern society. However, because he was able to read the Christian bible for himself, he dramatically reversed the trajectory of his life and started moving towards establishing an independent Chinese church rather than remaining beholden to the Western missionaries.

When intellectuals attacked Chinese Christians like Wang Mingdao during the anti-Christian movement of the 1920s, accusing them of being de-nationalized and de-culturalized, they do not seem to have understood how the gospel, at that very moment, was taking firm root in Chinese culture and society. Again, I find it particularly ironic that intellectuals, who had learned Marxism in Paris, accused Chinese Christians like Wang Mingdao of being the "running dogs" of capitalism and the West. On the contrary, it was Wang's deep commitment to the bible that empowered him to chart an independent course.

After his dismissal from the school in Baoding, Wang returned home. However, many people who knew him were disturbed by his decision as they could not imagine that he would give up his teaching job and bright future to pursue baptism by immersion. He could not find a job, possibly because potential employers may have considered him erratic. Unemployed, he used his time to read the bible, and to read the bible again. Having forfeited his opportunity to go to university or to seminary, Wang insisted he received all the education he needed by reading his bible.

On May 4, 1919, Wang Mingdao's contemporaries stormed Tiananmen Square; but although he was in Beijing at the time, it seems, according to my research, as though Wang remained at home reading his bible during the protest. Throughout the 1920s, May Fourth intellectuals desperately tried to identify a viable path that might save China, and they searched the world for an alternative ideology that would work in China, but Wang Mingdao, quietly reading at home, believed he had found the answer to save China in the bible. As the years went by, Wang became ever more convinced that the gospel provided the only hope for each individual person, and, further, it offered the only hope for the nation.

The May Fourth era of the 1920s, with its free-flowing ideas and plethora of ideologies, created an ideal context for Wang Mingdao to advocate the truths arising from the bible and the gospel message. Among the many activists participating in the marketplace of ideas, Mao Zedong and the Chinese Communist Party have often been credited for most effectively wielding the political, social, and cultural levers available in the 1920s and the 1930s to successfully build their communist movement. Wang Mingdao also endeavored to build a movement, an indigenous Chinese church, and although he was not as successful as the CCP at the time, he effectively used the same levers to build the Chinese church. Like the CCP, Wang utilized public speaking, writing, and organizing.

In 1923, emerging from his self-isolation and personal bible study at home, Wang began to preach publicly, and his gift for speaking was quickly recognized. By 1926, when he was still only twenty-six years old, he proved to be a popular preacher, and he was invited to speak to large audiences in Nanjing and other cities. He spoke in Mandarin, the dialect common to Beijing, using plain language and a direct style that communicated fundamental and straightforward bible truths with power. He preached in the growing urban centers in the Republican period from the 1920s to the 1940s. He soon grew far too popular to meet the demand for his speaking invitations, so he began to write down and to publish his sermons in a quarterly journal. He launched his self-published journal, *Spiritual Food Quarterly* (靈食季刊), in 1927, and the journal was printed quarterly without interruption until 1955.

In both his speaking and writing, he focused on the bible and applying the truths from the bible to the lives of the people. One central theme Wang emphasized was that people must be "born again." He was convinced that social reform, along with all the ideas promoted by the intellectuals and modernist Christians, were doomed to failure as those proposals only attempted to change people from the outside. Wang strongly believed that the human heart was corrupt, and therefore, if China were to be saved, then the heart of the Chinese people must be transformed. They must be born again. Wang carefully avoided discussion of politics and party associations, but he spoke boldly and prophetically about the sins he observed in society, and he became a champion and advocate of biblical principles, as well as those Chinese traditions and practices that he found in harmony with Scripture. In accordance with the theory of Lamin Sanneh referred to earlier, Wang Mingdao provided a prophetic and independent voice in May Fourth and Republican China.

The intellectuals generally dismissed Wang and his proposals as irrelevant to the national discourse, often criticizing him, and all fundamentalists, for their focus on spiritual rather than material and concrete problems. They assumed that Wang's diagnosis of the root problem of Chinese society was ludicrous, so they did not bother to engage critically with his ideas or the solutions he offered, and, further, they even questioned his patriotism and his commitment to the modern project of nation building.

Field Notes: On Nationalism and Patriotism

In my PhD program, I dialogued many times with my professors about the patriotism of Wang Mingdao and his commitment to nation building. They challenged my suggestion that Wang's biblical and fundamentalist perspective should be taken seriously in the context of building a society and seeking national salvation. They agreed instead with Wang's contemporary critics who believed that Wang was not particularly relevant to discussions of politics and culture, and that he should probably not be considered a

*"nationalist." My discussions with my advisors forced me to think exten-
sively about the question, "Did Wang Mingdao love the nation?"*

*I agreed that he might not be a "nationalist" by the common defini-
tion of nationalism in the 1920s and 1930s, or as defined by the Chinese
Communists in the 1950s. However, I strongly objected to the notion that
he was "anti-nationalist," leading one of my professors to suggest that
Wang might be considered "a-nationalist." That is, he was neither "nationalist" nor "anti-nationalist." I disagreed, because any reading of the
autobiography and sermons of Wang Mingdao clearly reveals his deep
empathy and enduring compassion for his Chinese compatriots, and he
worked tirelessly to bring an uplifting message to his people. In my dissertation on Wang Mingdao and the Chinese fundamentalists, I argued
that the fundamentalists, even though they focused on the spiritual, did
endeavor to provide concrete proposals for real change to China.*

*One central plank in my argument about the methodology and
goals of Wang Mingdao and the Chinese fundamentalists was inspired
by the ideology and successful program of the Chinese Communist Party
in the 1920s and 1930s. The CCP successfully used speaking, such as
standing on a soapbox on the street corners; writing, such as publishing
and distributing Marxist and communist tracts; and, most importantly,
organizing. The Communists displayed a brilliant aptitude for building a
cohesive organization that would attract new members, build a community (such as large labor unions), spread to various parts of the country,
and eventually seize control of the central government. I believe Wang
Mingdao possessed a similar vision for bringing fundamental change to
China based on his faith in the kingdom of God and his belief in church
planting. Change could only occur by first persuading people to join the
movement through public speaking (preaching and evangelism), writing
and distributing literature (Wang's printed sermons that were distributed
broadly throughout China and even overseas), and organizing (the planting of indigenous Chinese churches). Wang Mingdao, I concluded in my
dissertation, did pursue a concrete program for truly transforming China.*

Like the Communists, Wang was determined to flesh out his ideals,
which for him were uniquely Christian, and put them into practice. Therefore, he planted his own church, the Christian Tabernacle (基督徒會堂),
in Beijing in 1933, and by the 1940s it had grown to become the largest
church in Beijing with an attendance of around 500 people. In his local
church in Beijing, Wang practiced the ideals of a Christian community, a
vision that started with the "new birth" of the Chinese individual and then

incorporated those individual Christians into a community, the church. Wang knew with utmost certainty that the proposals of the intellectuals for social and political transformation were impotent, but that China could be transformed through Christian preaching and the ever-growing impact of the body of Christ.

Wang's ministries of preaching, writing, and church planting grew and prospered during the Nanjing Decade, from 1927–1937, but with the outbreak of the Sino-Japanese War in 1937, and then the Japanese occupation of Beijing during World War II, he faced several harsh challenges. A particularly note-worthy episode occurred which tested Wang's resolve and dedication during these times. Japanese authorities in charge of occupied Beijing demanded that all foreign magazines and periodicals in China print four pro-Japanese slogans on the cover of each issue. The Japanese occupation authorities considered everything Christian to be "foreign," and so they targeted not only Western missionary publications, but also indigenous Chinese Christian journals such as Wang Mingdao's *Spiritual Food Quarterly*.

Wang expressed his indignation, maintaining that his church and his journal were thoroughly indigenous. He was adamant that his journal should not be regulated under the new rules governing "foreign" publica-tions as he had no foreign ties, and his church and the journal had never received foreign funding. Confident that his church and ministry were decisively independent, he prayed for courage, and, after preparing to be arrested, he set out for an interview with the Japanese authorities in Bei-jing to explain why he refused to publish the four pro-Japanese slogans. He did not receive permission to exclude the propaganda, but he was also not arrested. Publication of many of the foreign and missionary-related pe-riodicals was suspended during World War II, but Wang Mingdao's truly indigenous journal continued its publication uninterrupted, even though Wang remained fearful and prepared himself for the possibility that the po-lice might arrive, pound on his door, and drag him to prison. Wang never compromised, and at the end of the occupation in 1945, he credited God for having protected him.

In 1950, Wang Mingdao published his autobiography, *These Fifty Years* (五十年來), in which he described his life and ministry up to his fiftieth birthday in simple, yet powerful, language. Ironically, at the age of fifty, he looked back at his life and identified the Japanese occupation as his most traumatic experience; he obviously did not yet know that he would become a world-renowned martyr for his long imprisonment several years later. In the early 1950s, after the CCP had come to power in 1949, he refused to join the new state-sanctioned Protestant church organization which would become the Three-Self Patriotic Movement (TSPM), arguing vigorously in the pages of *Spiritual Life Quarterly* that he was determined to remain independent. He argued that he had started his ministry independent from the Western missionaries and Imperial powers, independent from the KMT and the Republican Chinese government, and independent from the Japanese occupation authorities. He was determined also to remain independent from the Chinese Communist Party. He pointedly asserted that in a church where he never posted any images, including images of Jesus, he certainly was not going to post a picture of Mao Zedong.

Throughout the early 1950s, Wang engaged in an extended and high-profile debate about his refusal to join the new government sanctioned organization with Bishop K. H. Ting (丁光訓) (who would later become the head of the Three-Self Patriotic Movement). In a fascinating and prolonged dialogue, Bishop Ting addressed Wang in articles published in the national Protestant journal *Tian Feng,* and Wang Mingdao directly replied in *Spiritual Food Quarterly,* which helped Wang emerge as a key national leader of the conservative Protestants in China and serve as a loud, independent voice resisting the encroachment of the CCP into all areas of Chinese life. (This public debate is further examined in Chapter 14.)

By the mid-1950s Wang was imprisoned, as was his wife, and he remained in prison until 1980. When he was released, after the death of Mao Zedong and the launching of the political and economic reforms of Deng Xiaoping, he was about eighty years old. His body was broken, but his mind remained strong. He enjoyed world renown, and in his new home in Shanghai, he entertained famous church leaders, including Billy Graham. He became a symbolic figurehead of the rapidly growing Chinese house church movement of the 1980s, and he was widely regarded around the world as a living martyr for Christ. He died in 1991, at ninety-one years of age.

Wang is still remembered as a martyr and a hero among the conservative Chinese Protestant churches, but in broader Chinese culture his patriotism is still questioned because of his resistance to the modern intellectuals and the CCP. Even today, he still bears the unfair taint of this perceived lack of patriotism and concern for the welfare of China. However, Wang Mingdao, who was never beholden to any political powers, stands in history as a fiercely independent preacher and pastor who fearlessly offered Christ and courageously helped to build the indigenous Chinese church.

JOHN SUNG

Born in 1901 in the Fujian province, John Sung (宋尚節) began to preach when he was only ten years old in the church where his father served as the local Methodist pastor, already exhibiting the dynamism and power that would later make him famous. In 1920, John Sung moved to the United States for his higher education, studying first at Ohio Wesleyan University and later at The Ohio State University. During his studies in Ohio, Sung accomplished everything at full speed, as was his wont. In just six years, he completed his undergraduate and master's degrees, and he also earned his doctorate in chemistry from Ohio State, graduating with many distinctions and honors. At the same time, during those same six years, he taught himself English, all the while supporting himself financially by doing manual labor. Throughout his life, John Sung seemed indefatigable.

Unfortunately, the breakneck pace of his studies took a toll on his childhood Christian faith. After receiving his PhD in 1926, he agreed to attend Union Theological Seminary in New York for postgraduate studies. At the time, Union was one of the foremost institutions of modernist theology, led by prominent modernist theologians such as Harry Fosdick, and Sung became involved in translating ancient Chinese religious texts such as the *Dao De Jing* of Laozi. The brilliant twenty-six-year-old academic Dr. John Sung, living halfway around the world, no longer seemed to be a budding indigenous church leader or potent Chinese evangelist.

Field Notes: On The Impact of the "Icebreaker"

John Sung (1901–1944) might be my favorite character from Chinese church history. And, I think, he was definitely a "character"! I wish we could hear recordings of his sermons, especially from the precocious young ten-year-old preacher! Several years ago, to help me gauge the impact of John Sung in China, I tried an experiment. In a class with about thirty Chinese students, I asked if any of them had any direct "spiritual connection" to John Sung. That is, had anybody in their family, such as their parents, grandparents, great-grandparents, or aunts or uncles, been converted or spiritually influenced by Sung at one of his evangelistic meetings?

I noticed several students were amused as if they felt the American teacher was quite naïve to ask this curious question about a man who had been dead for over fifty years. Nonetheless, I waited, and a hand went up. The student told the class how her grandmother had been dramatically converted at a John Sung meeting. Since then, in many of my classes, at least one or two students have raised their hands and have been able to offer a testimony from their family. Remarkably, the stories of John Sung are passed from generation to generation.

In a recent biography, Daryl Ireland has produced a carefully researched account of John Sung. His narrative is compelling, and it may eventually inform popular perceptions of Sung; I highly recommend it. However, it is the mythology of John Sung that has inspired generations of Chinese Christians. The disparate stories, according to Ireland, arose from John Sung's own ever-changing retelling of his biography, and from his admirers who have distributed the legends around the world. Sung might be forgiven for generous use of dramatic license, however, as he often preached three times a day for several hours, employing Bible exposition, dramatic readings, innovative props, a variety of media, song, and personal testimony. Understandably, he might vary his stories over the years as he told them in different contexts. The recollections of his multitude of listeners might also differ.

One night in 1926, John Sung was walking the streets in New York City when he heard preaching from a doorway near the street. When he peeked in, he saw a teenage girl sharing her Christian testimony. Intrigued by her childlike faith, Dr. Sung decided to return the next night to listen again, and soon, through her simple speaking and testimony, he recommitted himself to his childhood faith in Jesus Christ. Around the same time, he began a struggle for good mental health, and in early 1927, he agreed to sign himself into a mental institution in New York. Popular mythology has suggested that the authorities at Union Theological Seminary had him committed because of his newfound fundamentalist faith, but in reality, the seminary provided him with benevolent funds to pay for his care, and they showed sincere concern for his condition.

Unfortunately, once admitted into the mental institution, he hated his time there. He could not bear the screaming of the other inmates at night, and at one point he managed to escape. With the help of dogs, he was recaptured and returned to the hospital. Of course, the attempted escape only made his situation worse, and he was incarcerated, eventually, for nine months. His diaries and letters show that he continued to struggle with severe mental illness. But he also used that time to read his Bible; he considered the nine months that he was in the hospital as his theological and biblical education. Because this is the unrelenting John Sung, he did not read his Bible only one time during his stay, but three or four times (in the popular retelling, he read the Bible forty times).

While traveling in New York City, his pastor from Ohio became aware of Sung's plight and negotiated his release. The benevolent funds had dried up, and the hospital was anxious to release Sung. In consultation with his pastor, the hospital, and Union Seminary, he agreed to leave the United States. Sung traveled by train to Seattle, where he boarded a ship to Shanghai, and upon arriving at the harbor in Shanghai, Dr. John Sung thoughtfully gazed at the view of the Chinese coast from the rail of his ship. He became convinced at that moment that God was calling him to preach the gospel to the Chinese people, and he believed God was also asking him to renounce his earthly accomplishments and serve him fully. Sung returned to his cabin, retrieved all the degrees and awards he had earned in the United States, and he carried them to the edge of the ship.

In a small but delightful twist, Dr. Sung did not throw *all* his awards and accomplishments into the ocean. Instead, in a meaningful Chinese contextualization of "offering one's all on the altar," Sung held onto one document. In deference to Chinese filial piety, and out of devotion to his mother, Dr. Sung lobbed all of his degrees and awards over the side of the ship, except for one—his PhD diploma, which he preserved in order to present it to his mother!

He spent the rest of his life in tireless devotion to preaching the gospel. He traveled ceaselessly, often preaching twice a day for two to three hours each time to thousands of people, all without modern electric amplification. He preached robustly and passionately, displaying an energetic flair that would leave his traditional Chinese robes soaked with perspiration. His athletic style of preaching is reminiscent of Billy Sunday, the well-known evangelist in the United States in the 1920s, and I wonder if John Sung was familiar with the ministry of Billy Sunday. Billy Sunday, the former professional baseball player, bounded athletically around the stage, using rural allusions and illustrations to aptly communicate biblical truths to the recent migrants in Chicago and other American urban centers. John Sung preached with the same passion, and he also enjoyed popularity with his audience in the rapidly growing urban areas in the 1930s.

John Sung supposedly traveled with two suitcases. One carried his belongings, and the other one carried prayer requests. After his meetings, he would remain in attendance, continue to pray for the special needs of the participants, and collect their prayer requests. Each morning, he would rise early and pray through the prayer requests carried in his second case.

Although he was known as a hero among the Chinese Christians for his ministry and spiritual power, his social skills lacked polish. One anecdote reports that when Sung stayed in the home of a Christian family, the hostess offered him a bowl of soup. Unfortunately, the soup did not conform to the particular requirements of his strict diet, and so, it is said, he unceremoniously dumped the contents of the bowl onto the floor. During his time in the United States, he suffered the onset of piles or hemorrhoids, a painful condition that consistently plagued him the rest of his life and may help explain his strict diet and his notorious ill-temper.

John Sung traveled through many parts of China, as well as Southeast Asia and Taiwan. He spoke the Fujian dialect and English, so when he traveled, he often preached with the help of translator. Not until later in his ministry, apparently, did he begin to attempt to preach in Mandarin. Unfortunately, the unrelenting schedule finally took a toll on his health. By the early 1940s, he was restricted to bed rest, and he succumbed to intestinal tuberculosis in 1944, apparently aggravated by exhaustion, at only forty-two years of age. Mr. Wang Mingdao conducted his funeral. His ministry only lasted about fifteen years, but he ignited a spark in many real lives as he helped set the foundation for an enduring indigenous church.

The Holy Spirit worked in mighty ways in China through the 1930s and 1940s, and China became a central part of the emerging global Christian church. By the end of the twentieth century, Christianity would be thriving in Asia, Africa, and Latin America. Nonetheless, before the miraculous revivals of the 1980s and 1990s, the Chinese churches were first to be tested by fire.

REFLECTION QUESTIONS

1. The Japanese occupation forces in Beijing required all foreign journals to print four slogans on the cover. Why do you think the Japanese authorities presumed Wang Mingdao's journal *Spiritual Food Quarterly* to be foreign? Do you consider it foreign or indigenous? Explain your answer.

2. Consider the following transitional periods in twentieth-century China. What social, political, and religious factors in each era would have touched the life and thinking of Wang Mingdao (1900–1991)? How did Wang, through his ministry and teaching, respond to each of these fast-moving phases of his life?

   - 1900–1910
   - 1920–1930
   - 1949–1955
   - 1980–1991

3. Why did Wang Mingdao, who did not oppose missions or the missionaries per se, want to break from the missionaries and create an independent church?

4. Why might the simple gospel message of John Sung have resonated so thoroughly in China during the 1930s?

SUGGESTED READING FOR CHAPTER 13

Harvey, Thomas Alan. *Acquainted with Grief: Wang Mingdao's Stand for the Persecuted Church in China*. Grand Rapids: Brazon, 2002.

Ireland, Daryl R. *John Song: Modern Chinese Christianity and the Making of a New Man*. Waco, TX: Baylor University Press, 2020.

Lim, Ka-Tong. *The Life and Ministry of John Sung*. Singapore: Genesis, 2012.

Lyall, Leslie. *Three of China's Mighty Men*. Robesonia, PA: OMF, 1973.

Tow, Timothy. *John Sung My Teacher*. Singapore: Christian Life, 1985.

Wang, Stephen. *The Long Road to Freedom: The Story of Wang Mingdao*. Kent, UK: Sovereign World, 2002.

PART FOUR

From 1949 to the Present, and Prospects for the Future (1949–Present)

EVANGELICAL CHRISTIANITY ARRIVED WITH Robert Morrison in 1807, and within one hundred years the church had taken root. Two offshoots emerged: the first told the story of the missionaries and the massive infrastructure they developed that modernized China. In 1949, that first story died abruptly. The second narrative told the story of the birth of the indigenous Chinese churches.

Part Four focuses on the narrative of the indigenous Chinese churches after 1949. After almost 150 years of missionary presence in China, all the missionaries had departed. But unlike at the end of the Tang Dynasty and the end of the Yuan Dynasty, Christianity had taken root.

The paradigmatic political shift created a new context for the churches. Chapter 14 shows how the new political environment brought the modernist–fundamentalist division to a breaking point. The Chinese Communist Party pressed the Protestant churches to coalesce into the Three-Self Patriotic Movement (TSPM), further deepening the schism. The modernists tended to welcome the new organization and assumed many of the leadership positions. The fundamentalists, on the other hand, preferred to remain separate from the government and resisted participating in an organization that included the modernists. Some of the contours of the division that lasted for decades were already apparent in the early 1950s, as we will discuss in an overview of the debate between Wang Mingdao and Bishop K. H. Ting.

The grand optimism of the early years of the CCP regime crashed quickly with the famine of the Great Leap Forward and the chaos of the Cultural Revolution. The political shocks of the 1960s and 1970s brought calamity for the entire population, and the churches experienced a prolonged period of testing. Chapter 15 tells the story of how the indigenous house churches proved they were genuine as they endured and then thrived through suffering. From the darkness of what appeared to be a tomb, a new vital Chinese church was born.

The political context for the churches changed again after the death of Mao Zedong. By the late 1980s and early 1990s, the reforms of Deng Xiaoping lifted millions of people out of poverty. By the turn of the century, it was apparent that China was rising to become a world power again. The urban areas were booming, and the face of Christianity also changed yet again. Chapter 16 looks at new urban house churches and considers the future directions for Christianity in China. Chinese Christians, even as they forge a new future, must continue confronting their past. They will need to construct a new self-identity as "Chinese Christians." After decades of persecution, they can now finally navigate their sensitive relationship with the state, and they can begin to envision a new Chinese culture that is informed by Christian truth.

As evangelicals, many of the Chinese Christians are activists as well. They want to do something for God. The last part of this book looks at their dream to pick up the baton of *missions* and advance the gospel to the ends of the earth.

SUGGESTED READING FOR PART FOUR

Cook, Richard R. "The Great Commission in Asia." In *The Great Commission: Evangelicals and the History of World Missions*, edited by Martin I. Klauber and Scott M. Manetsch, 149–63. Nashville: B & H, 2008.

Kindopp, Jason, and Carol Lee Hamrin, eds. *God and Caesar in China: Policy Implications of Church–State Tensions*. Washington, DC: Brookings, 2004.

Li, Huaiyin. *Village China under Socialism and Reform: A Micro-History, 1948–2008*. Stanford: Stanford University Press, 2009.

Liao, Yiwu. *God Is Red: The Secret Story of How Christianity Survived and Flourished in Communist China*. Translated by Huang Wenguang. New York: HarperOne, 2011.

Lozada, Eriberto P., Jr. *God Aboveground: Catholic Church, Postsocialist State, and Transnational Processes in a Chinese Village*. Stanford: Stanford University Press, 2001.

Mariani, Paul P. *Church Militant: Bishop Kung and Catholic Resistance in Communist Shanghai*. Cambridge: Harvard University Press, 2011.

Xi, Lian. *Redeemed by Fire: The Rise of Popular Christianity in Modern China*. New Haven: Yale University Press, 2010.

Yang, Fenggang. *Religion in China: Survival & Revival Under Communist Rule*. New York: Oxford University Press, 2012.

Yang, Mayfair Mei-hui, ed. *Chinese Religiosities: Afflictions of Modernity and State Formation.* Berkeley: University of California Press, 2008.

Yao, Xinzhong, and Yanxia Zhao. *Chinese Religion: A Contextual Approach.* New York: Continuum, 2010.

14

A Land without Missionaries
The Rise of the Chinese Communist Party

THE MISSIONARIES, AFTER CLOSE to one hundred and fifty years of presence in China, disappeared almost overnight. China became a land without missionaries once again. On October 1, 1949, masses of people again flooded into Tiananmen Square. On that memorable day, Mao Zedong proclaimed the founding of the People's Republic of China, and, according to many records, asserted, "The Chinese people have stood up." The misery of the past century was over, he declared, and the Communists came to power with the promise to bring a socialist revolution and justice for all. They hoped to build a strong and independent nation which could participate as an equal partner in international affairs; they also intended to bring new prosperity to the people and healing from the many social ills in China. This moment of optimism proved short-lived, but in the initial euphoric years, many segments of Chinese society, including many of the Chinese churches, were willing to support the new government.

Field Notes: On The Communist Reforms of the 1950s

When I teach American students Modern Chinese History, I find it helpful to provide context for the popularity of the new government in the 1950s. They did provide real relief for many people, which is sometimes forgotten. For instance, I came across one story of a woman who was in her early 30s when the CCP came to power in 1949. She was interviewed

---

around 1980, and, even after the harrowing years of the Great Leap Forward and the Cultural Revolution, she maintained her appreciation for the Communists. This is her story.

She was born to a poor family, and her parents could not afford to raise her. When a stranger from the city visited their village, they sold her to the man with the promise that he would arrange a job for her in a modern factory. When she arrived at the city, and she asked about the factory, she was assured that she would not be required to do manual labor. Instead, she had been sold into a brothel. She was only thirteen years old when she was put to work, and over the next twenty years she developed a drug addiction and became riddled with diseases.

By the time the Communist government came to power, she had grown to hate herself. When she and the other prostitutes were rounded up by the police, she did not expect any change. She assumed that she would be quickly released and sent back to the streets, as had happened in the past with new governments. Instead, they put her in a drug rehabilitation program, taught her to sew, and provided her with a job. The day she received her first paycheck, her first honest earnings, she wept. She declared, over thirty years later, that she would always be thankful to the CCP.

After 1949, the missionaries experienced ever-increasing pressure. In fact, as the CCP consolidated its control over the entire nation in the first two to three years after it assumed control, the missionaries gradually realized they were creating an impossible and awkward situation for the Chinese churches. With heavy hearts, they departed from China forever. The missionaries, like many Christians in the West, assumed the fragile young Chinese churches would collapse and that missions would need to start over in the future. They resigned themselves to the reality that, like it or not, for good or bad, Chinese Christians would have to survive on their own.

The rise of the Chinese Communist Party, which promised radical social transformation as it came to power, also brought a curious challenge to the modernist wing of the Protestant churches. The CCP insisted that the missionaries and Christians were no longer necessary in China, as the Party itself would carry out all the necessary social reforms. For decades, the modernists had accused fundamentalists such as Wang Mingdao of being "otherworldly" and therefore unable to offer concrete solutions to real and present problems. The modernists had emphasized the so-called social implications of the gospel, and they were critical of the fundamentalists who particularly focused on evangelism and discipleship. Not surprisingly, the modernists were now compelled to respond to the new Communist regime with arguments that the government could only address social and material issues, but that the problems in China were also spiritual.

In the early 1950s, a new issue emerged regarding the conflict within the Protestant churches. The modernists generally desired to work within the new government structures, but many of the fundamentalists and conservative Protestants, led by Wang Mingdao in Beijing, resisted government interference in their churches. In accordance with standard Marxist dogma, the CCP assumed that all religions would eventually perish, but they would allow an official "patriotic" space for religious followers who were willing to submit to the government's authority. One of the most prominent and lively church debates in the early 1950s emerged between Bishop K. H. Ting (1915–2012) (Ding Guangxun), the future head of the Three-Self Patriotic Movement (TSPM), and Wang Mingdao. This protracted debate was mentioned previously in Chapter 13.

The debate was waged through articles written in the TSPM's national publication *Tian Feng* (*Heavenly Wind*) and Wang's own journal *Lingshi* (*Spiritual Food*). In the pages of *Tian Feng*, Ding Guangxun regularly addressed Wang Mingdao and the conservatives, and Wang quickly emerged as the leader of the "faction" that would not cooperate with the TSPM, the "Wang Mingdao faction" (*Wang Mingdao pai*). In response, Wang reproduced large sections of the *Tian Feng* articles and then meticulously countered each point in his journal, *Spiritual Food*.

Ding emphasized the importance of unifying the nation to bring equality and justice to all. He argued that the unified Protestant churches could play a significant role in assisting the government achieve its noble goals. Wang responded, as he often did, with colorful and provocative language. He was determined to remain independent from the state government, and, if necessary, he would defy their mandates. He believed that God would protect him and his church in Beijing, just as God had protected them during the Japanese occupation.

Furthermore, he was adamant that he would never join an organization that would unite him with the Protestant modernists, or "unbelievers." For years, he had denigrated the "modernists" by employing a pun in Chinese. Rather than calling them *xinpai* (新派) (modernists), as they were generally known, which might be translated more literally "New Party," he referred to them as *buxinpai* (不信派) which might be translated "Party of Unbelievers." He was candid in his skepticism that the modernists were "born again" or even Christian at all, and he would not join them in any association.

Remarkably, the back-and-forth of dueling articles persisted for several years in the early 1950s. In one typical exchange, Wang Mingdao responded to a direct challenge from Ding Guangxun. Ding had quoted Romans 14:3–4, which admonishes Christians not to judge one another, to coax Wang and the conservative churches to seek Christian unity within the government-sponsored Protestant organization. Wang began by directly quoting Ding's article: "Lastly, Mr. Ding refers to a Scripture passage that says, 'God has accepted him. Who are you to judge someone else's servant, to his own master he stands or falls. And he will stand, for the Lord is able to make him stand.'"[1]

Then Wang thoroughly explained, based on a careful examination of the Romans passage, why he completely disagreed with Ding. First, Wang charged that Ding had misrepresented the biblical passage: "This [Romans 14] truly is a precious teaching, but unfortunately Mr. Ding has not put the passage into proper context. Let us now look at the entire passage."[2] Since Ding had referred to Romans 14:3–4, Wang went on to quote the entirety of Romans 14:1–12. This interaction with Ding, and the whole article, was quite lengthy. After copying out all twelve verses into the article, Wang then explained that the verses Ding quoted did not command him, Wang, not to criticize the modernists and the TSPM, because in those verses Paul was referring to tolerance toward Christians. The modernists, on the contrary, who did not believe the fundamental doctrines of the faith, were not Christians. Wang wrote:

> After reading this passage, we see clearly that Paul is writing this passage because in that day in the church at Rome there were those who had different opinions concerning food or special dates . . . These passages are written to those believers. These people were all people who truly believed in Jesus. They were not at all like the "non-believing party" [modernists], who do not believe that Jesus was born of a virgin, do not believe that Jesus redeemed people from sin, do not believe Jesus was resurrected in the body, do not believe that Jesus will come again. The believers in Rome were all people who had faith, and furthermore they had the same faith. They only differed in their opinion as to food in special days, so Paul encourages them not to judge one another.[3]

---

1. Cook, "Fundamentalism and Modern Culture," 111.
2. Cook, "Fundamentalism and Modern Culture," 112.
3. Cook, "Fundamentalism and Modern Culture," 112.

Wang concluded with a harsh condemnation of Ding and the other modernists, whom Wang considered to be false brethren and false prophets. Wang finished:

> It is completely wrong to apply this passage to the false brethren and false prophets who oppose true doctrine. In fact, when we speak of these people we should not use Romans 14, but rather 2 John 1:9–11. "Anyone who runs ahead and does not continue in the teaching of Christ does not have God; whoever continues in the teaching has both the Father and the Son. If anyone comes to you and does not bring this teaching, do not take him into your house or welcome him. Anyone who welcomes him shares in his wicked work."[4]

Wang could not, based on this passage in 2 John, unite with the modernists or the TSPM or, he believed, he would be sharing in the "wicked work" of those that do not have God.

Shortly before Wang Mingdao's journal was shut down in 1955, he concluded a lengthy article with this challenge to the CCP. He wrote:

> We will not unite in any way with these unbelievers, nor will we join any of their organizations . . . Our attitude in matters of faith is this: all truths that are found in the Bible we accept and hold . . . [F]or our loyalty to God we are ready to pay any cost that is required. We shall shrink from no sacrifice . . . We take our stand on Christian doctrine . . . We—for the sake of faith![5]

On August 7, 1955, Wang Mingdao was arrested and sentenced to fifteen years' imprisonment as an anti-revolutionary.

The division between the two factions persisted beyond the 1950s, and the "Wang Mingdao Faction" became known as the "underground" or house church movement. These independent churches, perhaps unexpectedly, displayed tremendous staying power. The government, like the retreating Western missionaries, had underestimated them. The churches no longer needed outside support for survival.

The churches showed a willingness and a readiness to stand alone without assistance from either the foreign missionaries or the central government. The CCP charged the Christians with complicity with foreign missions and imperialism, but, in fact, it was their independence that made them formidable. Independent churches such as the Little Flock, the Jesus Family, and the True Jesus Church could survive even after the withdrawal

---

4. Cook, "Fundamentalism and Modern Culture," 112–13.
5. Cook, "Fundamentalism and Modern Culture," 108.

of foreign missionary aid, and they could afford to ignore the dictates of the Chinese Communists Party.

The government initially offered Wang and some of the other dissenters a small amount of latitude; all of that latitude ended by 1957. By that time, not only Wang but many other Christians had been imprisoned, as well as a growing number of intellectuals. Although conflicting evidence exists surrounding the reason for Wang's imprisonment, I believe Wang was not arrested ultimately because he was a Christian or because he refused to join the TSPM. Rather, like other strong-minded dissenters, he was apprehended because he rejected the CCP's single narrative of national salvation. He refused to mindlessly endorse the government mandates for the people. Most importantly, in the early 1950s, as a Christian pacifist, he would not support China's participation in the Korean War. The government demanded submission, and they called into question the "patriotism" of any dissenting voices.

By the late 1950s, the initial enthusiasm for the Revolution waned, and slowly some voices of opposition arose. In 1957, the Anti-Rightist Movement violently suppressed those early expressions of dissent. The "bamboo curtain" descended over China, and news about what was really going on inside China became very scarce. The country entered a dark era, punctuated by the Great Leap Forward and the Cultural Revolution of the 1960s and 1970s. Many pastors, both modernists and fundamentalists, were arrested, forced to endure "struggle sessions," and publicly humiliated. The missionaries were gone, the infrastructure had been usurped, and the indigenous Christians entered a period of even more intense testing.

The fledgling church in China had not survived beyond the end of the Tang Dynasty, nor had it endured the rise of the Ming Dynasty at the end of the Yuan. Could the young roots of the indigenous churches remain fast in the coming storm of the 1960s and 1970s?

REFLECTION QUESTIONS

1. What ideas from Marxism and the Chinese Communist Party reflected biblical truth and values?

2. Some scholars have identified "nationalism" as the key common ideology that the CCP used to unite China and come to power in 1949. Should Christians support the nationalism promoted by the CCP?

3. Should the Christians have supported the social goals of the CCP in the 1950s?

4. Why would the CCP want to unite all Christians into a single organization? Why might Christians, even those who believe in the unity of the body of Christ, oppose this kind of association?

SUGGESTED READING FOR CHAPTER 14

Domenach, Jean-Luc. *The Origins of the Great Leap Forward: The Case of One Chinese Province.* Translated by A. M. Berrett. Boulder, CO: Westview, 1995.

Wickeri, Philip L. *Reconstructing Christianity in China: K. H. Ting and the Chinese Church.* Maryknoll, NY: Orbis, 2007.

Yan, Yunxiang. *Private Life under Socialism: Love, Intimacy, and Family in a Chinese Village.* Stanford: Stanford University Press, 2003.

15

A Land without Christians
Victory from the Tomb

WHEN I BEGAN TO research the churches in China as a college student in the early 1980s, I believed the churches had died for the most part. I believed that missionaries like me would need to launch another great missionary movement to the massive nation. Given that we thought the church had not survived the deprivation of the communist era, the researchers and missiologists I read at the time often asked the question, "What did the missionaries do wrong?" Why didn't an indigenous church take root after more than a century of intensive Protestant missionary activity? Some experts suggested, for instance, that perhaps the missionaries had failed to create a properly contextualized church and indigenous leadership, or maybe they had expended too much effort in education and medicine rather than concentrating on church planting.

Throughout the 1980s, however, news from China began to trickle out, gradually revealing that the churches had not only survived the Cultural Revolution, but that they were experiencing an unprecedented revival. Researchers and missiologists had to formulate new questions such as, "What did the missionaries do *correctly*?" Researchers and historians no longer highlighted only the errors of the missionary movement; instead, they focused on trying to make sense of the unprecedented revivals in the 1980s.

The period between 1950 and 1990 contained two paradoxical realities that are difficult to juxtapose in one brief chapter: both the unspeakable series of tragedies that rained down on the nation and the miraculous survival of the churches which culminated in the spiritual revivals of the 1980s. A church that seemed to be pushed toward the brink of death experienced a profound resurrection victory from the depths of the tomb.

This chapter will first look at the historical context, the Great Leap Forward, and the Cultural Revolution. I will then share my personal journey of how I came to learn of the marvelous work of God during those difficult years, and I will retell the stirring testimony of one faithful Chinese pastor I had the privilege to meet. The chapter closes with a brief description of the sweet worship and intense spiritual hunger that characterized the indigenous house churches of the 1980s and early 1990s.

THE GREAT LEAP FORWARD
AND CULTURAL REVOLUTION

The Communist Party, even as it came to power in 1949, was not fully unified, and Mao Zedong bore the difficult task of trying to unify the various factions. The urban intellectual elites, who dated back to the founding of the party in the 1920s, comprised one of the major factions. These elites had learned Marxism in Europe and in the universities. The other major faction included those who had grown up in the rural areas and who followed a less orthodox and more practical form of Marxism. Chiang Kai-shek targeted the urban communists for destruction when he unified China under the KMT in the 1920s and 1930s, forcing the CCP to go into hiding in the rural areas, and Mao subsequently emerged as the key leader of the rural Communists. Mao harbored an abiding distrust of the intellectuals within the urban communist elite, and they, for their part, questioned Mao's orthodoxy and his capacity to lead the Party and the nation.

The educated leaders naturally assumed many positions of government power in Beijing and in the large urban areas within China after 1949. Mao, growing increasingly suspicious of these leaders, launched a purge of the Party in 1957 called the Anti-Rightist Movement. This movement led to the denunciation of many party members and increased pressure on all segments of society opposed to the CCP, such as the Christian churches. Perhaps due in part to the inexperience and incompetence of the CCP leaders who wrested control of the government in the late 1950s, the CCP adopted a cluster of disastrous economic and agricultural policies, known as the Great Leap Forward, that created widespread famine between 1959 and 1961. Between 20 and 40 million people perished as a direct or indirect result of these devastating policies.

The CCP had slowly led the country out of the worst of the crisis by 1965, but Mao again suspected the leaders who were controlling the government, and so he launched yet another effort in 1966 to purify the Communist Revolution and the Chinese Communist Party. He called this effort the Cultural Revolution. Red Guards, mostly college and high school aged students, were given free rein, in the name of Mao, to pursue all elements of society that were deemed inadequately pure. They first violently targeted their schoolteachers and then increasingly directed their attention to all strata of society. This initial stage triggered a response. The victims of the first stage, such as the youth from families that had been attacked, united with other young people whose families had lost their prestige and privilege in 1949. Together, this group of younger people embarked on a counterattack. They seized the opportunity to unequivocally proclaim their allegiance to Chairman Mao, and they established their own groups of Red Guards.

Violence flared around the country, and the Party was forced to mobilize the Red Army to put down the insurrections. The top levels of the CCP also experienced deadly turmoil. By the late 1960s, millions of urban dwellers were "sent down" to the countryside in order to "learn" from the simple rural people, and the chaos lingered until the death of Mao in 1976. The tragedy of the Cultural Revolution resulted in the deaths of perhaps 20 million more Chinese people. Deng Xiaoping, who had himself been purged, emerged as the supreme leader in 1978 and again, as he had in the early 1960s, attempted to pursue less ideological and more practical and professional policies that could reform the government and bring economic prosperity to the nation.

Field Notes: On Gallows Humor

The volatility within the leadership of the CCP during these early decades was legendary, with the regular purging and then restoration of many of the most prominent leaders in the nation. The tense dangers from shifting political allegiances is perhaps best captured in a joke which allegedly circulated in China in the 1980s. Three men were sitting in a prison in Beijing lamenting their misfortune, and the first man complained, "I am in prison because I supported Deng Xiaoping." The second man exclaimed, "That is remarkable, because I am here for opposing Deng Xiaoping." The third prisoner panned, "I am Deng Xiaoping."

The death of Mao did bring opportunity for radical transformation, and the reforms under Deng Xiaoping achieved rapid success; the country began its now well-known path toward recovery and prosperity, lifting hundreds of millions of people out of poverty.

WHISPERS OF REVIVAL—1980s

I journeyed to China for one week in 1982 as a college student without knowing much about the country, which had been deeply hidden by the Bamboo Curtain for decades. I had little notion of the tragedies of the Great Leap Forward or the Cultural Revolution, but I believed I was called by God to serve as a missionary in this nation. Back home in college, I began to study Mandarin Chinese. As I prepared to become a missionary to China, my friends would often remind me that China was a "closed country," and even if I could serve there, church planting would need to begin again from the ground up. If the churches were not dead already, they must be close to it.

I read as much material on China and the Chinese churches as I could find, discovering articles and anecdotal evidence that the churches were not dead, and, in fact, some China-watchers were beginning to suggest that the church might actually be growing. Unsubstantiated reports of revival began to leak out, and rumors circulated about the possibility of incredible church growth. When I would share this information with my friends in Chicago, they would frown and shake their heads, assuring me that the churches were dead. Nonetheless, I gradually began to believe a miracle.

In about 1984, I visited a church to hear an American speaker who had been born to missionary parents in China and later served with the China Inland Mission during the late 1940s. The speaker's name was J. Herbert Kane, and several years later he became one of my instructors in seminary. He and his family had been forced from China in 1950 when he was a young man, but after thirty years of living in the United States, he had recently returned to visit his birthplace. He proceeded on his journey with the awareness that some estimates reported that 20 to 40 million Christians might currently live in China, up from one million in 1950. He acknowledged that he doubted those extraordinary estimates prior to his travel.

He was therefore absolutely stunned to witness, with his own eyes, a revival in the city where he had been born! Of course, he had only seen one city, and he conceded that he did not know if there was a broader revival, but he was optimistic. I left that meeting with the belief that God might truly be moving in China. The revival in that city, we now know, was not an isolated case, but was part of a larger, widespread, apparently spontaneous revival in numerous parts of China. The churches were not dead; they were experiencing resurrection from the depths of the tomb.

GRANDPA YEYE—A STORY

In 1991, during yet another visit to China, I had the privilege to meet a Chinese church leader who had lived through many of the crises of the twentieth century. I heard that he had suffered severely for his faith, to include prison time of over twenty years, and he was willing to tell us his story. For security reasons, I slipped into his apartment secretly, where four of us listened raptly as he bared his soul and "put flesh" onto the story of twentieth-century China. We called him *Yeye*, or "Grandpa" in Chinese, so in English I liked to call him Grandpa Yeye. Grandpa Yeye's story embodied the tragedy of twentieth-century China, dramatized the unexpected growth of the churches, and displayed the incomprehensible glory of God.

The day we met him, we waited in a dingy bedroom with a single bed and four small chairs for several minutes before Grandpa Yeye, frail and bent with a slightly hunched back, quietly entered. He sat on the edge of the bed, and I noticed that he looked much older than his seventy-five years as his wrinkled face betrayed years of persecution and suffering. But, even more striking than his aged look, I beheld the life and the spark in his eyes. As he opened his mouth, I remember thinking that my many years of struggling to learn Mandarin were all worth it as that struggle enabled me to absorb his amazing story.

In 1933, he was a just teenager when he attended an evangelistic meeting. At that meeting, he accepted Christ and experienced a thorough conversion. Three years later, in 1936, he attended another meeting where the young people were challenged to give their lives to serve Jesus. Gesturing dramatically with his hands as he spoke, Grandpa Yeye related that at that gathering he was challenged "to offer his hands, his feet, his head, and his heart . . . all to Jesus." He desired to dedicate his life to take the gospel to all parts of China, and so, during the altar call, he emphatically stood up and moved toward that destiny. I looked into the eyes of Grandpa Yeye, and I tried to imagine the young man he had been: talented and smart, nearing his twentieth birthday and filled with zeal for God and with passion for the evangelization of China.

One year later, in 1937, the Sino-Japanese War broke out and, by 1940, he was placed in a Japanese prison, like many Chinese pastors. (As he began to speak about his incarceration, I could not help but think of the well-known Olympian and China missionary, Eric Liddell, whose memorable story and death in a Japanese internment camp in China was portrayed in the movie *Chariots of Fire*.) I sat in stunned silence as I listened to Grandpa Yeye describe, with an astounding memory, the horrific details of the deprivations and suffering he encountered in the internment camp. In 1945, when the prisoners were all set free at the end of the war, he remarked sadly that he was one of only a handful of men who were still alive. Almost all his fellow inmates had perished.

He returned home for two years, but when war erupted between the KMT and the Communists in 1947, he, his wife, and his young children had to flee several times as they attempted to avoid the fighting. They experienced a brief respite in 1949 when the Chinese Communist Party achieved victory. Interrupting his story, we asked him if he considered leaving China at that time. He chuckled and then answered that he and his wife had six children by that time, and they never considered leaving.

Spellbound, we listened as Grandpa Yeye went on to tell us that he was arrested again in 1957, this time by the CCP. He was warned that he would be incarcerated unless he pledged his allegiance to the state and denied his faith in Jesus. He refused and was subsequently imprisoned. Then, about a year later, his wife was also imprisoned. He would remain in prison over twenty years, until 1980.

He then turned to the story of the Great Leap Forward, and he related in excruciating detail about the widespread famine and suffering during the early 1960s. I had long been aware that almost everybody in China suffered during the Great Leap Forward, and that millions of vulnerable people died, but it had not occurred to me that the prisoners were particularly hard hit. We listened in tears as he chronicled his horrific experiences, such as the many weeks he was so famished and frail that he could not rise up from his pallet. We wondered how God could allow this kind of suffering to afflict his children. Grandpa Yeye broke down at this point in his story, teared up, and slowly began to sing a few words from the song, "God Never Changes" (神永不改變). I will always treasure the memory of his sweet and pure voice singing those words through his tears.

Grandpa Yeye regained his composure and managed to complete his recollection of the Great Leap Forward. As he began speaking about the mid-1960s, I became alert as I anticipated hearing about his experiences during the Cultural Revolution. I had read many books about the Cultural Revolution, but this was to be the first time I heard a personal first-hand account of someone who had lived through the event. I was especially eager because Grandpa Yeye possessed such an astonishing memory and had shown himself to be so open and honest about his life. He did not hesitate to tell us everything, and I knew we would hear something unforgettable.

He continued: "Then in 1966, that was the beginning of the Cultural Revolution." As I looked in his eyes, I thought I could see the memories flutter through his mind, but he halted abruptly. With tears forming, he stopped altogether and apologized. He expressed sorrowful regret that even though so many years had passed since the Cultural Revolution, he still could not bring himself to speak of the unspeakable terrors he witnessed and experienced. After that heart-rending apology, he then skipped ahead in his story to the mid-1970s.

With the rise of Deng Xiaoping, many of the religious and political prisoners were set free in the late 1970s, and Grandpa Yeye and his wife were both released and had returned home by 1980. He was old, beyond the age of retirement, and his body was broken. He was an ex-prisoner and therefore unemployable. He and his wife were forced to eke out a living day by day, and it was tremendously difficult, but even through that extreme hardship, he assured us that God had been gracious.

Looking at the old, broken gentleman before me, I thought back to 1936. I again pictured the young, vigorous man standing up and dedicating his life to bring the gospel to all of China. I could not help but feel like weeping, wondering what had gone wrong. What happened to his life? If not for the tragedies of twentieth-century China, what might he have accomplished for the kingdom of God? We will never know.

Before we left, one of my colleagues asked Grandpa Yeye, "Of all your experiences, what would you say was the hardest?" I found the question puzzling because there seemed to be far too many painful stories to choose just one, but Grandpa Yeye did not hesitate. He immediately answered the question, replying that the hardest part of his life was that his children could not believe in Jesus. He went on to explain.

When he was arrested in 1957, his young children experienced a crisis of faith. How could they believe in a God who would allow their parents, two people who had been so faithful, to suffer incarceration? How could they believe in a God who would allow the disintegration of their family? On the other hand, his children also witnessed other pastors, the parents of their friends, who were arrested but then released because they had pledged their allegiance to the government and compromised their faith in Jesus. Grandpa Yeye sighed, wondering aloud how his young children could have been expected to understand, having grown up enduring shame and unimaginable hardship as un-parented children of criminals. That his own children could not believe in Jesus, Grandpa Yeye stated decisively, was the hardest experience of all.

Later that evening, I had the opportunity to hear his daughter, whom I believe was in her mid-40s at the time, give her testimony. She disclosed to us the horror of witnessing the arrests of her parents, and although they maintained their unshakeable faith in Jesus, she watched them being dragged off to prison. She also saw some of her friends' parents, those who had denied Jesus, as they were released and not forced to suffer shame and separation. She asked, "As a young child, how could I believe that God was true, and that God was good?"

She continued, moving forward in time to relate when she finally saw her parents after their release. They returned home in the early 1980s and lived near her and her family. She observed that although they were broken and destitute, and they had every reason to be bitter, they displayed instead an inexplicable spirit of joy. And, she marveled, they *prayed*, especially her mother, every day for their six children. Grandpa Yeye's daughter testified to us that evening, that through the powerful testimony of the suffering and survival of her parents, she came to believe that God was true. She testified that she, and all her brothers and sisters, had come to trust in Jesus.

So many years before, in 1936, Grandpa Yeye had consecrated himself to bring the gospel to China. I dare not presume to know the ways of God, but I suspect a connection existed between the many faithful suffering servants of God in the early days of the indigenous Chinese churches, men like Grandpa Yeye and Wang Mingdao, and the revival of the Chinese churches in the 1980s and 1990s. The blood of the martyrs certainly seemed to have seeded a massive revival and extensive church growth. Grandpa Yeye's greatest passion in 1936 was for the conversion of Chinese people to Jesus, particularly his own family and especially his own children, and although he never could have expected how God might use him and his suffering to achieve this dream, I believe God did use him, and many faithful martyrs of his generation, to build a flourishing church in China.

THE HOUSE CHURCHES OF THE 1970s AND 1980s

The Holy Spirit animated the warm fellowship described in Acts 2, and that same spirit seemed to permeate the initial burst of growth in the house churches. The churches of the late 1970s and 1980s, like the early church, were characterized by prayer, love for the Word of God, signs and wonders, warm fellowship, and rapid growth. The TSPM still survived, maintaining a tenuous link between Christianity and the government. The TSPM experienced modest growth, but the conservative evangelical house church-es appeared to drive the revivals.

Perhaps the house churches can be best understood through their worship. A new indigenous sound of praise whispered across the land. The house churches needed to worship quietly and remain out of the public eye, but their zeal was infectious. Lü Xiao Min (呂小敏) emerged as a popular song writer. She was born in 1970 to a peasant family in Henan, and after her conversion as a teenager she began to write indigenous hymns. She was not trained in music, and she credited her inspiration and gift to the Holy Spirit. Writing a few hymns every week, she soon had a collection of sev-eral hundred songs that were gathered into the *Canaan Hymns*. Outside of China, she is also known as "Sister Ruth." Her simple songs captured the deep suffering and the sweet spirit of the churches. As Chloe Starr observed, "These are genuinely inculturated hymns, with a folk lilt, Chinese harmo-nies, and an imagery that blends rural China with biblical themes."[1] Perhaps most famous was Xiao Min's song, "Five O'clock in the Morning in China." An excerpt shows her heart for China:

> Five o'clock in the morning of China,
> rises the sound of prayers.
> Prayers bring revival and peace,
> bring harmony and victory . . .

> Five o'clock in the morning of China,
> rises the sound of prayers,
> spreading across mountains and rivers, melting icy heart and soul.
> No more bondage, no more war.
> Bringing about blessings, turning around destiny, this is a year
> of harvest.[2]

A passion for learning the bible characterized the churches at this time as well. Extended worship services of singing and preaching could last for hours, and young leaders were responsible for feeding ever-growing net-works of believers. Chinese Christians outside of mainland China, mostly ethnic Chinese people from Hong Kong, Taiwan, and the United States, quickly picked up the task of providing bible training. By the late 1980s, the demand for training outstripped the supply. To help meet the demand, Chinese church researcher Dr. Jonathan Chao established mission training centers in Hong Kong and Taiwan. The centers needed to train more young

---

1. Starr, *Chinese Theology*, 265.
2. Ho, trans., "Five O'clock in the Morning in China," by Xiao Min, para. 4.

Mandarin-speaking missionaries to meet the cry for help from the house churches, and this became their goal.

Field Notes: On Teaching in Taiwan

I graduated seminary in 1990 and joined the training center that Dr. Jonathan Chao had established in Taiwan in 1988. As a foreigner, opportunities for me to serve in missions in China were severely restricted, so I jumped at the chance to participate in training young ethnic Chinese missionaries in Taiwan. When I arrived, I was delighted to learn that our seminary also attracted Korean and other Asian missionaries who desired to serve the house churches. I could not go when our Chinese faculty visited the mainland several times each year, but I began to hear innumerable first-hand accounts of the revivals when the faculty returned.

The seminary president in the early 1990s arranged a special fact-finding trip to the house churches for several American missionaries, and he invited me to participate. My colleague, Rev. Woo, was tasked with leading our tour of seven American missionaries. We were not able to visit the churches during worship, but Rev. Woo arranged for numerous key house church leaders to meet us at restaurants and other secure locations. Most memorable was a midnight meeting with about fifteen house church leaders in the middle of nowhere.

In Shanghai, the eight of us squeezed into a rented bus. The rural village was only six hours away, but our veteran bus driver could not find the obscure location, and we arrived four hours late. We were scheduled to have dinner with a group of house church leaders, but we did not even arrive until after 10 PM. To our surprise, the wonderful brothers and sisters had waited patiently. We were tired and hungry, and we simply wanted to eat and then sleep. However, they assured us the delay was fine, and that while we ate dinner they would continue to wait.

We departed the tiny village after 11 PM on three-wheeled pedicabs they had hired. For the American missionaries, the scene was surreal. Four Chinese drivers pedaled furiously into the dark and quiet night, as we, riding with two people per cycle, wondered where we might end up. When we spotted a motorcycle gang silhouetted in the distance, we thought we might be doomed. Instead, the motorcyclists turned out to be the house church leaders who were anticipating our visit. Dispatching our pedicab operators, we rode another ten minutes on the back of the motorbikes along narrow paths in the darkness. We began our meeting with about fifteen house church leaders a little bit after midnight.

We sat in a circle, and each person offered a brief introduction. They were delighted to find that the missionaries from Taiwan could all speak Chinese. Our delight surpassed theirs when we learned the extent of their ministries. The men and women, mostly in their 20s or 30s, informed us they led a network of churches comprised of several thousand believers. We inquired about their preparation to lead such a vast ministry, including preaching and bible teaching. We learned that one brother had a sixth-grade education, but they assured us that was unusual. Most of them only made it to first or second grade, and some of them had no formal education at all! Stunned, we asked them to tell us their greatest need. They said bible teaching. They needed to know the Word of God in order to feed the thousands of believers.

At about 2 AM, Rev. Woo asked if we could share a time of prayer for one another. After prayers, he stood up to lead us away. One brother grasped the arm of Rev. Woo and asked him when he would return. To our shame, we missionaries had presumed the house church leaders were so anxious to meet with the seven of us, even staying up through the middle of the night, because they had never met foreigners before. Now we truly learned why they had been so patient. They insisted that Rev. Woo must return soon, but they requested that he bring Chinese bible teachers next time, not a group of foreigners.

In a heartbreaking scene, we watched as he tried to explain that he would not be able to return. We learned later that our leadership in Taiwan had determined that our seminary could no longer supply teaching for this particular network. With limited resources, we could not meet the rising demand. But the brother would not let go of the pastor's arm. Finally, Rev. Woo relented, and he arranged for a date and time when he would return with another teacher.

No sooner had the first brother released Rev. Woo, when a second man caught his arm. He explained that he was not actually part of this fellowship, but he was responsible for a similar group of several thousand believers in the next valley. His churches, and their leaders, unlike this group, had no help in bible training at all. He had learned of this meeting and had ridden his bicycle for several hours that day to come and request teachers. This time, Rev. Woo had to disappoint him. He said, using a phrase that our seminary colleagues often repeated in situations like this, "Let us pray together that God will supply your need."

CONCLUSION: CHINA AND GLOBAL CHRISTIANITY

The growth of the Chinese churches in the 1980s and 1990s certainly resulted from God's blessing, but it also thrived as a byproduct of the external circumstances. The missionaries had first built a viable foundation, the churches were then released to survive on their own, and finally they were tested by persecution. The revivals revealed the health of the roots of the indigenous churches. To the surprise of many, those roots were healthy, and the churches were thus bearing much fruit.

Beyond the setting in China, however, Chinese Christianity also emerged in a broader worldwide context as the transformation of the global face of Christianity began with the remarkable growth of the churches in Asia, Africa, and Latin America. The church in China today cannot be understood apart from the emergence of Christianity in the global South, as God worked mightily not just in China but in many parts of the world.

Global Christianity had its own extraordinary story, as described in Chapter 11. When the Western imperial powers departed after the end of World War II, the indigenous churches did not collapse, but thrived in an unexpected and exponential way. In the West, at the same time, the churches stagnated, and secularization theory predicted the demise of religion. Many observers, oblivious to the growth of the indigenous churches in Asia, Africa, and Latin America, surmised and pontificated that Christianity might be declining worldwide. However, victory from the tomb became apparent. By the early 2000s, the fantastic growth of the churches could no longer be ignored. No longer would the West be able to assert a distinctive claim to Christianity; Christianity had become truly global. And the Chinese churches were poised to secure a central role in this expanding, global Christianity.

REFLECTION QUESTIONS

1. Could the suffering of the persecuted Christians from the 1950s to the 1970s be interpreted as part of the plan of God to grow the churches in China? How might persecution help the growth of the church? Explain your answer.

2. Why might a church under persecution, like the house churches in China in the 1970s and 1980s, experience sweet worship and exhibit a strong desire for the Word of God? What influences are you aware

of that would arise in China later, in the 1990s and 2000s, to weaken that enthusiasm?

3. What "preparations" for the reception of gospel existed in China? How would you compare these eras?

   - In the Tang Dynasty?
   - In the late Qing Dynasty (1810–1900)?
   - In the 1980s and 1990s?

4. To unite the country and maintain popular support, the CCP seems to have been emphasizing nationalism and economic development since the 1980s.

   - In what ways can Christians support the CCP in these goals?
   - In what ways should the church provide a prophetic voice challenging the government?

SUGGESTED READING FOR CHAPTER 15

Dikotter, Frank. *The Cultural Revolution: A People's History, 1962–1976.* New York: Bloomsbury, 2016.

———. *Mao's Great Famine: The History of China's Most Devastating Catastrophe, 1958–1962.* New York: Walker, 2010.

Lambert, Tony. *China's Christian Millions: The Costly Revival.* Rev. ed. London: Monarch, 2006.

Liao, Yiwu. *God Is Red: The Secret Story of How Christianity Survived and Flourished in Communist China.* Translated by Huang Wenguang. New York: HarperOne, 2011.

Mariani, Paul P. *Church Militant: Bishop Kung and Catholic Resistance in Communist Shanghai.* Cambridge: Harvard University Press, 2011.

Van Houten, Richard, ed. *Wise as Serpents, Harmless as Doves: Christians in China Tell Their Story, Interviews by Jonathan Chao.* Pasadena: William Carey Library, 1988.

16

Out of the Dark Shadows,
into the Light of the Global Stage

I AM SOMETIMES ASKED to predict what will happen next for the Chinese churches, and although I am an historian and not a prophet, I will do my best to address three key questions in this chapter.

What has happened to the Chinese churches since the year 2000?
I will suggest, first, that 2003 marks a critical transformation for the young indigenous churches, as that year the Chinese churches intentionally came out of seclusion and out of the shadows, desiring to play a significant part in global Christianity.

What are the central issues facing the Chinese churches?
Second, as the church matures, Chinese theologians will need to continue to develop a contextual theology that speaks to the Chinese people today, and I will briefly suggest three fundamental questions that I believe may occupy the attention of Chinese Christian thinkers for the next several generations.

What is next for the Chinese churches?
Third, and finally, I will present the dream of many within the missions movement that a mighty missionary force will arise within China. Today, a small vanguard of Chinese church leaders is effectively disseminating this missionary vision, and, as far as I can tell, the vision is beginning to sweep through the churches.

OUT OF THE SHADOWS,
THE CHINESE CHURCH GOES GLOBAL

In 2003, I attended a Chinese Christian conference with about 2,000 participants, and the moderator invited the Caucasian Christians in the audience to stand and be recognized, so, 196 years after Robert Morrison arrived in China in 1807, I awkwardly stood up with about thirty other Caucasian Christians to the thunderous applause from the Chinese Christians. I was exceedingly embarrassed (was I supposed to take a bow?), but I appreciated that the moment had nothing to do with me or the others who were standing; the Chinese Christians merely desired to praise God for his grace and express their appreciation for the long-suffering sacrifice of the Western missionaries. I also believe the standing ovation epitomized a historical transformation for the Chinese churches.

In an article published in February of 2005 in *Christianity Today*, titled "Behind China's Closed Doors: Newly Confident House Churches Open Themselves up to the World," I argued that 2003 proved to be a watershed year and a turning point for the Protestant Chinese churches, because in that year the house churches began to make a concerted effort to join the global church. The three significant occurrences that year, which would have been unimaginable even two or three years earlier, can best be appreciated by first understanding the developments of the house churches during the twenty-five years preceding 2003.

Growing but Discreet Churches before 2003

Throughout the 1980s, information regarding the churches in China remained sparse, hotly contested, and confused; no one could even agree on how many Christians dwelt in China, while some observers maintained that the churches had not grown at all since 1949. Even inside China, Chinese Christians could only know for certain what was happening in their own local areas due to the continued repression which limited communication. Minimal news existed about the overall size, condition, and health of the churches.

China still did not allow missionaries in at this time, but gradually more Christians could visit, and throughout the late 1980s and early 1990s, those visitors begin to paint a picture of a vibrant and growing church in numerous locations around the country. The initial missionary efforts focused on smuggling bibles into China as organizations learned of the large number of Christians there. As knowledge expanded regarding the needs of

the Chinese churches, missions organizations and churches began to prepare bible study and discipleship materials and to send short-term teaching
teams to the house churches. Caucasian people could only provide limited
direct ministry within China, but overseas ethnic Chinese from Taiwan, the
United States, and other parts of the Chinese diaspora began to take up the
task of providing short-term training for rural house church leaders.

Korean missionaries, who can be considered one of the first fruits of
the phenomenal explosion of global Christianity in the twentieth century,
also joined the growing missionary force in China. At the beginning of the
twentieth century, the small Korean church experienced heavy persecution,
but it exploded with growth through the 1970s. By the 1980s, particularly
after the 1988 Seoul Olympics resulted in loosened travel restrictions on
Korean citizens, Korean Christians grew anxious to join the global missionary movement. They formed a new and mighty force, streaming to all parts
of the world, specializing in unreached peoples and preferring the most
dangerous parts of the world. China, sitting on the Korean doorstep, proved
a natural draw for many workers.

The influx of more international Christians into China created greater
awareness of the situation, and these Christians gradually confirmed the
early reports of the revivals from the 1980s. They also provided additional
verification of ongoing church growth. I assumed, along with many observers at the time, that the period of rapid church growth in China would be
short-lived, and therefore we needed to mobilize rapidly to take advantage
of this brief window of opportunity. Missionaries were not permitted in
China, so foreign Christians entered as Mandarin language students, as
English teachers, and as professionals in an array of occupations with the
goal to evangelize and disciple Chinese friends to Christ.

The Tiananmen Square incident of 1989, with the brutal government
suppression of student demonstrations in Tiananmen Square, shocked the
world while solidifying the CCP control over China, but it did not interrupt
the revivals. On the contrary, church growth accelerated and perhaps even
expanded into additional segments of society, particularly among the overseas and urban intellectuals who had led the demonstrations in 1989. Again,
I assumed the rapid church growth would be short-lived, perhaps only lasting several years, but I was wrong, as the boom in church growth continued
past the year 2000.[1] Foreign Christians also continued to flow into China,
and information about the development of the churches flooded out.

At the same time, by the late 1990s, China boasted one of the fast-
est growing economies in the world. The cities, with their massive building

1. Cook, "Windows of Opportunity in China," 22–30.

projects, transformed themselves from the ground up, becoming almost unrecognizable from just ten years earlier. The 1990s also brought a loosening of the residence regulations imposed on the rural dwellers, and more and more struggling peasants migrated to the burgeoning urban centers. The cities became centers of activity for the Chinese churches as well as the economic world.

I had long been curious, as an observer of the Chinese churches throughout the 1980s and early 1990s, about one peculiar characteristic of the Chinese churches that seemed to set it apart from the revivals in other parts of global Christianity. In Africa and other parts of Asia, the global revival of the churches arose from the urban centers, but in China the revivals came out of the countryside. The key house church leaders were often rural, and in many cases, they were not well-educated. That unusual pattern of church growth led many outside organizations to focus their church training efforts on the smaller towns and villages in the 1980s and early 1990s, and I now suspect that certain government regulations against migration, such as unusually restrictive household registration policies, bottled up the emerging church leaders in those rural areas. In other emerging economies, ambitious and capable rural residents moved *en masse* to take advantage of the vibrant economic opportunities in the cities. This type of migration drew the greatest talent, Christians and non-Christians, out of the villages and into the metropolitan areas.

As the CCP finally began to relax their strict migration policies, rural migrants, including the determined and gifted church leaders, poured into the cities, creating a new urban workforce, a new urban underclass, and new social instability. The migration gutted the rural churches of their most promising talent, the same type of church leaders who would have left a generation earlier if not for the restrictions. This influx from the country areas created a new a disparity in the urban churches. The Christian conversion of a growing number of college-educated intellectual elites after the 1989 Tiananmen Square incident, along with the arrival of newly converted Christian academics returning from the West, introduced even more complexity and tension in the urban churches. The center of gravity of the house churches, and the source of dynamic activity and spiritual zeal, moved into the cities. It is true that even now, the urban Christians will most likely dominate the future of Chinese Christianity, pushing forward in areas such as developing a Chinese theology and promoting global missions. In 2003, the Chinese churches were primed to make their mark on global Christianity.

Three Events in 2003

The churches, after decades of operating in a discreet manner, emerged from the shadows in 2003. Just as China gained confidence on the global stage, so did its churches. China was in the process of negotiating entrance into the World Trade Organization, for instance, and they planned to host the 2008 Olympics in Beijing. A signal of the new confidence of the house churches arrived in the form of a book written by David Aikman in 2003, titled *Jesus in Beijing*. Shortly after that, China Soul for Christ Foundation in Los Angeles released its DVD series *The Cross: Jesus in China* by Yuan Zhiming. These two events helped to mark the public debut of the house churches in China.

I wrote at the time in *Christianity Today*:

> Both of these journalistic works put names and faces on the house-church movement. Previously, a veil of secrecy covered the movement. *Jesus in Beijing* introduces Western readers to the key house-church leaders, based on interviews and research in China by the former Beijing bureau chief for *Time*. *The Cross* is a powerful collection of interviews and testimonies, taped on location in China, of Christians from all walks of life, collected across three years. Yuan brilliantly combines his talents as a filmmaker, philosopher, and apologist as he weaves the dozens of stories into a coherent montage.[2]

Later, in a third event, Christian Life Press hosted the Chinese Christmas Conference in December of 2003 in Chicago. The speakers at the conference included many of the prominent church leaders featured in the book and the videos, essentially a "Who's Who" of the Chinese house churches, and it was the first time an all-star lineup of speakers was invited directly from mainland China. I was delighted to meet some of these prominent leaders, and I used my Aikman volume as a kind of cheat sheet, to help me keep track of the biographies of the major personalities in attendance.

These three events occurred independently of one another, but some overlap did exist among the leaders featured. Even before 2003, these leaders were generally known and recognized in their small Christian circles, but now they seemed confident enough to reveal themselves and their stories to the world. At my seminary in Taiwan in the years from 1990 to 2003, all of us had been familiar with these leaders, but we would only speak about them privately, and even then, only in whispers. It seemed repression and persecution followed them closely. I was stunned to see them speaking

2. Cook, "Behind China's Closed Doors," 70–73.

publicly in Chicago, and I concluded that the churches in China had indeed entered a new era.

It was at this Christmas conference in 2003 that the organizers singled out the thirty or so Caucasian missionaries and asked us to stand. Thereupon, the sea of Chinese Christians, which included some of the most prominent and long-suffering leaders of the Chinese house churches, rose to their feet in a rousing ovation. I listened and watched as these humble servants applauded *us*, feeling utterly unworthy and embarrassed to receive the applause for Robert Morrison, Hudson Taylor, and the martyrs of the Boxer uprising. As I experienced this outpouring, I was convinced that the Chinese churches stood ready to assert themselves on the global stage.

The conference did raise one note of concern in my mind, however. I wondered if the maturing of the Christian movement might also mark a new era of the gradual decline of spiritual vitality. One humorous anecdote stood out to me. Among the prominent leaders, the prolific hymn writer Lü Xiao Min (Sister Ruth) was invited to speak. She mentioned having recently visited a rural house church where she taught them her popular song "Five O'clock in the Morning in China." During a break, she was approached by one of the older sisters of the congregation. The woman warmly assured her that she appreciated the beauty of the song, but she earnestly queried Sister Ruth, "Do we really have to get up at 5 AM? It is so early!"

Indeed, I suspect the churches have lost some of their fire since those "coming-out" events of 2003. I have overheard some Chinese Christians lament the loss of passion and even suggest that a new persecution of the churches might be needed. I believe some may have even quietly welcomed the growing restrictions on the churches after the ascension of Xi Jinping to paramount leader of China in 2012.

ONGOING QUESTIONS FOR THE CHINESE CHURCHES: SELF, NATION, AND CULTURE

Newly self-confident churches in China, and churches throughout the Global South, will gradually integrate and contextualize their Christian faith. Inspired by concepts from church historian Mark Noll concerning global evangelicalism, I have identified three primary questions the young churches in China must address:

Self: Who are we?

Nation: What is our relationship to the nation?

Culture: What is our relationship to Chinese culture?

Self

Chinese Christians will need to negotiate who they are within the larger Chinese society as they move forward in developing their unique identity. Are they Chinese, just like every other Chinese, or are they called out to be a "peculiar people" within a broader Chinese society? Do they identify as Christian first: "Chinese Christians," or as Chinese first: "Christian Chinese"? Do Christian Chinese have a primary loyalty to the nation, or to the global Christian church?

These questions involve complexity and extreme sensitivity when considering the self-identity of various diaspora and minority populations. Christians in Hong Kong and Taiwan have complex identities, as do the non-Han Chinese peoples. For instance, a believer with a Muslim background from a minority ethnic group in western China might have multiple layers of conflicting identities and loyalties. These questions have the potential to rip apart the body of Christ, and the way in which Christians in China answer these questions will have an impact on the whole of their society, as well as on Christian communities, Christian families, and Christian individuals.

Nation

The relationship between church and state, dating from the time of the early church in the Roman Empire, has generated debate among citizens, created division within the church, and caused friction between the church and the government. Christians, it is often assumed, should offer a positive contribution to society and the nation. But when the church is a small and persecuted minority of the population, then the churches can, with some justification, strive to avoid interaction with the government. After 1949, the churches in China endeavored to keep a low profile and to avoid antagonizing government authorities, much as the early church did. In the 1970s and 1980s, many young burgeoning churches around the world operated from the same defensive position. However, in some countries, such as South Korea, the churches grew rapidly into a significant percentage of the population. These churches which enjoyed growing influence and clout in the nation needed to assess what role they should play in society and in politics.

What role *should* the church play in society and politics? Can the churches remain uninvolved in a nation where the government institutes unjust policies that discriminate against their congregations? When marginalized and vulnerable people in the culture are exploited, at what point must the church speak on their behalf? Should the church speak out in areas of foreign policy, particularly if the nation takes advantage of weaker peoples? Should the church, with its prophetic voice, remain outside government, or should it also involve itself in the day-to-day politics and governing of the nation? If the government itself proves fundamentally corrupt, what role does the church play in that circumstance? Should the churches address these problems piecemeal and at the local level, or should they seek to bring large-scale reform to the central political powers? (For example, should the church simply seek to feed the hungry, or should the church promote specific government policies designed to relieve poverty? Even more radically, should the church address the underlying sources of poverty?) Can and should the church support revolution against an autocratic and corrupt government? Finally, is the goal of the church to build a Christian state and a Christian nation? If so, then what should that state look like? If not, then why not?

These fundamental matters will be addressed by the Chinese churches and theologians in the coming decades, but the issues will not be discussed in a vacuum. The historical baggage in both China and in the Chinese churches will surely influence the direction of the relationship between the church and state. A consensus will almost certainly never be reached on the proper role of the church in the political sphere, and so discussion of these questions is likely to add tensions and divisions to the churches. There are numerous hot button issues in China today, such as:

- Belt and Road Initiative
- Foreign policy and global prestige
- Border disputes with India and other neighboring nations
- Relations with Islamic nations
- Interaction with Muslims in China and other minority populations
- Population control measures
- Hong Kong and Taiwan
- Censorship of the Internet and other media

Chinese Christians, like all Chinese people, will likely adopt wildly divergent opinions about these issues; but thoughtful Christians can surely impact these sensitive and crucial debates in a positive and prophetic way that will not only influence China, but also the world.

Field Notes: On Christian Influence

As Chinese power and global reach expand in the twenty-first century, and China wrestles with these complex issues, I cannot help but wonder if China will become more sympathetic to British imperialism in the nineteenth century. If so, might that lead to a reevaluation of China's harsh critique of Britain's global empire? My hope is not so much that China would be more sympathetic to British imperialism, but that they also would seek to recognize how peoples might interpret (or misinterpret) their ambitions in the twenty-first century. China claims to want to help strengthen struggling nations by establishing mutually beneficial relationships, a vision that might be reminiscent of nineteenth-century Britain. But perhaps history teaches us that not all international involvement proves benevolent or benign. Most of all, I hope Chinese Christians can influence and help temper Chinese aspirations around the world.

Culture

The hardest question may be the third one related to Chinese culture. As the great church father Tertullian asked in the second century, "What does Athens have to do with Jerusalem?" Today, the Chinese "church fathers" will need to continue asking, "What does Confucius have to do with the teachings of Jesus?" A consensus has not been reached on the topic, and there could be many generations of debate.

This timeless question regarding the church's connection to culture and civilization holds special relevancy in China, with its grand history spanning thousands of years. An underlying question must be answered first: is China more a "nation," or a "civilization"? As we discussed more extensively in Part 3, "nationalism" only emerged as a concept in China around 1900. Before that, the Chinese more commonly thought of themselves as *Tianxia* ("All Under Heaven" 天下), or all that is civilized; everything and everywhere else is "not China," or uncivilized, or barbarian. The conception of China as a "nation" only materialized around 1900, and the KMT (The Nationalist Party) promoted the idea in the early twentieth century. The CCP subsequently, and sometimes violently, imposed nationalism on the people.

The issue is even further complicated in the current context, as contemporary China, rooted in modernism and communist ideology, is in many ways disconnected from traditional and Confucian Chinese culture. In a turn that I did not expect, the Chinese Communist Party founded the

Confucius Institute (孔子学院) in Beijing in 2004, with the goal to promote Chinese culture around the world. The first Confucius Institute opened in South Korea in 2004. Hundreds of institutes which are now open in dozens of nations around the world indicate that, as China interacts with the outside world, the Chinese Communists have decided to present traditional Chinese culture as the face of the nation.

If a widespread, vigorous conversation about the meaning and history of China arises in a way which includes the long historical record, the numerous philosophical and religious contributions, and the unique stories of the many distinct ethnic groups, will the churches be ready to join in that discourse? Is it enough for Christians to follow and understand the debates? Or, perhaps, should Christian theologians prefer to be on the cutting-edge, envisioning and proposing a new self-understanding of China? If, in the coming decades, Chinese Christian scholars and theologians can seize a prominent role in shaping the future of Chinese civilization, then I am confident that the old adage of, "one more Christian, one less Chinese" will be lost to history.

WHAT IS NEXT FOR THE CHINESE CHURCHES?

Global missions might be the future of the Chinese churches. With growing self-confidence inside of China, the Chinese churches will continue to boldly step out in missionary work.

Field Notes: On a Missions Professor and a Missions Student

A young student in 2005 burst into my office. The precocious American excitedly announced that he had recently returned from China where he studied Mandarin for two years, and, aware of my background in China, he wanted to meet me. He asked me my story, and as I always enjoy speaking with a kindred spirit, I enthusiastically launched into my testimony. I described to him my short one-week visit to China in 1982, a week that changed my life and caused me to fall in love with the country. Starting with my trip in 1982, I described to him a world that seemed completely foreign to him. With a wry smile, I explained, "When I first went to China, I was the only person I knew who had ever been there!" My friends could barely believe that I was going to China, as it had been closed for forty years. Sino–US relations had only been reestablished in the late 1970s, and everything there was exotic to American eyes. China had just emerged from the Cultural Revolution, and almost everybody still wore their drab gray or blue Mao suits and seemed to move in a slow-motion mass. Even in the large cities the people were not accustomed to seeing foreigners, and in most places, they avoided eye contact with our group of Americans.

Believing God had called me to China, I began to seek out international students when I arrived back home at my university. However, the international students from China of the early 1980s were quite different from the students who would begin to pour into the US universities in the 1990s. Most of them were older men in their 40s and 50s, generally dressed in a pair of poorly fitted black slacks and a long-sleeved white dress shirt. They did not look anything like the vibrant young students from Taiwan and Hong Kong, and I joked at the time that you could spot the people from the PRC from a mile away. They formed a very select group, approved by the government to go overseas, and the several I befriended in 1983 and 1984 had arrived severely underfunded. One friend told me the government had not estimated correctly how much money they would need in the United States. He showed me his cramped and dreary two-bedroom apartment, in a poor neighborhood in Chicago, where he lived packed together with ten or twelve other older male "students" from China. They maintained a cautious attitude in general, and I imagine they even harbored suspicion toward one another, but they expressed eagerness at the opportunity to speak English with an American friend.

My student listened attentively as I explained that I belonged to an eccentric group in the university, the small cohort who took Mandarin classes and courses on Korean, Japanese, and Chinese politics and history. At the time, when I explained to one Chinese history professor my interest in Christian missions, he nodded with understanding and informed me that his students were all peculiar and generally fell into three categories. There were the Christian missionaries, the former military personnel who had been stationed in Asia, and the students who were learning martial arts. An occasional student also expressed an interest in Eastern religions, such as Buddhism and Taoism. We represented an odd hodgepodge of individuals, but together we created a tightknit community on campus. We shared a passion for China.

Wrapping up my story of how God had worked in my heart, and how he had given me a distinct call to a faraway and mysterious land, I assumed my mesmerized student could relate to my experience. After a momentary silence, he looked at me, smiled, and candidly blurted, "My story is nothing like yours."

Startled, I listened thoughtfully as he shared his experience. He had arrived in China in 2002, just a short twenty years after my first visit, but the world of 1982 that I had described had vanished. I listened and I came to the realization that, just as China had transformed dramatically, his generation of missionaries looked strikingly different from mine.

He explained that God had called him to missions, but not necessarily to China or any specific place. As an extroverted person with an entrepreneurial spirit and a passionate desire to make a difference in the kingdom of God, he had begun his missionary career by strategically investigating data on economics, church growth, missions, and unreached people groups. He wanted to identify the place where he could have the greatest impact. At the time, in the early 2000s, the BRIC nations, Brazil, Russia, India, and China, were experiencing rapid economic growth and were constantly in the news, and so he focused his research on those countries. When he learned of the phenomenal church growth in China, he concluded that the confluence of rapid economic growth together with unprecedented church growth allowed China the potential to become one of the great missionary powerhouses in church history.

He grinned again at me, and he declared he wanted to be "in on the action"! And the most action, he determined, would be in China. So, after college, he traveled to China to learn Mandarin, and then, at the time that I met him, he enrolled in seminary to prepare for missions. He planned to return to China to mobilize and train Chinese missionaries.

As he finished his story, I reflected on his words, astonished to realize the differences in our stories. When I was called to China in the early 1980s, I could never have imagined that China would ever be considered "strategic." China was still a global backwater, mostly closed and extremely isolated. When I journeyed to China, I did not go because of its potential relevance; China boasted no significance at the time, but now this bright and ambitious young missionary, with a strong entrepreneurial spirit, picked China as the single most strategic place on earth to serve and change the world for Jesus.

I agree with that student; China is currently poised to change the face of global missions.

In the new world of twenty-first century missions, missionary movements continue to arise and build momentum in the Global South, particularly in places like Korea, China, Brazil, and Nigeria. I only hope that the churches in the West and in the United States will remain relevant. In fact, with a myriad of ethnic churches, the United States could potentially serve as a partner and a kind of "force multiplier" to the emergence of missions from China and other parts of the world.

In theological circles, some experts today speak of "South-South" dialogue. The belief states that as the churches in Asia, Africa, and Latin America come in closer contact with one another and begin to discover one another, they will initiate fruitful theological dialogue. In the past, these churches tended to see the church in the West as their dialogue partner, but that is changing. The churches in the Global South may soon find that they hold more affinity with other non-Western churches. The study of theology will be deeply enriched by meaningful theological conversations across various national and ethnic lines.

In those global theological discussions, I hope missions will be at the center of the agenda. Since the fall of Adam and Eve and the selection of Abraham to be a blessing to all peoples, God has relentlessly pursued the nations. Today, many people groups are coming to Jesus, and the younger churches are putting their hands to the plow in the remaining task of missions.

Profound influence can arise from strategic positioning, and the Chinese churches and Chinese Christians currently hold that strategic position. The Chinese economy booms at home, while Chinese entrepreneurs circle the globe. Further afield, in many parts of the world, the Chinese diaspora thrives, and the ethnic Chinese churches flourish. The dynamic situation we witness today did not spring up overnight; something profound has been happening in the last two hundred years. I mourn the pain and suffering of so many Chinese people through the nineteenth and twentieth centuries, and yet, I sometimes pause and wonder if God did not have a strategic and intricate plan for China and the Chinese people. God perhaps brought the Chinese churches through the dark experience of the tomb and then out of those shadows to serve as a light to the world.

In 1792, William Carey published *An Inquiry* in Great Britain. The book resonated with his audience because for Great Britain at that moment, it was "the fullness of times" for the people of God to do his work in the nations. The churches were experiencing revivals, the people were enjoying stability, and the nation was embarking on a trajectory to build one of the most powerful global empires in history. William Carey, foreseeing that coming Empire, urged the churches not to build a political kingdom, but to bring true change by boldly preaching the gospel to the non-Christian peoples.

Today, is this the "fullness of times" for China?

REFLECTION QUESTIONS

1. Of the three issues Chinese Christian will face—self, nation, and culture—which do you believe is most important? Which is most urgent? Why?

2. What role could China potentially play in missions during the next 50 to 100 years? What assets do Christians in China and the Chinese diaspora bring to global missions? What words of caution might we offer to the churches in China as they embark on global missions?

3. When Chinese people go to various parts of the world:

    - What are the perceptions the local populations have of Chinese individuals and Chinese missionaries? (Consider the United States, Europe, Asia, Africa, and Latin America.)

    - Can God use Chinese missionaries in a unique way?

4. What will be the role for non-Chinese Christians and missionaries residing in China over the next 10 to 50 years?

5. What was the best twenty-five-year period in all Chinese history? When would have been the best time to live in China? Why?

SUGGESTED READING FOR CHAPTER 16

Bell, Daniel A. *China's New Confucianism: Politics and Everyday Life in a Changing Society.* Princeton: Princeton University Press, 2008.

Cao, Nanlai. *Constructing China's Jerusalem: Christians, Power, and Place in Contemporary Wenzhou.* Stanford, CA: Stanford University Press, 2011.

Cook, Richard R., and David W. Pao, eds. *After Imperialism: Christian Identity in China and the Global Evangelical Movement.* Studies in Chinese Christianity. Eugene, OR: Pickwick Publications, 2011.

Goossaert, Vincent, and David A. Palmer. *The Religious Question in Modern China.* Chicago: University of Chicago Press, 2011.

Hamrin, Carol Lee, and Stacey Bieler, eds. *Salt and Light: More Lives of Faith that Shaped Modern China.* Studies in Chinese Christianity. Eugene, OR: Pickwick Publications, 2011.

Xi, Lian. *Redeemed by Fire: The Rise of Popular Christianity in Modern China.* New Haven: Yale University Press, 2010.

Lozada, Eriberto P., Jr. *God Aboveground: Catholic Church, Postsocialist State, and Transnational Processes in a Chinese Village.* Stanford: Stanford University Press, 2001.

Nedilsky, Lida V. *Converts to Civil Society: Christianity and Political Culture in Contemporary Hong Kong.* Waco, TX: Baylor University Press, 2014.

Shambaugh, David. *China Goes Global: The Partial Power.* New York: Oxford University Press, 2013.

Stanley, Brian. *The Global Diffusion of Evangelicalism: The Age of Billy Graham and John Stott.* Downers Grove, IL: IVP Academic, 2013.

Sunquist, Scott W. *The Unexpected Christian Century: The Reversal and Transformation of Global Christianity, 1900–2000.* Grand Rapids: Baker Academic, 2015.

Wang, Zheng. *Never Forget National Humiliation: Historical Memory in Chinese Politics and Foreign Relations.* New York: Columbia University Press, 2012.

Bibliography

Aikman, David. *Jesus in Beijing*. 2nd rev. ed. Oxford: Monarch, 2006.

Batchelor, Robert K. *London: The Selden Map and the Making of a Global City, 1549–1689*. Chicago: University of Chicago Press, 2014.

Bays, Daniel H. *A New History of Christianity in China*. Blackwell Guides to Global Christianity. West Sussex, UK: Wiley-Blackwell, 2012.

Bell, Daniel A. *China's New Confucianism: Politics and Everyday Life in a Changing Society*. Princeton: Princeton University Press, 2008.

Brashier, K.E. *Ancestral Memory in Early China*. Cambridge: Harvard University Asia Center, 2011.

Brockey, Liam Matthew. *Journey to the East: The Jesuit Mission to China, 1579–1724*. Cambridge, MA: Belknap, 2007.

Brook, Timothy. *Vermeer's Hat: The Seventeenth Century and the Dawn of the Global World*. New York: Bloomsbury, 2008.

Broomhall, A. J. *Hudson Taylor and China's Open Century*. 7 vols. London: Hodder & Stoughton, 1985.

Cao, Nanlai. *Constructing China's Jerusalem: Christians, Power, and Place in Contemporary Wenzhou*. Stanford: Stanford University Press, 2011.

Charbonnier, Jean-Pierre. *Christians in China: A.D. 600–2000*. Translated by M. N. L. Couve de Murville. San Francisco: Ignatius, 2007.

Chouvy, Pierre-Arnaud. *Opium: Uncovering the Politics of the Poppy*. Cambridge: Harvard University Press, 2010.

Clark, Anthony E. *Heaven in Conflict: Franciscans and the Boxer Uprising in Shanxi*. Seattle: University of Washington Press, 2015.

Cohen, Paul A. *History in Three Keys: The Boxers as Event, Experience, and Myth*. New York: Columbia University Press, 1997.

Cook, Richard R. "Behind China's Closed Doors." *Christianity Today* 49.2 (February 2005) 70–73.

———. "Fundamentalism and Modern Culture in Republican China: The Popular Language of Wang Mingdao, 1900–1991." PhD diss., University of Iowa, 2003.

———. "The Great Commission in Asia." In *The Great Commission: Evangelicals and the History of World Missions*, edited by Martin I. Klauber and Scott M. Manetsch, 149–63. Nashville: B & H, 2008.

———. "Overcoming Missions Guilt: Robert Morrison, Liang Fa, and the Opium Wars." In *After Imperialism: Christian Identity in China and the Global Evangelical*

Movement, edited by Richard R. Cook and David W. Pao, 35–45. Studies in Chinese Christianity. Eugene, OR: Pickwick Publications, 2011.

————. "Windows of Opportunity in China." *Evangelical Missions Quarterly* 31 (1995) 22–30.

Cook, Richard R., and David W. Pao, eds. *After Imperialism: Christian Identity in China and the Global Evangelical Movement*. Studies in Chinese Christianity. Eugene, OR: Pickwick Publications, 2011.

Daily, Christopher A. *Robert Morrison and the Protestant Plan for China*. Hong Kong: Hong Kong University Press, 2013.

Dikotter, Frank. *The Cultural Revolution: A People's History, 1962–1976*. New York: Bloomsbury, 2016.

————. *Mao's Great Famine: The History of China's Most Devastating Catastrophe, 1958–1962*. New York: Walker, 2010.

Domenach, Jean-Luc. *The Origins of the Great Leap Forward: The Case of One Chinese Province*. Translated by A. M. Berrett. Boulder, CO: Westview, 1995.

Dorsett, Lyle W. *Billy Sunday and the Redemption of Urban America*. Grand Rapids: Eerdmans, 1991.

Doyle, G. Wright. "Maria Dyer Taylor." In *Biographical Dictionary of Chinese Christianity*. (2005–2020). http://bdcconline.net/en/stories/taylor-maria-dyer.

Duara, Prasenjit. *Rescuing History from the Nation: Questioning Narratives of Modern China*. Chicago: University of Chicago Press, 1995.

Dunch, Ryan. *Fuzhou Protestants and the Making of Modern China, 1857–1927*. New Haven: Yale University Press, 2001.

Esherick, Joseph W. *The Origins of the Boxer Uprising*. Berkeley: University of California Press, 1987.

Fairbank, John King, and Merle Goldman. *China: A New History*. 2nd ed. Cambridge, MA: Belknap, 2006.

Fontana, Michela. *Matteo Ricci: A Jesuit in the Ming Court*. Translated by Paul Metcalfe. New York: Rowman & Littlefield, 2011.

Ganss, George E., ed. *Ignatius of Loyola: The Spiritual Exercises and Selected Works*. New York: Paulist, 1991.

Gernet, Jacques. *China and the Christian Impact: A Conflict of Cultures*. Translated by Janet Lloyd. New York: Cambridge University Press, 1985.

Gilmartin, Christina Kelley. *Engendering the Chinese Revolution: Radical Women, Communist Politics, and Mass Movements in the 1920s*. Berkeley: University of California Press, 1995.

Girardot, Norman J. *The Victorian Translation of China: James Legge's Oriental Pilgrimage*. Berkeley: University of California Press, 2002.

Goldman, Merle, ed. *Modern Chinese Literature in the May Fourth Era*. Cambridge: Harvard University Press, 1977.

Goossaert, Vincent, and David A. Palmer. *The Religious Question in Modern China*. Chicago: University of Chicago Press, 2011.

Grieder, Jerome. *Hu Shih and the Chinese Renaissance*. Cambridge: Harvard University Press, 1970.

Gützlaff, Karl F. A. *Journal of Three Voyages Along the Coast of China in 1831, 1832, & 1833*. Elibron Classics, 2005. Facsimile of the first edition. London: Frederick Westley and A. H. Davis, 1834.

Hamrin, Carol Lee, and Stacey Bieler, eds. *Salt and Light: More Lives of Faith That Shaped Modern China*. Studies in Chinese Christianity. Eugene, OR: Pickwick Publications, 2011.

Hancock, Christopher. *Robert Morrison and the Birth of Chinese Protestantism*. New York: T. & T. Clark, 2008.

Harrison, Henrietta. *The Missionary's Curse and Other Tales from a Chinese Catholic Village*. Berkeley: University of California Press, 2013.

Harvey, Thomas Alan. *Acquainted with Grief: Wang Mingdao's Stand for the Persecuted Church in China*. Grand Rapids: Brazos, 2002.

Hattaway, Paul. *Back to Jerusalem*. Waynesboro, GA: Gabriel, 2003.

Hayford, Charles W. *To the People: James Yen and Village China*. New York: Columbia University Press, 1990.

Ho, Anita, trans. "Five O'Clock in the Morning in China," by Xiao Min. "Xiao Min Introduction" (web page). *China Soul for Christ Foundation* (website). https://www.chinasoul.org/en_US/xiaomin-introduction/.

Hunter, Jane. *The Gospel of Gentility: American Women Missionaries in Turn-of-the-Century China*. New Haven: Yale University Press, 1984.

Ireland, Daryl R. *John Song: Modern Chinese Christianity and the Making of a New Man*. Waco, TX: Baylor University Press, 2020.

Jen, Yu-wen. *The Taiping Revolutionary Movement*. New Haven: Yale University Press, 1973.

Kemp, Geoffrey. *The East Moves West: India, China, and Asia's Growing Presence in the Middle East*. Washington, DC: Brookings, 2010.

Kessler, Lawrence D. *The Jiangyin Mission Station: An American Missionary Community in China, 1895–1951*. Chapel Hill: University of North Carolina Press, 1996.

Kindopp, Jason, and Carol Lee Hamrin, eds. *God and Caesar in China: Policy Implications of Church–State Tensions*. Washington, DC: Brookings, 2004.

Kwok, Pui-lan. *Chinese Women and Christianity, 1860–1927*. Atlanta: Scholars, 1992.

Laamann, Lars Peter. *Christian Heretics in Late Imperial China*. New York: Routledge, 2006.

Lambert, Tony. *China's Christian Millions*. Rev. ed. London: Monarch, 2006.

Latourette, Kenneth S. *A History of Christian Missions in China*. Taipei: Ch'eng Wen, 1973.

Lewis, Mark Edward. *China's Cosmopolitan Empire: The Tang Dynasty*. Cambridge, MA: Belknap, 2009.

Li, Dun Jen, ed. *China in Transition, 1517–1911*. New York: Van Nostrand Reinhold, 1969.

Li, Huaiyin. *Village China under Socialism and Reform: A Micro-History, 1948–2008*. Stanford: Stanford University Press, 2009.

Liao, Yiwu. *God Is Red: The Secret Story of How Christianity Survived and Flourished in Communist China*. Translated by Huang Wenguang. New York: HarperOne, 2011.

Lim, Ka-Tong. *The Life and Ministry of John Sung*. Singapore: Genesis, 2012.

Lindley, Augustus F. *The Project Gutenberg Ebook of Ti-Ping Tien-Kwoh*. Vol. 1, 2012. http://www.gutenberg.org/files/39180/39180-h/39180-h.htm.

Lozada, Eriberto P., Jr. *God Aboveground: Catholic Church, Postsocialist State, and Transnational Processes in a Chinese Village*. Stanford: Stanford University Press, 2001.

Lu, Xun. *Diary of a Madman and Other Stories*. Translated by William A. Lyell. Honolulu: University of Hawaii Press, 1990.

Lutz, Jessie G. *Opening China: Karl F. A. Gützlaff and Sino-Western Relations, 1827–1852*. Grand Rapids: Eerdmans, 2008.

Lyall, Leslie. *Three of China's Mighty Men*. Robesonia, PA: OMF, 1973.

Madsen, Richard. *China's Catholics: Tragedy and Hope in an Emerging Civil Society*. Berkeley: University of California Press, 1998.

Mariani, Paul P. *Church Militant: Bishop Kung and Catholic Resistance in Communist Shanghai*. Cambridge: Harvard University Press, 2011.

Menegon, Eugenio. *Ancestors, Virgins, and Friars: Christianity as a Local Religion in Late Imperial China*. Cambridge: Harvard University Asia Center, 2009.

Michael, Franz, and Chung-li Chang. *The Taiping Rebellion: History*. Vol. 1. Seattle: University of Washington Press, 1966.

———. *The Taiping Rebellion: History and Documents*. Vol. 2. Seattle: University of Washington Press, 1971.

Michener, James A. *Hawaii*. New York: Fawcett Crest, 1959.

Millward, James A. *Eurasian Crossroads: A History of Xinjiang*. New York: Columbia University Press, 2007.

Moffett, Samuel Hugh. *A History of Christianity in Asia: Beginnings to 1500*. Vol. 1. Maryknoll, NY: Orbis, 1998.

———. *A History of Christianity in Asia: 1500 to 1900*. Vol. 2. Maryknoll, NY: Orbis, 2005.

Mungello, D. E. *The Catholic Invasion of China: Remaking Chinese Christianity*. Critical Issues in World and International History. Lanham, MD: Rowman & Littlefield, 2015.

———. *The Great Encounter of China and the West, 1500–1800*. Critical Issues in History. Lanham, MD: Rowman & Littlefield, 2009.

Nedilsky, Lida V. *Converts to Civil Society: Christianity and Political Culture in Contemporary Hong Kong*. Studies in World Christianity. Waco, TX: Baylor University Press, 2014.

Neill, Stephen. *A History of Christian Missions*. New York: Penguin, 1964.

———. *A History of Christian Missions*. 2nd ed. New York: Penguin, 1986.

Noll, Mark. *The New Shape of World Christianity: How American Experience Reflects Global Faith*. Downers Grove, IL: InterVarsity, 2009.

O'Mally, John W. *The First Jesuits*. Cambridge: Harvard University Press, 1993.

Perdue, Peter C. "The Cause of the Riots in the Yangtse Valley (1891)." *Massachusetts Institute of Technology Visualizing Cultures*. 2014. https://visualizingcultures.mit.edu/cause_of_the_riots/cr_intro.html.

Piper, John. *Let the Nations Be Glad! The Supremacy of God in Missions*. 3rd ed. Grand Rapids: Baker Academic, 2010.

Polachek, James. *The Inner Opium War*. Cambridge: Harvard University Asia Center, 1991.

Polo, Marco. *The Travels of Marco Polo*. New York: Penguin, 1958.

Rahav, Shakhar. *The Rise of Political Intellectuals in Modern China: May Fourth Societies and the Roots of Mass-Party Politics*. Oxford: Oxford University Press, 2015.

Reilly, Thomas H. *The Taiping Heavenly Kingdom: Rebellion and the Blasphemy of Empire*. Seattle: University of Washington Press, 2004.

Ricci, Matteo, SJ. *On Friendship: One Hundred Maxims for a Chinese Prince*. Translated by Timothy Billings. New York: Columbia University Press, 2009.

———. *The True Meaning of the Lord of Heaven (T'ien-Chu Shih-I)*. Translated by Douglas Lancashire and Peter Kuo-chen Hu. St. Louis: Institute of Jesuit Sources, 1985.

Ross, Andrew. *A Vision Betrayed: The Jesuits in Japan and China, 1542-1742*. Maryknoll, NY: Orbis, 1994.

Ruokanen, Miika, and Paulos Huang, eds. *Christianity and Chinese Culture*. Grand Rapids: Eerdmans, 2010.

Said, Edward W. *Orientalism*. New York: Vintage, 1978.

Sanneh, Lamin. *Translating the Message: The Missionary Impact on Culture*. 2nd rev. and ex. ed. Maryknoll, NY: Orbis, 2009.

Schwarcz, Vera. *The Chinese Enlightenment: Intellectuals and the Legacy of the May Fourth Movement of 1919*. Berkeley: University of California Press, 1986.

Shambaugh, David. *China Goes Global: The Partial Power*. New York: Oxford University Press, 2013.

Sheridan, James E. *Chinese Warlord: The Career of Feng Yu-Hsiang*. Stanford: Stanford University Press, 1966.

Spence, Jonathan D. *God's Chinese Son: The Taiping Heavenly Kingdom of Hong Xiuquan*. New York: Norton, 1996.

———. *The Memory Palace of Matteo Ricci*. New York: Penguin, 1983.

———. *The Search for Modern China*. 3rd ed. New York: Norton, 2012.

Stanley, Brian. *The Bible and the Flag: Protestant Mission and British Imperialism in the 19th and 20th Centuries*. Trowbridge, UK: Apollos, 1990.

———. *The Global Diffusion of Evangelicalism: The Age of Billy Graham and John Stott*. A History of Evangelicalism. Downers Grove, IL: IVP Academic, 2013.

Starr, Chloe. *Chinese Theology: Text and Context*. New Haven: Yale University Press, 2016.

Sunquist, Scott W., David Wu Chu Sing, and John Chew Hiang Chea, eds. *A Dictionary of Asian Christianity*. Grand Rapids: Eerdmans, 2001.

Sunquist, Scott W. *The Unexpected Christian Century: The Reversal and Transformation of Global Christianity, 1900–2000*. Grand Rapids: Baker Academic, 2015.

Tang, Xiaobing. *Global Space and Nationalist Discourse of Modernity: The Historical Thinking of Liang Qichao*. Stanford: Stanford University Press, 1996.

Tawney, R.H. *Land and Labor in China*. Boston: Beacon, 1966.

Ten Elshof, Gregg A. *Confucius for Christians: What an Ancient Chinese Worldview Can Teach Us about Life in Christ*. Grand Rapids: Eerdmans, 2015.

Thong, Chan Kei, and Charlene L. Fu. *Finding God in Ancient China: How the Ancient Chinese Worshipped the God of the Bible*. Grand Rapids: Zondervan, 2009.

Tow, Timothy. *John Sung My Teacher*. Singapore: Christian Life, 1985.

Towery, Britt. *Christianity in Today's China: Taking Root Downward, Bearing Fruit Upward*. Bloomington, IN: 1st Books Library, 2000.

Uhalley, Stephen Jr., and Xiaoxin Wu, eds. *China and Christianity: Burdened Past, Hopeful Future*. Armonk, NY: Sharpe, 2001.

Van Houten, Richard, ed. *Wise as Serpents, Harmless as Doves: Christians in China Tell Their Story, Interviews by Jonathan Chao*. Pasadena, CA: William Carey Library, 1988.

Wakeman, Frederic, Jr. *The Fall of Imperial China*. New York: Free Press, 1975.

Walls, Andrew F. *The Cross-Cultural Process in Christian History*. Maryknoll, NY: Orbis, 2002.

———. *The Missionary Movement in Christian History: Studies in the Transmission of Faith*. Maryknoll, NY: Orbis, 1996.

Wang, Stephen. *The Long Road to Freedom: The Story of Wang Mingdao*. Kent, UK: Sovereign World, 2002.

Wang, Zheng. *Never Forget National Humiliation: Historical Memory in Chinese Politics and Foreign Relations*. New York: Columbia University Press, 2012.

Weatherford, Jack. *Genghis Khan and the Making of the Modern World*. New York: Three Rivers, 2004.

Wickeri, Philip L. *Reconstructing Christianity in China: K. H. Ting and the Chinese Church*. Maryknoll, NY: Orbis, 2007.

Wigram, Christopher E. M. *The Bible and Mission in Faith Perspective: J. Hudson Taylor and the Early China Inland Mission*. Missiological Research in the Netherlands 42. Zoetermeer: Boekencentrum, 2007.

Wolferstan, Bertram. *The Catholic Church in China: From 1860 to 1907*. London: Sands, 1909.

Wong, Sik Pui. *In Remembrance of Martyrs a Century Ago: Last Words and Letters from the Missionary Martyrs of the 1900 Boxed Incident*. Hong Kong: CCM USA and OMF Hong Kong, 2009.

Woodberry, Robert D. "The Missionary Roots of Liberal Democracy." *The American Political Science Review* 106 (2012) 244–74. http://dx.doi.org/10.2307/41495078.

Wylie, Alexander. "Translation of the Nestorian Inscription." (2019). https://en.wikisource.org/wiki/The_Nestorian_Monument:_An_Ancient_Record_of_Christianity_in_China/Translation_of_the_Nestorian_Inscription.

Xi, Lian. *Re-deemed by Fire: The Rise of Popular Christianity in Modern China*. New Haven: Yale University Press, 2010.

Yan, Yunxiang. *Private Life under Socialism: Love, Intimacy, and Family in a Chinese Village*. Stanford: Stanford University Press, 2003.

Yang, Fenggang. *Religion in China: Survival & Revival under Communist Rule*. New York: Oxford University Press, 2012.

Yang, Mayfair Mei-hui, ed. *Chinese Religiosities: Afflictions of Modernity and State Formation*. Berkeley: University of California Press, 2008.

Yao, Kevin Xiyi. *The Fundamentalist Movement among Protestant Missionaries in China, 1920–1937*. Dallas: University Press of America, 2003.

Yao, Xinzhong, and Yanxia Zhao. *Chinese Religion: A Contextual Approach*. New York: Continuum, 2010.

Yeh, Wen-hsin, ed. *Becoming Chinese: Passages to Modernity and Beyond*. Berkeley: University of California Press, 2000.

CPSIA information can be obtained
at www.ICGtesting.com
Printed in the USA
JSHW032118150822
29286JS00004B/11